NEW
CHINESE
COOKERY
COURSE

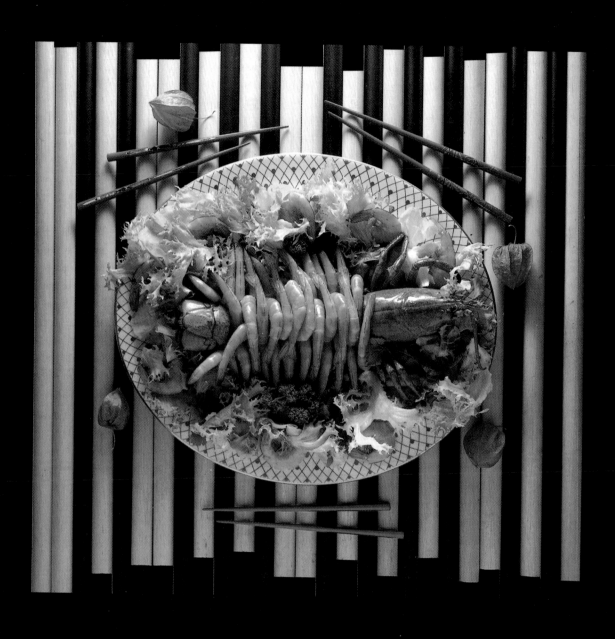

NEW
CHINESE
COOKERY
COURSE

Kenneth Lo

Macdonald Illustrated

新開辦中餐烹飪學校

A Macdonald Illustrated Book
Copyright © Quarto Publishing Ltd, 1985
First published in Great Britain in 1985
by Macdonald & Co (Publishers) Ltd
London & Sydney
A member of Maxwell Macmillan Pergamon Publishing
Corporation

Reprinted 1989, 1991

British Library Cataloguing in Publication Data
Lo, Kenneth
    Kenneth Lo's New Chinese Cookery Course
    1. Cookery, Chinese
    I. Title
    641.5951   TX724.5.C5
    ISBN 0-356-17663-0

This book was designed and produced by
Quarto Publishing Ltd
The Old Brewery, 6 Blundell Street
London N7 9BH

Senior Editor Tessa Rose
Editor Barbara Croxford

Art Editor Nick Clark
Design Penny Dawes
Photographers David Burch and Jon Wyand

Art Director Alastair Campbell
Editorial Director Jim Miles

- The publishers wish to thank Scott Ewing, Hazel
Edington and Candice Burch for their help; and
Cheong-Leen Supermarkets for loaning groceries,
equipment and utensils.
- Special thanks are extended to Reject China Shops for
their kind assistance.

Typeset by Text Filmsetters Ltd, Orpington
Colour origination by Universal Colour Scanning Ltd,
Hong Kong
Printed by Lee Fung Asco Printers Ltd, Hong Kong

Macdonald & Co (Publishers) Ltd
Orbit House
1 New Fetter Lane
London EC4A 1AR

CONTENTS

RECIPES

★★★★★
Recipes have been graded according to ease of preparation and cooking, on a scale from ★ to ★★★★★.
★ denotes a dish that requires few and simple skills.
★★★★★ denotes a dish for which mastery of certain techniques is required.

MSG
MSG is monosodium glutamate, white crystals which enhance the flavor of food. The use of MSG is optional.

INTRODUCTION

The speed at which the taste for Chinese food has spread throughout the Western world over the last 25 years is truly remarkable. Yet despite the enormous popularity of Chinese food, the practice of Chinese cooking is still regarded by many Westerners as being difficult and requiring some special talent of those who attempt it. This is mainly because the techniques used are so different from those of Western cuisines, but this does not mean that they are any more complex.

In Western cooking, individual foodstuffs are conditioned by heat until they are ready for consumption: meat is roasted or grilled; vegetables are boiled or fried. But, essentially, it is the nature of the initial ingredient that determines the character of the dish. Chinese cooking is dominated by compound dishes. Ingredients are mixed and cooked in different ways. It is this method – rather than the ingredients themselves – that determines the nature of the final dish. There is much more flavour- and texture-blending involved in Chinese cooking, which is where the fun starts.

Once you have grasped the implications of this radical new approach to cooking,

the rest is simple. Most of the techniques used in Chinese cooking are the same as those used in the West, and those that are different can be categorized into a few set patterns of using heat and marrying ingredients. The only completely new skill that needs to be mastered is stir-frying. Other techniques employed are quick, open steaming, steaming in a closed container and slow simmering. These methods are used when fresh, prime ingredients are not available, but the end result is often as tasty as if first-rate ingredients had been used. Red-cooking is simply slow-stewing in soya sauce. Each of these techniques is well known to cooks in the West.

The exotic ingredients required should present no problem either. Over 80 per cent of Chinese dishes can be prepared with no more than a handful of specifically Chinese ingredients, which are easily obtained from foodstores everywhere. If you examine the recipes in this book, you will find that in a majority of cases the dishes can be easily prepared and cooked. The essential point is to regard Chinese cooking as fun-cooking. Once you have done that you will find that the techniques are soon mastered, leaving you free to fully enjoy and explore the creativity that Chinese cooking allows.

Kenneth HS Lo

Equipment for the Chinese Kitchen

THE WOK WAS INVENTED about two thousand years ago and is definitely the most useful piece of equipment for Chinese cooking. Its thin metal and deep, curved sides and bottom make it perfect for frying: less oil is needed for deep-frying, and for stir-frying bite-sized ingredients can be quickly tossed without spilling out. Because wok-cooking is so quick, several dishes can be prepared one after another in the same wok which saves cooking space and washing up time.

The best woks are traditional ones made of iron or carbon steel, with one long or two wooden side handles. The first is excellent for stir-frying since the cook can hold the wok yet is far away from the very hot oil, using a long-handled spoon, chopsticks or wok scoop to toss the ingredients. The two-handled wok is better for deep-frying or for steaming food because it is steadier to move when full of liquid. When buying a wok the important thing is that yours has deep sides, is fairly large, about 35cm/14 inches in diameter, and the metal is not too thin or stir-fried food will burn easily. Make sure your wok has a good fitting domed lid to use when steaming.

▓ SEASONING AND CLEANING A WOK ▓

It is very important to season a wok before first cooking in it. Scrub it well to remove any protective coating, rinse, then dry it well. Place the wok over low heat, wipe it lightly with vegetable oil and let it heat for about 10 minutes. When cool, wipe the wok with absorbent kitchen paper to remove the dark film. Repeat the process until the paper wipes clean. Clean a seasoned wok in plain water without soap; never scrub it. Let the wok dry thoroughly over low heat before storing it. If the metal ever rusts, clean it with a scouring cream or fine sandpaper, rinse, dry and season it again.

▓ OTHER EQUIPMENT ▓

A **wok brush** is a stiff bundle of thin bamboo splints that is good for cleaning a wok.
A **wok stand** is necessary for wok cooking when deep-frying and steaming as it provides a steady base for the pan. The stand is also used with a two-handled wok for stir-frying. If cooking over gas, be sure to use a solid wok stand that has ventilation holes. It gives the wok stability and prevents the flame from going out.
Bamboo steamers are placed on a metal or bamboo trivet over water. When the food is in place, the wok can be covered with its lid or with the steamer's own tight-fitting bamboo lid, which is necessary when more than one type of food, each in its own steamer, is stacked on top of the other. When new, wash then put the empty steamer over water and let it steam for 5 minutes.
Metal steamers can be placed directly on the heat, fit snugly and have a tight-fitting lid. To prevent food sticking, place it on cheesecloth or in a heatproof dish.

With able-bodied men and women engaged in food production in China, it's the old and the young who operate the food stalls. Here the old woman is cooking some stir-fry delicacy to accompany the rice gruel or congee cooking in the large pot. The picture was taken in a market in Sian, where the famous Terracotta Warriors were discovered.

Left: double wooden-handled wok with wok brush; *right:* single-handled wok on wok stand with long-handled metal sieve and smaller perforated ladle; *below:* long wooden chopsticks for cooking on chopstick stand and soft brush for cleaning woks.

Above: base and lid of a metal steamer; *below:* Chinese bamboo steamer with lid and ornate wooden cooking chopsticks.

Left: Chinese
earthenware
cooking pot
with basket
ladle; *right:*
Mongolian
hot pot with
long-handled
wire baskets
for cooking.
(Recipe page 211.)

Resting on a
chopping
board, *above:*
small chopper
(cleaver);
below: heavier,
large chopper.

EQUIPMENT FOR THE CHINESE KITCHEN

EATING CHINESE STYLE

A simple Chinese table setting including a soup bowl and spoon, a small shallow bowl for dip sauces, chopsticks and a small, deeper bowl for holding rice and other foods added from the several communal main dishes.
Below left: to eat with chopsticks, hold the bowl close to the mouth to facilitate and grace the movements.
Below: to use chopsticks, hold one chopstick towards its base between your thumb and index finger and against the middle of the fourth finger at its tip. This chopstick remains stationary. Hold the second chopstick similarly against your index finger, supporting it with your thumb like a pencil. The two thinner tips should be kept level, with the first or lower chopstick kept steady while you manipulate the second or upper chopstick to pick up the food.

Top: metal ladle. *Left to right:* bamboo sieve, basket ladle; wok scoop; glazing brush; larger wok scoop; whisk.

Electric rice cookers cook and keep rice warm during the meal, but they are not essential and may be expensive unless you cook a lot of rice.

Chinese earthenware cooking pots, also known as sand pots, come in a variety of shapes and sizes, all with unglazed exteriors and lids. They can be used over low heat, as in making soup, but not in the oven. Caution: they will crack if hot and put on a cold surface or an empty pot is heated. Any heavy casserole makes a satisfactory substitute.

Mongolian hot pots, or fire-pots, heat stock or soup at the table from glowing charcoal under and in the middle of the pot. Small long-handled wire baskets or bamboo sieves or chopsticks are used to add and remove ingredients from liquid.

Long-handled sieves and perforated ladles are useful for lifting food from hot oil, when steaming or straining noodles. A **wok scoop** is a long-handled metal disc perfect for stirring and serving up stir-fried food. A long-handled wooden spoon or metal spatula can also be used.

Chinese choppers, or cleavers, come in two sizes: heavy ones for chopping through bones and tough ingredients and smaller, thinner and lighter ones for cutting vegetables and slicing meat.

Chopping boards should be fairly thick and either hard wood or white acrylic. A wooden board needs regular oiling. An acrylic board is easier to clean.

Miniature rolling pins are used for rolling out dough for making dim sum.

Chopsticks for cooking are wooden and long so they don't conduct heat and distance the cook from hot fat and steam. For eating, chopsticks can be wood, plastic or especially for special occasions, ivory. Chopstick stands are useful for resting chopsticks on and make a decorative addition to a Chinese meal.

Ingredients for Cooking Chinese

SOME INGREDIENTS IN Chinese cooking, like egg noodles, peppers, soya sauce and rice, will be familiar to the Western cook. Others may be new. It is these items, many of them imported dried or canned from China, which give the cuisine its distinctive character.

China is such a large country that sometimes these same ingredients are also bought dried and others, like hundred year old eggs, are prized because of the way they are preserved. Some can be kept almost indefinitely and will help you to try new oriental dishes in future.

On the other hand, if you do find fresh ingredients like water chestnuts when shopping, try them. Their superior flavour will be well worth any extra effort. Some Chinese ingredients are now sold at supermarkets, but nearly all of them are available from Chinese markets and grocery stores.

■ DRIED FOODS ■

Chinese mushrooms, known as shiitake in Japanese, add a smoky flavour and chewy texture to dishes. Whether the finer brown ones with blackish spots or the darker less expensive ones, they are always sold dried and must be reconstituted by soaking them in hot water for about 25 minutes.

Chinese wind-dried sausages are fatty, very highly flavoured, slightly sweet sausages made of pork liver or pork and duck liver. They should be steamed for about 20 minutes before slicing and adding to dishes.

Cloud ears are a dried fungus smaller than wood ears which must also be soaked in hot water. They are used in stir-fried dishes to add texture and a delicate flavour.

Dried chilies are thin and reddish, and about 1cm/½ inch long. They are sold in Chinese supermarkets, usually in small plastic bags.

Dried shrimp are small to very small and are sold cleaned, shelled and whole, with or without heads and tails. They add a salty, savoury seasoning to dishes.

Golden needles are the dried golden-brown buds of lily flowers. Soaked before use, they are added for their texture and unique flavour.

Hair seaweed is a hair-like, dried variety of black sea moss that is used mostly in vegetable dishes. Reconstitute in warm water before using.

Lotus leaves are soaked in lukewarm water, then used as an aromatic wrapping for steamed food.

Purple flat seaweed is sold dried. Rehydrated it is used in vegetable soups.

Red dates are the dried, prune-like fruit of the jujube tree. About the size of a kidney bean, they have a sweet taste and must be soaked before using.

Tangerine peel is the sun-dried peel of the fruit that, when soaked, has a tangy flavour. It is often used with Sichuan peppercorns and star anise.

In free markets in China agricultural produce can now be bought and sold. This reversion to the trading ways of the West has accounted for a huge expansion in food production in recent years. Famines are a thing of the past and China is now self-sufficient in food, despite its one billion population.

中
餐
烹
飪
材
料

Wood ears are a dried tree fungus exported from China. Reconstitute them in hot water, then wash repeatedly in cold water, picking over them to remove any grit.

■ RICE AND NOODLES ■

Egg noodles are made from wheat flour, water and egg, and are used fresh or dried.
Glutinous rice is shorter and plumper than long grain rice. It becomes very sticky when cooked and is used in both sweet and savoury dishes.
Long grain rice has been hulled and polished, the basis of most Chinese meals.
Pea starched noodles are fine, snowy-white, almost transparent dried noodles made from mung beans. They are soaked for 5 minutes and added to soups and braises.
Rice flour noodles are thin white, usually dried noodles made from rice flour. They come in a variety of shapes. Soak the dried ones in warm water until they are soft, then drain them to use in dishes.
Spring roll skins are fresh, very thin square or round sheets of flour and water dough. Different from egg roll skins, they come in packs of 10–25 skins. Store them sealed and covered in the refrigerator or freezer.
Wheat flour noodles are made from flour and water and used fresh or dried.

■ VEGETABLES AND FRUIT ■

Baby corn are miniature ears of corn used whole in meat and vegetable dishes. Rinse them before using.
Bamboo shoots are available canned, either whole or sliced. Used for their texture.
Bean sprouts are sprouted mung beans, highly nutritious and prized especially for their crunchy texture.
Chillies used in Chinese cooking are about 5–7.5cm/2–3 inches long and are sold fresh, both red and green, at Chinese grocers.
Chinese flowering cabbage is one of the favourite vegetables of the Chinese. It needs only brief boiling, steaming or stir-frying.
Chinese spinach has broad oval, rather than arrow-shaped leaves. Sometimes it has red markings. Cooked like western spinach, its taste is mild.
Chinese turnip, also called 'daikon radish', is a large, crisp and juicy vegetable with a slightly sharp flavour. It is eaten raw or cooked.
Chinese white cabbage has succulent, thick, long, white stalks and small green leaves. Both are delicious.
Fresh root ginger is an essential Chinese ingredient used to remove or cover objectionable flavours and odours in other ingredients. Choose pieces that are uniformly pale-skinned, firm and round.
Garlic is used to sweeten cooking oil and is removed before stir-frying.
Green oriental radish is similar in flavour and texture to the Chinese turnip, or daikon, but pale green in colour inside and out.
Kumquats are an orange-coloured, juicy, acidic fruit, 2.5–4.5cm/1–1¾ inches in diameter, with few seeds and an edible sweet rind.
Lichees are a succulent, white-fleshed fruit which, when fresh, must be peeled before eating.
Longons, or 'dragons' eyes', are similar to lichees, but they have a smooth yellowish skin. Their season is short, but they are sold canned and dried.
Lotus roots are large and thick with naturally occurring holes. Sold canned in thick slices, they are used in stews and vegetable dishes.
Mange tout can be eaten in the pod. Choose young tender ones, topping and tailing them to pull away the strings.

continued page 26

Chinese wind-dried sausages,
whole and sliced, displayed on dried
lotus leaves. *Left:* pork and duck
sausages; *right:* pork liver sausages.
When steamed, the sliced sausages
add rich savouriness to blander dishes
like steamed or stir-fried vegetables.
Once soaked, the reconstituted
lotus leaves make an especially
flavourful parcel in which to steam
cooked rice mixtures.

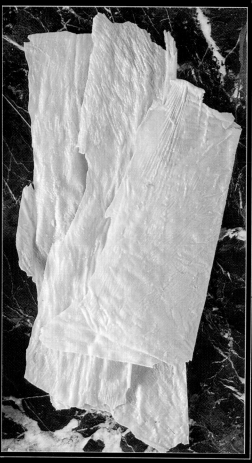

Above: dried bean curd skin. *Right, above from left to right:* wheat flour noodles; pea-starched noodles; rice flour noodles; glutinous rice; *below, from left to right:* egg noodles; wonton skins; spring roll skins; long grain rice.

From the top, left: sesame seeds; star
anise; fresh coriander; pine nuts;
from the middle, left: five spice
powder; ground ginger; ground
and whole Sichuan peppercorns;
from the bottom, left: cashew nuts;

From the top, left: dried shrimps;
golden needles; hair seaweed; *from
the middle, left:* wood ears; tangerine
peel; purple flat seaweed; *from the
bottom, left:* red dates; chestnuts,
shelled and dried; Chinese

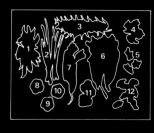

1, mange tout; 2, spring onions; 3, bean sprouts; 4 garlic cloves and whole pods; 5, fresh root ginger; 6, Chinese flowering cabbage; 7, Chinese turnip (daikon radish); 8, longons, canned; 9, kumquats, preserved in syrup; 10, lichees, canned; 11, peppers; 12, lotus roots, dried.

1, Chinese spinach; 2, chillies, fresh; 3, pickled mustard green, preserved in brine, has a tangy, bitter flavour prized in soups and in fresh vegetable dishes; 4, dried turnip; 5, water chestnuts, canned; 6, baby corn; 7, straw mushrooms, canned; 8, Chinese white cabbage; 9, bamboo shoots, canned.

Peppers, or capsicums, are familiar to Westerners. They are a flavourful ingredient used in Chinese cooking.

Spring onions are an essential ingredient in Chinese cooking. The green and white parts are often cooked separately in the same dish.

Straw mushrooms are grown on rice straw. They have a meaty texture and a savoury, rich fragrance. When canned, drain and rinse them before using.

Water chestnuts are a crunchy root vegetable. Their black skin must be peeled off when they are fresh. The canned ones must be drained. Store them covered in water in the refrigerator, changing the water daily.

Water spinach tastes like a milder version of Western spinach and, when cooked, gives a much-prized contrast between its crunchy stems and limp leaves.

◼ HERBS AND SPICES ◼

Coriander is a thin and flat-leaved plant sold in bunches. It is used as a garnish and seasoning, especially with fish.

Chilli powder is made from dried pulverized chillies.

Dried ginger is dried pulverized root ginger.

Five spice powder is a sharp-smelling mixture of ground fennel seeds, star anise, Sichuan peppercorns, cloves and cinnamon. It is used sparingly.

Sichuan peppercorns are not as pungent as familiar black or white peppercorns. Often used with star anise, they have a slightly numbing effect on the tongue.

Star anise is a highly scented, licorice-tasting spice that should be ground or crushed just before using.

◼ SOYA BEANS AND BEAN-BASED PRODUCTS ◼

Bean curd is made from the curdled liquid of soaked, pulverized and strained soya beans. Cut into squares, it is sold fresh covered in water. Store it in the refrigerator, covered in water. Change the water daily and the curd will keep for up to three days. It needs only brief cooking.

Bean curd cheese is made of fresh bean curd which is either 'white' – fermented with or without chilli – or 'red' – fermented with rice wine and salt. Sold in small jars or cans, it tastes like salty cheese.

Bean curd skin is the thin skin which forms on top of freshly made bean curd. Preserved by drying, it must be soaked in water before use.

Salted black beans are cooked, salted and fermented whole soya beans. Mash them with other ingredients or mix into dishes for colour and flavour.

Sichuan chilli paste is yellow soya bean paste mixed with dried chillies and their seeds, sugar and garlic.

Soya bean paste is made of crushed soya beans mixed with sugar, salt and chilli.

Sweet bean paste is made from cooked, puréed, sweetened red beans.

Yellow bean paste is made of fermented, salted puréed yellow beans with salt, flour and water.

◼ EGGS ◼

Hundred year old eggs are ducks' eggs 'pickled' by wrapping them in a straw, mud and lime compost. Shell before using them in dishes.

Marbled tea eggs are hen's or duck's eggs hard boiled, then finely cracked all over and simmered in a tea, anise and cinnamon mixture to marble them.

Quails' eggs are tiny eggs, usually hard boiled, sold fresh or preserved in liquid.

Salted eggs are ducks' eggs preserved in charcoal brine, so they have a salty flavour.

Above, from the left: quails' eggs surrounding a duck's egg; hundred year old eggs, halved, surrounding marbled tea eggs; soya eggs.

Left: fresh bean curd (tofu), drained.

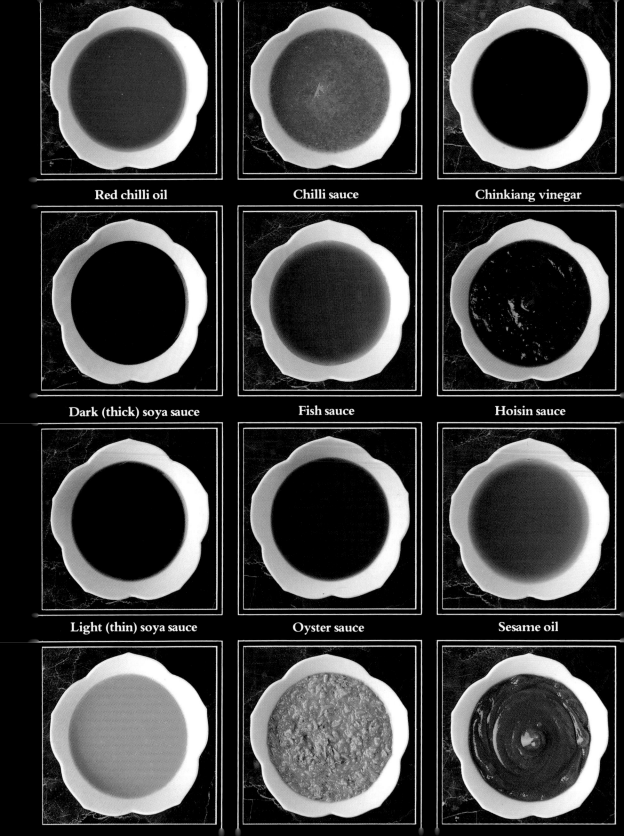

Red chilli oil

Chilli sauce

Chinkiang vinegar

Dark (thick) soya sauce

Fish sauce

Hoisin sauce

Light (thin) soya sauce

Oyster sauce

Sesame oil

The yolk is solid, but the white remains liquid. Scrape off the black shell coating and cook the eggs before eating them.

Soya eggs are hard boiled eggs reboiled, in their shells, in soya sauce. They are brown in colour and the salt in the soya helps them keep. The Chinese take them on picnics.

■ SAUCES, OILS, VINEGARS AND WINES ■

Chicken fat is slowly rendered (melted) and strained.

Chilli oil is made by marinating or frying chopped red chillies in vegetable oil.

Chinkiang vinegar has a rather sweet flavour and is used in many Yangtze recipes. Add a little sugar to white or rice wine vinegar as a substitute.

Dark soya sauce has been aged longer so it is thicker, darker and heavier than light soya sauce. It is used to give a dark colour and rich flavour to long-cooked dishes.

Fish sauce is a transparent, golden brown sauce made from fish, water and salt. It has a strong salty, savoury flavour.

Hoisin sauce is a dark thick 'fruity' sauce made of puréed soya beans, sugar, salt, chilli, vinegar and sesame oil.

Lard is rendered, strained pork fat which is used in meat and vegetable recipes.

Light soya sauce is thin and salty and is the finest grade of soya sauce. Made from yeast-fermented soya beans, wheat, salt and sugar, it is used as a final seasoning in dishes and as a table condiment.

Mei Kwei Lu wine is a highly alcoholic, fragrant spirit flavoured with rose petals. Gin or vodka are satisfactory substitutes.

Moutai wine is a clear spirit made from sorghum and wheat. Made in western China, it is drunk with food.

Oyster sauce is a slightly sweet, richly flavoured oyster-based sauce.

Plum sauce is a sweet sauce used as a dip, especially for crispy or fatty foods.

Sesame oil is used in small quantities in many Chinese recipes to add an aromatic nutty flavour.

Sesame paste is thick and made from roasted, ground sesame seeds and sold in jars. Do not use tahini instead. Use peanut butter as a substitute.

Shrimp sauce is strongly flavoured and made from shrimps. Use it sparingly.

Yellow rice wine, or Shaoshing wine, is made from glutinous rice fermented with yeast and is drunk with meals. In cooking, medium dry sherry can be substituted.

■ NUTS AND SEEDS ■

Cashew nuts are used especially in Cantonese stir-fried dishes.

Lotus seeds are candied for use in sweet dishes and are available canned.

Pine nuts are the soft white seeds of certain pine trees. The seeds' bland, slightly pine flavour improves when they are briefly grilled or fried.

Sesame seeds, both black and white, have the same distinctive nutty flavour. They are used whole or ground, often lightly toasted.

■ PICKLES ■

Salted, or pickled, cabbage is preserved in brine and canned. Rinse, drain before using.

Sichuan hot Ja Chai pickle is preserved in salt, then pickled with ground chilli in cans. Rinse it before using.

Snow pickle is a salted, canned green pickle used especially in stir-fried dishes.

Winter pickle is a very savoury, yellowish-brown pickle usually sold in jars.

Basic Preparations

Cutting, Slicing and Shredding

BECAUSE MOST CHINESE FOOD is eaten with chopsticks, it is cut into bite-sized pieces, usually before it is cooked. This is time-consuming, but it allows the ingredients to be cooked evenly and quickly so that they retain their natural flavour and texture, yet are enhanced by the oil and seasonings in the dish.

Visual appeal is another important part of Chinese cooking. Vegetables especially are cut so that their shapes as well as their colours appear in attractive contrast to other ingredients. Chinese slicing techniques are few and easily mastered with variations in style accomplished by subtle changes in the angle of the cutting blade. The Chinese always use a cleaver, or chopper, for slicing as its weight and sharpness make it a speedy and efficient tool though a sharp knife may be used instead.

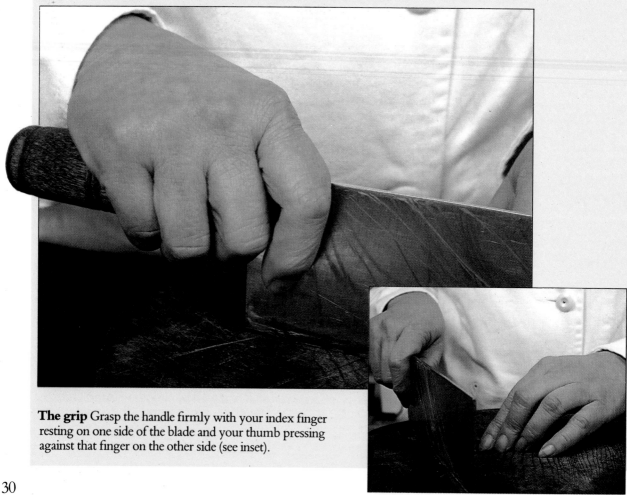

The grip Grasp the handle firmly with your index finger resting on one side of the blade and your thumb pressing against that finger on the other side (see inset).

1 **Shredding cabbage** Cut the tough central vein out of each leaf, making a tapering slice on either side of the vein.

2 Fold half the leaf over lengthways then, starting at the bottom, roll up the leaf.

For recipe see Crispy 'Seaweed' with Almonds, p. 84

3 Resting the cleaver against the knuckles, cut the leaf into fine shreds or ribbons, never lifting the blade higher than the knuckles.

1 **Slicing mushrooms** Hold each mushroom by its springy cap, pressing it against the cutting board, and slice away the stalk at the point it meets the cap.

2 For attractive horizontal slices, steady the mushroom with the free hand, hold the blade at an angle almost parallel to the cap and slice three or four times.

3 Always resting the blade against the knuckles, slice downwards on the cap. Regulate the thickness of the slices by adjusting the position of your knuckles.

基
本
準
備
：
：
切
、
薄
切
和
切
碎

1 **Root ginger** Smash slices of fre root ginger with the side of a chopper or heavy knife.

2 Holding the piece of ginger firmly in one hand, carefully peel away the thin skin with a sharp knife.

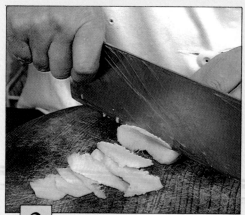

3 Slice the peeled ginger thinly, guarding and guiding the blade with the knuckles of the free hand.

4 Arrange the ginger slices on top of one another, then cut the stack into thin shreds.

5 Gather the ginger shreds into a bundle, then cut across them at short intervals to chop.

6 Top: sliced; smashed; chopped. Bottom: shredded.

1 **Bamboo shoot** Slice the bamboo shoot lengthways into several wedges.

2 Cut each wedge lengthways into thick slices.

3 Cut the slices across into cubes.

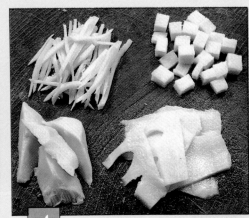

4 Top: shreds; cubes. Bottom: thick wedges; thin slices.

1 **Peppers** Carefully cut the seeds and white pith away from the pepper (*left*). Cut the pepper flesh into rectangles, then cut diagonally across them for triangles (*above*).

基
本
準
備
：
切
、
薄
切
和
切
碎

1 **Spring onions** Cut the spring onion across into 2.5cm/1in sections.

2 Cut each section in half lengthways.

3 Place each section cut-side down and slice it lengthways into fine shreds.

4 Roll cut thick spring onions by firmly holding the green part, then cutting the white part diagonally.

5 Roll the spring onion a quarter turn and make another diagonal cut.

6 Continue rolling and cutting until the green end is reached.

蔬菜‥添飾配菜

GARNISHES
To the Chinese, food is a foundation of life, for both physical and aesthetic sustenance. Attractive presentation of food is therefore very important, sometimes having symbolic significance. A dish's appearance should be given as much consideration as the freshness of the ingredients used in it.

Attractively sliced vegetables such as the carrot, radishes, cucumbers and lemon shown above are common garnishes, chosen for their colour and flavour along with parsley and fresh coriander, to complement the various dishes with which they may be served.

Though these garnishes may seem elaborate, all of them are made with a succession of simple, careful cuts and folding or a soaking in ice water to make the carrot and radish flowers open. With a sharp knife (or chopper), fresh crisp vegetables, a steady hand and a little practice, such decorations are available to everyone.

MEAT AND POULTRY

Chinese cooking involves a great deal of cutting and slicing because meat, poultry and other ingredients are usually cut into bite-sized pieces for rapid, even cooking. Chinese cooks deftly use a chopper, or cleaver, for this. A large knife can be used instead, but with a little practice you will find that the weight of the chopper and its sharp cutting edge makes the few Chinese slicing, cutting and chopping techniques even easier. Because the knuckles of your free hand are used to guide the chopper as you slice and cut, the chopper's size makes positioning the blade safer than if a knife were used.

Chicken, duck, pork, fish and shellfish and offal are so tender that it does not matter at which angle their flesh is sliced. Beef and lamb, on the other hand, should always be cut across the grain of the fibres to make the meat more tender when it is cooked. This is most important when quickly cooking as in stir-frying for which prime cuts are recommended.

When slicing meat very thinly, it is advisable to firm it up by freezing it for one to two hours beforehand.

1 **Chicken** Guarding and guiding with one hand, cut the chicken breast lengthways into strips or more thinly into slivers.

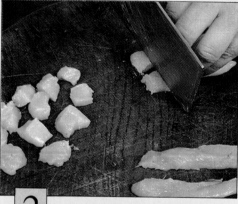

2 Cut the strips across into cubes or more finely into dice.

3 Alternatively, hold the chopper blade at an angle to cut the breast lengthways into thin slices.

4 Top: cubed; Bottom: shreds; thin slices.

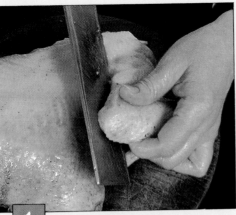

1 **Dismembering chicken and reassembling it for serving.**
Pulling the wing gently from the body, cut through the joint where it attaches to the body.

2 Similarly, pull the thigh and leg away from the body and cut down through the thigh joint.

Reassemble the meat pieces into a chicken shape, using the first wing joints for wings and the second wing joints for 'legs'.

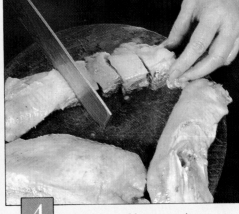

3 Holding the body with the tail-end upright, carefully and firmly cut down through the backbone.

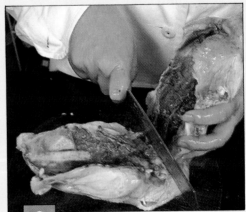

4 Cut the boned breast sections across into pieces.

基本準備：切、薄切和切碎

1 **Beef** Cutting across the grain while guarding and guiding with the other hand, cut the beef into slices about 0.5cm/¼in wide.

2 Lay each slice flat and cut the meat into double-size matchstick shreds.

3 Cut shredded meat into small pieces, then chop them finely, repeatedly gathering them into a pile and turning it over as you chop.

4 Top: slices; chopped. Bottom: shreds.

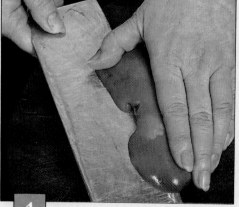

1 **Kidneys** Gently pressing the kidney with one hand, slice the kidney in two horizontally. (Cut each slice in half again if necessary.)

2 Cut away the core and connecting fat.

For recipe see Stir-fried Diced Beef with Kidneys, prawns and Mushrooms, p. 198

38

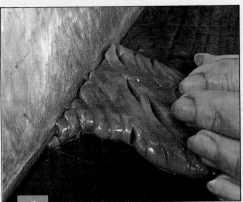

3 Make diagonal cuts or score half-way through the kidney, about 0.5cm/¼in apart, holding the chopper blade at a slight angle. Repeat on the opposite diagonal.

4 Cut the scored kidney into bite-sized pieces.

5 Left: poached; right: raw.

Duck Secure the deep-fried duck with chopsticks or a fork and tear the meat with a fork into shreds.

Pork Cutting thick, boneless slices of the meat into large bite-sized pieces.

For recipe see Sweet and Sour Pork, p. 197

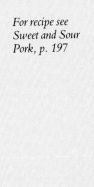

基本準備‥切、薄切和切碎

FISH AND SEAFOOD

Fish and shellfish are always eaten in China as fresh as possible – almost alive – and cooked lightly to preserve their natural flavor and delicate texture. Freshness and rapid cooking should also be your prime considerations when preparing these delightful foods. Unlike meat, fish does not improve with keeping and shellfish perishes extremely quickly. Though the prime aspect of freshness will be lost, frozen fish and shellfish, cooked as soon as it defrosts, is far better than fish and shellfish which has been kept too long so that its flesh has deteriorated.

Fish and shellfish need little cooking because their flesh is so tender, and everything for quick-cooked dishes must be prepared beforehand. The fish, shellfish, vegetables, noodles, rice and any condiments should be cut and measured, ready for a lightning stir-fry and hungry mouths poised to eat. Steaming is another technique the Chinese use for quickly cooking fish and shellfish. They are especially fond of it because a whole fish can be cooked at one time, usually on a heatproof dish from which the fish is served in its own juices, decoratively garnished.

Prawns are a joy to the Chinese, who cook them ever so briefly to protect their succulent sweetness and tenderness. In China often only the legs are removed before cooking and people at the table expertly remove the shell in their mouth, then discard the shell.

For recipe see Quick-fried Crystal Prawns, p. 143

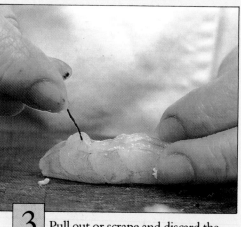

1 Peel the shell away from the body, then pull away the legs.

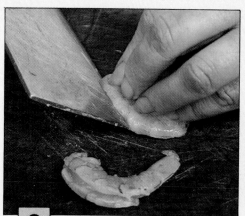

2 Holding the tail, make a shallow cut ¾-way down along the centre of the prawn's back.

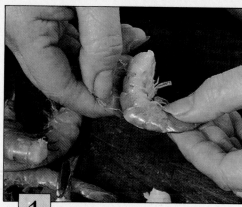

3 Pull out or scrape and discard the black vein from the shallow cut.

40

Preparing fish Once fish is scaled, gutted, washed and dried, it is often cooked whole to preserve as much of its natural goodness as possible. The tender flesh absorbs flavour quickly from marinades and/or seasonings which can enhance its flavour. A common way of doing this is by making cuts in whole fish *(see above)* so that the marinade or condiments reach the flesh more easily and the fish is ready to eat that much sooner.

Alternatively, make 5–6 diagonal cuts in the top of the gutted, cleaned fish to allow more seasoning flavours to reach the flesh.

For recipe see Quick Fry of Three Sea Flavours, p. 260

1 **Squid** Make light diagonal cuts or score part-way through the raw cleaned squid, guarding and guiding with the other hand.

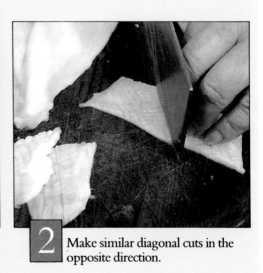

2 Make similar diagonal cuts in the opposite direction.

Methods and Techniques of Cooking

STIR-FRYING IS THE MOST popular Chinese cooking technique as it cooks ingredients very quickly in only a small amount of oil so they retain much of their flavour, texture and colour. Though not essential, a wok is best for stir-frying as its metal body, preferably carbon steel, gets hot very quickly, when the heat is lowered. The wok's very shape facilitates using little oil as well as the vigorous stirring and tossing needed to ensure even, rapid cooking.

It is important to heat the wok or pan until it is very hot before adding the oil in order to prevent meat, fish and other ingredients from sticking when stir-frying. Experienced cooks can feel when the empty wok is hot enough by holding the palm of one hand above the heating metal. Another way is to wait until you see a wisp of smoke rising from the bottom of the empty wok. When it is hot enough, pour in the oil carefully and gently tip the wok or pan to spread the oil evenly before adding the ingredients. (Remember, if using a frying pan, choose a large one.)

Large woks are easier to use than small ones, provided they have deep sides so they hold more food and allow more room for tossing and stirring. Woks can also be used for more gently shallow frying and for deep-frying, provided they are placed on steady wok stands and watched carefully.

One method of testing the temperature of a wok is by holding the palm of one hand over it and feeling the heat rising – for experienced cooks only

Sweet and sour pork is an excellent example of wok cooking, using it for deep- and stir-frying. The battered pork is first submerged in hot deep oil to fry it crisply. The pineapple and pepper pieces are stir-fried in a separate wok or skillet, then the sweet and sour sauce is stirred in. When the sauce thickens, the fried pork is added, to turn and toss in the sauce.

1 Roll the pieces of pork in cornflour on all sides.

2 Coat the pieces well in a smooth egg and cornflour batter.

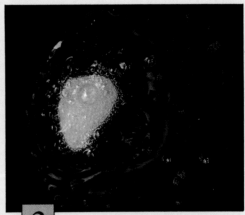

3 To test if the oil is hot enough, drop in a slice of peeled ginger – Chinese style. It should bubble instantly. Or see deep-frying on page 45.

4 Lower the battered pork into the oil with a slotted spoon and deep-fry. When cooked, remove, drain them on absorbent kitchen paper and keep warm.

5 Stir-fry the vegetables quickly.

43

6 Stir the sweet and sour sauce into the vegetables.

7 Add the battered, deep-fried pork to the sweet and sour sauce. Turn and stir for 1 minute.

For recipe see Sweet and Sour Pork, p. 197

Deep-frying For deep-frying, food is totally immersed in hot oil or fat. To obtain best results, the correct temperature is vital. Oil should just 'move' when hot enough; if it begins to smoke it is too hot. A thermometer is the best way to check the temperature – add to the wok or other deep-fryer, half-filled with oil, and heat until the thermometer registers the required temperature. If you have no thermometer, use a bread cube to test the temperature. The oil will be at 180°C (350°F) when the bread browns in about 60 seconds. Dry food thoroughly before deep-frying to prevent splattering. Carefully lower the food into the oil using a spatula, strainer, tongs or chopsticks. When cooked, remove food with a slotted spoon or strainer, drain over

Approximate deep-frying temperatures

	°C	°F
Meat	180-185	360-370
Poultry	170	350
Fish	185	370
Vegetables	180-185	360-370
Spring rolls	185	370

the wok and place on absorbent kitchen paper.

Deep-frying, properly carried out, seals the surface of the food and prevents the flavours of the food escaping into the oil; the cooked food itself will be crisp and non-greasy.

For recipe see Aromatic and Crispy Duck, p. 174

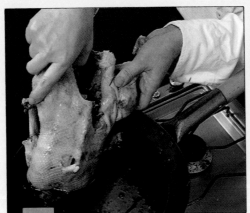

1 Aromatic and Crispy duck. Carefully lower the steamed ıck into the hot oil.

2 Ladle hot oil repeatedly over the part submerged duck to ensure even crisping.

1 Blanched noodles stir-fried in seasoned oil. Add the cooked, drained noodles to the oil in the wok.

2 Turn the noodles frequently to ensure even cooking.

烹
飪
方
法
與
技
巧

Reducing sauce Concentrating the flavour in a Chinese dish is often achieved by reducing the marinade or cooking liquid into a thick sauce to pour over the ingredients. Sometimes this is done as they cook, sometimes after they are cooked and removed.

1 Soya sauce and the other marinade ingredients are poured over the spare ribs.

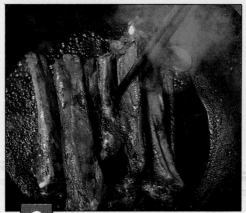

2 The sauce reduces and concentrates as it simmers.

3 The reduced sauce gives the ribs a rich glaze.

For recipe see Barbecue Spare ribs, p. 193

Onion pancakes Popular in Peking, these pancakes from northern China, shown here made as one large pancake, have a strong spring onion flavour with an occasional sharpness of salt crystals in the fried crispy dough. Easy to make, they are a good example of Chinese pastry making and a tasty alternative to plain boiled rice (see also p.250 for special regional version).

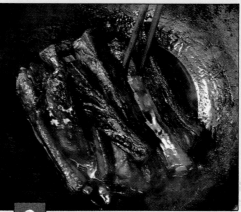

1 Folding up the salt and spring onion sprinkled pastry.

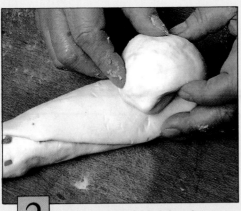

2 Rolling up the folded dough into a wheel.

3 Forming the wheel into a smooth mound.

4 Rolling out the dough again into a pancake.

5 Dusting the pancake with flour.

6 Above: frying the pancake. Left: the finished pancake.

烹
飪
方
法
與
技
巧

Rice is a staple food throughout China, especially in the south and west. White, long grain rice is preferred to short or glutinous varieties for most meals as long, properly cooked, fragrant grains are a perfect complement to other dishes served. To enjoy it at its best, be sure to use ordinary long grain rice that needs to be washed before cooking in preference to instant or pre-cooked varieties which lack flavour.

The Chinese are adept at estimating the proportions of water and rice for proper boiling. They do this by adding water to the first knuckle – or about 2.5cm/1in – above the rice level in a cooking pot. To cook smaller amounts of rice, measure the rice and water according to recipe instructions on page 68.

1 **Egg-fried rice** Frying in the beaten eggs until barely set.

2 Adding plain boiled rice to the egg.

3 Adding spring onions and other ingredients to the mixture.

4 Seasoning with soya sauce.

5 Turn and mix over low heat before serving.

STEAMING

Steaming food is popular throughout China because it brings out a delicate quality in ingredients, especially if they are very fresh, and steam is readily available in Chinese kitchens. The steam's moist heat circulates freely around the food, cooking it quickly and, provided the food is not over-steamed, enhancing the ingredients' subtle blend of flavours. Steaming can be done with or without a wok.

When using a wok as a steamer, the base of a bamboo steamer is usually used as a stand for food placed on a heatproof cooking dish. Water is added to below the dish. The wok is covered with a lid or foil and the simmering water replenished as necessary. An appropriate-sized bamboo steamer with one or more stacked baskets and topped with its bamboo lid can also be used in a wok to steam one or more dishes at a time.

Metal steamers are used without a wok, but be sure to cook meat, poultry, seafood or fish or mixtures containing them on a heatproof dish, or wrap them in muslin to prevent them sticking to the metal.

Steaming fish The Chinese steam almost all types of food including bread and dim sum, but they prize whole steamed fish above all. Served on its cooking dish, the fish juices blend with the seasonings and any marinade flavourings.

1 Sprinkle the seasoning mixture inside the fish and rub in.

For recipe see Steamed Fish with Garnish, p. 126

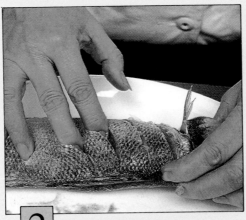

2 Make sure the seasoning gets well inside the slits, and leave for the flavour to develop.

3 Season the outside of the fish.

烹飪方法與技巧

4 Spread the spring onion and ginger garnish over the steamed fish.

5 Pour soya sauce along the length of the fish. Repeat the process with dry wine or sherry. Finally, pour smoking hot oil over the fish to finish cooking.

Poultry is another food the Chinese like to steam. Because of the relative speed of the process and the resulting delicacy of flavour, fresh, cleaned and not previously frozen poultry, either whole or in pieces should be used. Often the meat is marinated or seasoned in some other way before steaming so that the cooking juices will be deliciously flavoured to serve either on their own or with the meat.

1 Once cleaned and patted dry, a variety of seasonings can be used to enhance the flavour of steamed poultry.

For recipe see Melon Chicken, p. 165

2 The seasonings are sprinkled liberally inside the cavity of whole birds. Then the seasonings are sprinkled over the skin and rubbed in.

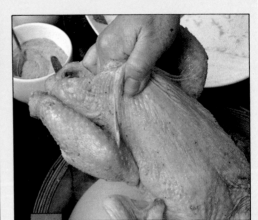

3 The seasoned bird is placed on a heatproof dish inside a bamboo or metal steamer to cook.

The Chinese use many distinctive techniques for modifying and enhancing the flavour and texture of foods. A grasp of these will help you identify what you may expect from each recipe.

■ TECHNIQUE FOR CONTROLLING TEXTURE ■

TECHNIQUE	SUBJECT	OBJECT	EXAMPLE
Air-drying	Chicken or duck	Drying skin to make it crisp.	Peking Duck. (See page 178.)
Blanching	Vegetables	To fix the colour and set the texture. Follow by rinsing in cold water and draining.	Madam Fei's Spinach and Radish Salad. (See page 89.)
Cutting across the grain	Beef	To make slices more tender.	Stir-fry sliced meat dishes.
Marinating in dry salt or sugar	Poultry, meat, vegetables	To extract water and improve crunchiness of vegetables or crispness of skin.	Salt-Buried Baked Chicken. (See page 156.)
Removal of skin and bones	Poultry	To prevent clash of textures.	Kou Shoa Deep-Fried Boneless Duck. (See page 171.)
Removal of tendons, membranes, ligaments and sheaths	Fish, poultry, pork, beef	To give homogeneity and smoothness of texture.	All chicken, pork, prawn dishes.
Slicing with the grain	Chicken, pork	To minimize reduction in cooking and preserve appearance.	Sliced meats with vegetables or noodle dishes.
Soaking in salt and wine	Kidneys, other offal	To extract juices that would otherwise form scum. To improve firmness of texture.	Most dishes using cooked offal
Trimming fat	Beef, pork	To remove membranes and keep stock clear.	Recipes where only tender, lean meat is required. Stir-fried sliced meat dishes.

■ INGREDIENTS USED TO ENHANCE TEXTURE ■

INGREDIENT	ADDED TO	OBJECT	EXAMPLE
Cornflour	Beef, pork, chicken	To add smoothness to meat dishes and bind juices of meat with seasonings.	Most fried and sliced chicken and meat stir-fry dishes.
Cornflour and egg white (1 egg white plus 1 level tablespoon cornflour)	Seafood, chicken, lamb	To protect the meat from hot oil to preserve texture.	Stir-fry meat, fish/prawns
Water or stock	Minced meat, seafood, vegetables	To keep dish moist and light.	Lion's Head Meat Balls. (See page 186.)
Water chestnut powder	Minced chicken, soups, sauces	To thicken. Similar to cornflour but with smoother texture.	Use in place of cornflour in most recipes.

■ INGREDIENTS USED TO MODIFY FLAVOUR ■

INGREDIENT	ADDED TO	OBJECT	EXAMPLE
Black pepper	Tripe, seafood, pork, pig's knuckles, offal	To accentuate zest and spiciness in dishes.	Salt and Pepper Pork Chops. (See page 192.)
Hoisin sauce	Meat	To impart richness of taste.	Capital Spareribs. (See page 196.)
Chicken, duck or pork fat	Minced chicken or prawn, meat balls	To add richness.	Lion's Head Meat Balls. (See page 186.)
Ginger, onions	Soups, stews, meat, seafood	To suppress or dissolve unwanted flavours. Brings out quality of blended flavours.	Marinated Lamb with Onions and Ginger. (See page 208.)
Monosodium glutamate	All ingredients except sweets and fruit	To intensify flavour. Use sparingly as if it were salt or pepper or not at all.	Mainly soups and vegetable dishes; Sichuan Braised Eggplant. (See page 96.)
Oyster sauce	Meat, vegetables, seafood, offal	To impart seafood savouriness.	Cantonese Stir-Fried Beef in Oyster Sauce. (See page 203.)
Salted black beans	Seafood, meat, vegetables	To add rich, earthy piquant flavour.	Sliced Beef in Black Bean and Chilli Sauce. (See page 201.)
Sesame oil	Lamb, soups, sauces, jelly-fish, marinated vegetables	Added after cooking to compound aromatic flavor.	Quick Stir-Fried Lamb in Garlic Sauce. (See page 206.)
Sesame oil	Seafood, soups	To improve aroma. Added during concluding stages of cooking.	Most soups.
Soya sauce	Meats, soups, stir-fry sauces	To improve meaty taste and add colour/flavour.	Most meat dishes.
Sugar	Fish, prawns, vegetables, mushrooms, poultry	To accentuate sweetness of fresh foods. Used in moderation.	All soya-braised red-cooked dishes; Red-Cooked Chicken. (See page 148.)
Vinegar	Hot, red peppers	To intensify hot taste.	Sichuan Hot Crispy Fried Shredded Beef. (See page 203.)
Wine	Seafood, poultry, meat	To suppress rank flavours and bring out aromatic qualities.	Long-Steamed Wine-Soaked Lamb with Tangerine Peel and Turnips. (See page 214.)

■ TECHNIQUES FOR ALTERING FLAVOUR ■

TECHNIQUE	SUBJECT	OBJECT	EXAMPLE
Blanching	Seafood, poultry, pig's trotters	To cook lightly, to preserve fresh flavour.	Cantonese Poached Shrimp. (See page 136.)
Breaking of marrow bones followed by –	Spare ribs, pork, duck, chicken bones	To expose marrow and enrich stock.	Duck Carcass Soup. (See page 179.)
Rapid boiling in water or stock	Fish head, marrow	To isolate fat deposits.	All dishes involved in rapid reduction of sauce; Shanghai Quick-Braised Chicken on the Bone. (See page 164.)
Sautéing	Ginger, spring onions, garlic, hot pepper	To season oil.	Sautéed Fish Steaks with Garnish. (See page 123.)
Steaming	Fish, poultry	To preserve sweetness and freshness of ingredients.	Steamed Fish with Garnish. (See page 126.)

SOUPS

Wonton Soup (*left*); see page 231.
Yellow Fish Soup (*above*); recipe page 62.

SOUPS

Soups are mainly drunk as a savoury beverage during a Chinese meal. Hence the majority of Chinese soups are clear, although they sometimes contain fairly large pieces of meat, seafood and vegetables. There are however a number of thick soups in the Chinese repertoire. During a multi-dish Chinese meal, these soups are treated more or less as another savoury dish to be consumed with rice. There may be several soups included in a large Chinese meal, which adds to the variety of dishes – an integral part and purpose of a Chinese menu.

1.5-1.75 kg/3-4 lb chicken (broiler if available) or duck carcass or spare ribs	
Scant 2 lt/3¼ pt water	
3-4 slices fresh root ginger	

■ GOOD STOCK ■

***

Cooking time: about 2 hours

Serves: about 12

Cooking method: long simmer

Time-consuming but useful part of many dishes, especially soups

Good clear stock is the basis of all Chinese soups. The making of good stock is sometimes an elaborate affair, but it can be made relatively simply in the following manner:

Remove the breast meat and the 2 legs from the chicken. Boil the remaining carcass of the chicken in 1.75 lt/3 pt of the water for 20 minutes. Remove from the heat and add 150 ml/¼ pt cold water. (The adding of the cold water causes the fat and impurities to cling together making them easier to remove.) Skim the surface of all scum which rises to the top. Add the ginger and continue to simmer gently for about 1½ hours. After about an hour of simmering, remove the chicken carcass from the stock. Mince the leg meat and the breast meat separately. Add the leg meat to the stock at this stage. Simmer for 10 minutes, then add the breast meat and simmer for about 5 minutes. Strain the stock through a fine sieve or muslin. The resultant stock will be both rich and clear, and can be made into many kinds of Chinese soups.

BEEF STOCK

2.25 kg/5 lb leg of beef

1.75 lt/3 pt water

3-4 slices fresh root ginger

salt and pepper to taste

Beef stock or broth is considered a strong nourishing soup in China. Although not used as extensively as a good chicken stock, it forms the basis of quite a number of soups. Good beef stock is made in much the same way as chicken stock.

■ PREPARATION AND COOKING ■

Cut about 1 kg/2 lb of beef into small cubes. Place the beef in a pan containing the water and ginger. Simmer gently for about 1½ hours to extract the richness from the beef. Add 675 g/1½ lb more beef and a little more ginger and simmer gently for 30 minutes to further enrich the stock. Finally, add another 675 g/1½ lb leg of beef to the stock and simmer for 15 minutes only to add an element of freshness to the stock.

To season the stock, add salt and pepper just before using. Once a good beef stock is obtained, the making of a beef soup becomes easy. Strain before using.

BEEF BROTH TOMATO SOUP

75 g/3 oz lean beef

1½ tsp salt

1½ tbsp cornflour

½ egg white

4 tbsp vegetable oil

6 firm medium tomatoes

2 spring onions

1.2 lt/2 pt good stock (see above)

3-4 slices fresh root ginger

1 chicken stock cube

1½ tbsp light soya sauce

pepper to taste

1 egg

1 tsp sesame oil

This is a tasty but light soup which is a suitable accompaniment to both spicy and plain cooked (boiled or steamed) dishes.

■ PREPARATION ■

Cut the beef into very thin slices. Rub with the salt and cornflour, then toss in the egg white. Heat the vegetable oil in a wok or frying pan. When moderately hot, gently fry the beef for 30 seconds, then drain. Cut each tomato into 6 pieces. Cut the spring onions into 1 cm/½ inch sections.

■ COOKING ■

Bring the stock to the boil in a wok or saucepan. Add the ginger, crumbled stock cube, beef, soya sauce, pepper, spring onion and tomatoes. Simmer for 2 minutes and then pour the beaten egg into the soup in a thin stream. Finally, add the sesame oil. Stir and serve immediately.

Hot and Sour Soup (*left*), a
popular soup especially in
winter; recipe page 63.
Egg-flower Soup (*above*),
garnish this light soup
with chopped spring onion;
recipe page 63.

2 chicken breasts

4 canned stalks asparagus

8-10 canned straw mushrooms

1 egg white

½ tbsp cornflour

vegetable oil for deep-frying, about 300 ml/½ pt

1.2 lt/2 pt good stock (see page 56)

½ tsp salt

¼ tsp MSG

¼ tsp sesame oil

CHICKEN AND STRAW MUSHROOM SOUP

■ PREPARATION ■

Cut the chicken into thin slices. Slice the asparagus into 2·5 cm/1 inch sections. Cut the straw mushrooms in half. Beat the egg white with the cornflour in a bowl. Add the chicken to the egg and cornflour mixture and toss together.

■ COOKING ■

Heat the oil in a wok or deep-fryer. When hot, cook the chicken over medium heat for ½ minute. Remove and drain, pour away the oil to use for other purposes. Bring the stock to the boil in the wok or a saucepan. Add the chicken, asparagus and straw mushrooms. Bring back to the boil, add the salt, monosodium glutamate, if using, and the sesame oil. Simmer for 2 minutes and serve.

★★★

Cooking time: about 8 minutes

Serves: 4-6

Cooking methods: deep-fry p.45 and simmer

Quick to prepare

1.75-2.25 kg/4-5 lb chicken (capon or duck)

1 Chinese white cabbage, 1-1.5 kg/2-3 lb

3 spring onions

4 slices fresh root ginger

3 tsp salt

2 chicken stock cubes

2 tbsp light soya sauce

4 tbsp dry sherry

WHOLE CHICKEN OR DUCK SOUP

This soup is frequently served in China partly because of the ease in which it can be made with the minimum of preparation. For a family dinner or informal party, there is sufficient soup to serve up to 12 people. For smaller groups of people, left-overs can be reheated for another meal. When reheating, add more Chinese white cabbage and 2 tablespoons light soya sauce, which will liven up the soup. Although a simple and straightforward soup to cook, it is important to bear in mind that in the majority of Chinese dishes the aim is to marry the rich, mature and seasoned flavours to the fresh. In this case, the richness of the chicken or duck with the freshness of the cabbage.

■ PREPARATION ■

Place the bird in a large heavy metal pot, casserole or earthenware pot, as in the past in China, with 2.25-2.75 lt/4-5 pt water. Bring to the boil and simmer for 20 minutes. Skim away the scum and impurities together with about 300 ml/½ pt of the stock. Meanwhile, cut the cabbage into 10 sections and the spring onions into 2·5 cm/1 inch sections.

■ COOKING ■

Add the ginger and salt to the simmering stock and reduce the heat to very low. Simmer gently for 1½ hours, turning the bird over carefully every 30 minutes. Add the crumbled stock cubes, soya sauce, sherry and spring onions. Lift out the bird, place the cabbage in the pot and place the bird back on top. Bring back to the boil, reduce the heat and simmer very gently for a further 20 minutes.

★★

Cooking time: 2-2½ hours

Serves: 6-12

Cooking method: slow simmer

Easy to prepare

Substantial centrepiece for family or party dinner

SERVING

Serve in a very large serving bowl or bring the casserole to the table. The meat of the bird will be tender enough to take to pieces with a pair of chopsticks. Ladle the soup, chicken meat and cabbage into individual rice bowls to consume with rice, each mouthful pepped up with a little good quality soya sauce or one or two dip sauces.

★★★★

*Cooking time:
8-10 minutes*

Serves: 4-6

*Cooking methods:
simmer and deep-
fry, p.45*

*Needs care to
prepare*

*Serve with meat
and/or vegetable
dishes*

CRACKLING CREAM OF MINCED FISH SOUP

Thick soups are called Kengs in China and are often eaten as warming savoury dishes.

■ PREPARATION ■

Place the fish in a pan of boiling water and simmer for 5-6 minutes. Drain and chop the fish into a paste or purée in a blender. Soak the dried mushrooms in hot water to cover for 25 minutes. Drain and discard the tough stalks. Dice the mushroom caps. Cut the tomatoes into similar sized pieces. Dice the bread into small cubes. Blend the chicken fat with the sesame oil. Roughly chop the ginger.

■ COOKING ■

Bring the stock to the boil in a wok or saucepan. Add the ginger, salt and fish paste, then the monosodium glutamate, if using, pepper, mushrooms, peas and tomatoes. Simmer for 2-3 minutes, then add the blended cornflour, top of the milk, blended chicken fat and finally the white wine. Continue stirring over medium heat for another 1-2 minutes until the soup begins to thicken. Keep the soup hot over a low heat. Meanwhile, heat the oil in a wok or deep-fryer. When hot, fry the cubes of bread until crisp. Transfer the croûtons to the bottom of a heated tureen and take it to the table. Pour the soup into the tureen at the table; the soup will make a crackling noise. Serve immediately.

150g/5oz white fish, eg, sole, cod, haddock, sea bass etc., any skins and bones discarded

4 large dried Chinese mushrooms

3 firm tomatoes

1½ slices of bread

1 tbsp melted chicken fat

1 tsp sesame oil

3 slices fresh root ginger

900ml/1½pt good stock (see page 56)

2 tsp salt

¼tsp MSG (optional)

pepper to taste

2 tbsp peas or petits pois

1½ tbsp cornflour blended with 4 tbsp good stock (see page 56)

2 tbsp top of the milk

3 tbsp white wine

vegetable oil for deep-frying

1 trout (sea bass or bream etc), about 675g/1½lb
2 tsp salt
1 tsp ground ginger
1 tsp pepper
150g/5oz leeks
4 slices fresh root ginger
50g/2oz canned bamboo shoots
vegetable oil for deep-frying
1.2lt/2pt good stock (see page 56)
1 tbsp drained, canned chopped snow pickles
2 tbsp light soya sauce
3 tbsp wine vinegar

YELLOW FISH SOUP (OR WHOLE FISH SOUP)

Called Yellow Fish Soup because this fish is most often used in China, being cheap and plentiful. Here in the West, fish such as trout, sea bass, bream, carp, herring etc. may be used. The fish is first seasoned and fried until golden and crispy. It is then simmered in good stock with vegetables.

■ PREPARATION ■

Clean the fish thoroughly. Rub the inside and outside well with salt, ground ginger and pepper. Leave to season for 20 minutes. Clean the leeks and shred. Shred the ginger and bamboo shoots.

■ COOKING ■

Heat the oil in a wok or deep-fryer. When hot, fry the fish for about 7-8 minutes until beginning to brown and become crispy. Remove and drain on absorbent kitchen paper. Heat the stock in an oval-shaped flameproof casserole, wok or similar pan. Lower the fish into the stock. Bring to the boil, add the leeks, ginger, bamboo shoots and pickles, and simmer for 5-6 minutes. Sprinkle on the soya sauce and vinegar, continue to simmer for a further 5-6 minutes.

■ SERVING ■

Ladle the soup and vegetables from the casserole into individual rice bowls and consume with rice and the fish.

★★★
Cooking time: about 20 minutes
Serves: 4-6
Cooking methods: deep-fry p.45 and simmer
Quick to prepare
Serve with meat or vegetarian dishes
Illustrated on p.55

225g/8oz spare ribs of pork
175g/6oz watercress
2 medium tomatoes
900ml/1½pt good chicken stock (see page 56)
2 slices fresh root ginger
¼tsp MSG (optional)
salt and pepper to taste
1 tsp sesame oil

WATERCRESS AND SPARE RIB SOUP

■ PREPARATION ■

Cut the spareribs into 4cm/1½ inch sections. Trim the watercress, wash and cut into 4cm/1½ inch lengths. Cut the tomatoes into eighths.

■ COOKING ■

Bring the stock to the boil in a wok or saucepan. Add the spare ribs and ginger and simmer for 35-40 minutes. Skim off any scum which rises to the surface. Add the tomatoes, watercress, monosodium glutamate, if using, salt and pepper to taste. Bring back to the boil for 1 minute, add the sesame oil and serve.

★
Cooking time: 35-45 minutes
Serves: 4-6
Cooking method: simmer
Easy to prepare

EGG-FLOWER SOUP

■ PREPARATION ■

Finely chop the garlic, ginger and spring onions. Lightly beat the egg with a fork for 30 seconds, then sprinkle with a pinch of salt and pepper.

■ COOKING ■

Heat the stock in a wok or saucepan. Add the garlic, ginger and crumbled stock cube. Bring to the boil and simmer for 3 minutes. Pour the beaten egg in a very thin stream, along the prongs of a fork, and trail it over the surface of the soup. When the egg has set, sprinkle the soup with spring onion, remaining salt and pepper and the sesame oil.

★★

Cooking time: about 6-8 minutes

Serves: 4-6

Cooking method: simmer

A simple, light soup

Illustrated on p.59

1 clove garlic
2 slices fresh root ginger
3 spring onions
1 egg
1 tsp salt
pepper to taste
1 lt/1¾pt good stock (see page 56)
1 chicken stock cube
1 tsp sesame oil

HOT AND SOUR SOUP

This is a popular soup especially in the winter. As the soup can be made from any left-over bits and pieces of meat and vegetables, I sometimes call it the 'Chinese Junk Soup' although it can be served in quite respectable company. An ingredient you need to produce the traditional version is bean curd (tofu).

■ PREPARATION ■

Shred the pork and bamboo shoot into 2.5 cm/1 inch strips. Soak the dried mushrooms and dried shrimps separately in hot water to cover for 25 minutes. Drain, reserving the soaking water. Discard the tough stalks from the mushrooms, then cut the caps into slices a similar size to the pork. Add the soaking water to the stock. Cut the bean curd into 1 cm/½ inch cubes. Beat the egg lightly with a fork for 15 seconds. Roughly chop the spring onions. Mix the hot and sour mixture together in a bowl.

■ COOKING ■

Bring the stock to the boil in a wok or saucepan. Add the pork, dried shrimps and mushrooms and simmer for 10 minutes. Add the fresh or frozen shrimps, bean curd, bamboo shoot, salt, crumbled stock cubes, monosodium glutamate, if using, peas and spring onions. Continue to cook for 3–4 minutes, then stir in the hot and sour mixture which will thicken the soup. Gently pour the beaten egg over the surface of the soup in a thin stream. Sprinkle the soup with sesame oil and serve immediately.

★★★★

Cooking time: about 15 minutes

Serves: 4-6

Cooking method: simmer

Needs a fair amount of preparation

A substantial soup which need not be accompanied by many courses

Illustrated on p.58

50-100g/2-4oz lean pork
25-50g/1-2oz canned bamboo shoots
4 medium dried Chinese mushrooms
1 tbsp dried shrimps
1-2 cakes bean curd
1 egg
2 spring onions
1.2lt/2pt good stock (see page 56)
3 tbsp fresh or frozen shrimps
1 tsp salt
2 stock cubes
¼tsp MSG (optional)
2 tbsp peas
1 tsp sesame oil
Hot and sour mixture:
2 tbsp soya sauce
3 tbsp vinegar
2 tbsp cornflour
4 tbsp water
pepper to taste

175g/6oz carton frozen spinach
4 medium dried Chinese mushrooms
75-100g/3-4oz ham
50-75g/2-3oz button mushrooms
2 tbsp cornflour
2 cakes bean curd
900ml/1½pt good stock (see page 56)
1½ tsp salt
pepper to taste
1 chicken stock cube
1 tbsp light soya sauce
1 tsp sesame oil

BEAN CURD, HAM, MUSHROOM AND SPINACH SOUP

■ PREPARATION ■

Thaw the spinach and roughly chop. Soak the dried mushrooms in hot water to cover for 25 minutes. Drain, reserving the soaking liquid. Discard the tough stalks and cut the mushroom caps into shreds. Cut the ham and fresh mushrooms into similar shreds. Blend the cornflour with the mushroom soaking water. Cut the bean curd into 4cm/1½ inch cubes.

■ COOKING ■

Bring the stock to the boil in a wok or saucepan. Add the fresh and dried mushrooms, bean curd, salt, pepper and crumbled stock cube. Bring back to the boil and add the spinach, ham, soya sauce and blended cornflour. Cook over gentle heat for 3-4 minutes. Sprinkle with sesame oil and serve.

★★

Cooking time: 6-7 minutes

Serves: 4-6

Cooking method: simmer

Quick to prepare

A substantial soup which need not be accompanied by many courses

6 medium dried Chinese mushrooms
1½ tbsp dried shrimps
100g/4oz fine rice noodles
2 tbsp minced or finely chopped chicken breast meat
1½ tbsp drained, canned chopped snow pickles
1½ tbsp drained, canned chopped Sichuan hot Ja Chai pickles
2 tbsp chopped fresh ginger root
1½ tbsp chopped spring onion
2 tsp salt
1½ chicken stock cubes
1.2lt/2pt good stock (see page 56)
3 tbsp vegetable oil
1 tsp sesame oil
2 tsp red chilli oil or chilli sauce
1 tsp chopped garlic
¼ tsp MSG (optional)

THE 'YUNNAN OVER THE BRIDGE' NOODLE SOUP

Yunnan is one of China's far western provinces, where this light soup is often served. One curious thing about the soup is that the ingredients are not actually cooked, they only have a very hot stock poured over them; and in the very last stage a small quantity of hot oil is added as a 'hot lid' to seal them.

■ PREPARATION ■

Soak the dried mushrooms and dried shrimps separately for 25 minutes in hot water to cover. Drain, discarding the tough mushroom stalks. Roughly mince or chop the mushrooms and shrimps. Shred the Chinese cabbage. Soak the rice noodles for 3-4 minutes in hot water to cover. Drain.

■ COOKING ■

Place the shrimps, mushrooms, chicken, pickles, 1½ tablespoons of the chopped ginger and the spring onion at the bottom of a large heatproof soup bowl, together with the salt and crumbled stock cubes. Bring the stock to the boil in a saucepan and pour immediately into the bowl on top of the ingredients. Leave the contents to stand in the hot stock for 5 minutes, stirring once or twice. Add the noodles and cabbage and submerge in the soup. Heat the vegetable oil, sesame oil and red oil in a small saucepan, together with the remaining chopped ginger, the garlic and monosodium glutamate, if

★★★

Cooking time: 5-6 minutes, plus standing time

Serves: 5-6

Cooking method: poach

Quick to prepare

Serve with any combination of dishes

using, until boiling. Pour the mixture immediately over the soup; the oil will spread over the entire surface, acting as a hot lid which imparts more heat to the soup. Leave to stand for an extra 5 minutes, then stir well and serve immediately.

PEKING SLICED FISH PEPPER POT SOUP

★★★
Cooking time: about 10 minutes

Serves: 4-6

Cooking methods: deep-fry p.45 and simmer

225g/8oz white fish fillets
1½tsp salt
1tbsp cornflour
1 egg white
2 slices fresh root ginger
1 clove garlic
2 spring onions
vegetable oil for deep-frying
900ml/1½pt chicken stock (see page 56)
½tsp salt
¼tsp MSG
3tbsp wine vinegar
½tsp pepper

PREPARATION

Cut the fish into 4 × 2.5 cm/1½ × 1 inch slices. Dust with the 1½ teaspoons salt and the cornflour, and wet with the egg white. Finely chop the ginger and garlic. Coarsely chop the spring onions.

COOKING

Heat the oil in a wok or deep-fryer. When hot, lightly fry the coated fish for 1 minute. Remove and drain, pour away the oil for other uses. Bring the stock to the boil in the wok or saucepan. Add the ginger, garlic, remaining salt and monosodium glutamate, if using, and bring back to the boil for 1 minute. Add the fish, vinegar and pepper and simmer for 3-4 minutes. Pour into a heated tureen, sprinkle with spring onions and serve.

VELVET OF CHICKEN, HAM AND SWEETCORN SOUP

★★
Cooking time: 5-6 minutes

Serves: 4-6

Cooking method: quick simmer

Quick to prepare

Quite a substantial soup that goes well with any combination of dishes

75g/3oz ham
150g/5oz chicken breast meat
2 egg whites
3tbsp top of the milk
1tbsp cornflour
1.2lt/2pt good stock (see page 56)
225g/8oz can creamed sweetcorn
2tsp salt
pepper to taste
¼tsp MSG (optional)
1tsp finely chopped spring onion

PREPARATION

Chop the ham. Coarsely mince the chicken. Beat the egg whites in a small bowl until frothy. Add the top of the milk and cornflour and beat again. Blend the minced chicken into the mixture.

COOKING

Bring the stock to the boil in a wok or saucepan. Add the sweetcorn, salt, pepper and monosodium glutamate, if using, and bring back to the boil. Stir in the egg white and minced chicken mixture. Finally, sprinkle, on the chopped ham and spring onion. Stir gently and serve immediately. A few tablespoons of fresh shrimps may be added with the ham to enhance the colour and taste of the dish.

RICE, NOODLES AND VEGETABLES

Colourful stir-fried selection of vegetables with Sweet and Sour Sauce; recipe page 197.

飯、麵與蔬菜

RICE AND NOODLES

Rice is not considered a dish in China, but is usually served as the bulk food to accompany the savoury dishes on the table. Noodles are served and eaten as snacks, albeit often large snacks, between meals but occasionally they are included as an item to bulk up the meal. When they are served as such, they are usually fairly plainly cooked, perhaps with one or two vegetables and a minimum amount of shredded meat added, for the sake of variation in texture.

Rice is normally eaten plain in China (boiled or steamed) and is only very occasionally made savoury (as in 'fried rice'), usually when there is a shortage of savoury dishes and there is an abundance of scraps available. Plain rice is ideal for absorbing the numerous flavours and ingredients to be found on the Chinese dinner table.

There are three main types of noodle, made from wheat flour, rice flour and pea starch. These are eaten in every part of China, but the various regions do have their favourites: wheat flour noodles predominate in the North while in the South rice flour noodles are more popular. Pea starched noodles are seldom cooked into bulk-food dishes, but more usually are used in soups or cooked with meats and seafoods in savoury dishes to consume with rice.

---

1 cup or bowl long grain white rice

1¼ cups or bowls water

PLAIN BOILED RICE

■ PREPARATION ■

Wash and rinse the rice, drain well. Place in a saucepan and add the water.

■ COOKING ■

Cover and bring to the boil. Reduce heat and simmer gently for 9-10 minutes. Remove from the heat and leave the rice to continue to cook and dry in its own heat for a further 10 minutes.

★

Cooking time: 10 minutes plus standing time

Serves: 2-4

Cooking method: simmer

Easy to prepare

Serve with all savoury dishes

BASIC FRIED RICE

★★

Cooking time:
6-7 minutes

Serves: 4

Cooking method:
stir-fry, p.42

Easy to prepare

Serve in
conjunction with
other dishes

■ PREPARATION ■

Peel and thinly slice the onions. Cut the bacon across the lean and fat into matchstick size strips. Cut the spring onions into 0.5 cm/¼ inch shreds. Lightly beat the eggs.

■ COOKING ■

Heat 2½ tablespoons of the oil in a wok or frying pan. When hot, stir-fry the onion and bacon over medium heat for 1 minute. Add the peas and continue to stir-fry for 45 seconds. Add the cooked rice and turn and toss for 45 seconds. Remove from the heat. Heat the remaining oil in a separate small wok or pan. When hot, add half the spring onions and stir over medium heat for 30 seconds. Pour in the beaten egg. Tilt the pan, so that the egg flows evenly over the bottom of the pan. After 1 minute, when the eggs have nearly set, sprinkle with the salt and the remainder of the spring onions. Stir and lightly scramble the eggs. When set, transfer the egg mixture to the rice. Stir and turn over medium heat for 1 minute.

Note: A suitable convenience food to eat with fried rice is, surprisingly, a can of sardines.

Ingredients
2 medium onions
2-3 rashers of bacon
2 spring onions
3 eggs
5 tbsp vegetable oil
3 tbsp green peas
2 bowls cooked rice (see opposite)
1 tsp salt

PLAIN COOKED RICE GRUEL OR CONGEE

★

Cooking time:
1½ hours

Serves: 4-6

Cooking method:
simmer

Easy, but takes
time to prepare

Serve with pickled
or salted foods for
breakfast or late
supper

Rice eaten at breakfast time in China is cooked with much greater quantity of water and for a much longer period of time. It is when this rice gruel or congee is cooked in the Chinese kitchen that the most steam is generated; this steam is largely utilized in producing China's numerous steamed dishes.

■ PREPARATION ■

Wash and rinse the rice, drain well. Place in a deep heavy pot or pan and add the water. Bring to the boil, reduce the heat and simmer very gently, uncovered, for 1½ hours, stirring occasionally. By this time, the rice will be fairly thick and porridgy; suitable for serving for breakfast or late supper.

■ SERVING ■

Serve accompanied by pickled or salted foods.

Ingredients
2 cups or bowls long grain white rice
10 cups or bowls water

1 recipe Basic Fried Rice (see page 69)
1 medium red pepper
50-75 g/2-3 oz bean sprouts
75 g/3 oz fresh or frozen medium or large prawns
50-75 g/2-3 oz canned straw mushrooms or 100 g/4 oz button mushrooms
1 medium courgette
2½ tbsp vegetable oil
2 tbsp sweetcorn
75 g/3 oz fresh or frozen shrimps
20 g/¾ oz lard or butter
1½ tbsp light soya sauce

YANCHOW FRIED RICE

This is the best known of all fried rice dishes, the only one permissible to be served at a party table. Yanchow Fried Rice is cooked in precisely the same manner as Basic Fried Rice, except that a few extra ingredients are added. (Yangchow is a famous river port on the Yangtze river.) The extra ingredients are all the foods which abound in the Lower Yangtze regions: namely, mushrooms, straw mushrooms (normally available canned), lotus seeds, red peppers, pimentos, bean sprouts, tomatoes, string beans and fresh water shrimps and prawns. We will endeavour to use some of these in the following recipe.

■ PREPARATION ■

Repeat the Basic Fried Rice recipe. Cut the red pepper into 0.5 cm/¼ inch pieces. Wash and dry the bean sprouts. Cut each prawn into 2-3 pieces. If using button mushrooms, quarter them. Cut the courgette into 8 sections, then further divide in quarters.

■ COOKING ■

Heat the oil in a wok or frying pan. When hot, stir-fry the pepper, mushrooms, bean sprouts, courgette, shrimps and prawns over high heat for 1½ minutes. Add the lard and light soya sauce and continue to stir-fry over medium heat for 1½ minutes. Turn the contents into the pan containing the fried rice. Reduce the heat to low, turn and stir together for 30 seconds.

★★

Cooking time: about 10 minutes

Serves: 5-6

Cooking method: stir-fry, p.42

Easy to prepare

Complements and provides bulk to a multi-dish meal

Illustrated on p.74

2 large sheets lotus leaf
225 g/8 oz long grain rice
225 g/8 oz glutinous rice
2 tbsp dried shrimps
1½ tbsp soya sauce
½ tsp salt
1½ tsp sesame oil
¼ tsp pepper
100 g/4 oz shelled shrimps
225 g/8 oz roast duck meat pieces
75 g/3 oz flaked crab meat
75 g/3 oz chopped ham

LOTUS LEAF SAVOURY RICE

This large savoury rice parcel can be made into small individual packages, simply by dividing the rice mixture into smaller portions, and wrapping and steaming in ¼ size piece lotus leaf.

■ PREPARATION ■

Soak the dried lotus leaves in warm water for 5-6 minutes to soften. Drain and wipe dry. Place and mix the two types of rice in a saucepan. Wash, drain and just cover with water. Bring to the boil and simmer for 6 minutes over very low heat until all the water has been absorbed. Soak the dried shrimps in 150 ml/¼ pint hot water to cover for 10 minutes. Pour the shrimps and soaking water into the pan containing the rice. Place the pan over low heat to simmer gently for 5 minutes. Remove from the heat, cover and leave the rice and shrimps to stand for 5 minutes to absorb the water. Add the soya sauce, salt, sesame oil and pepper and turn them over a few times. Add the duck meat, shelled shrimps, crab meat and chopped ham to the mixture, blend evenly. Wrap the savoury rice

★★★★

Cooking time: 15 minutes

Serves: 6-7

Cooking methods: simmer and steam, p.49

Lotus leaf packages take time to prepare, but cooking is straightforward

Interesting dish to serve as a dim sum

Illustrated on p.225

mixture in the double layer of lotus leaves, tying them firmly with string into a secure parcel.

■ COOKING ■

Place the lotus leaf parcel in a steamer and steam vigorously for 15 minutes.

■ SERVING ■

Bring the parcel to the table, open and the diners serve themselves.

GOLD AND SILVER RICE GRUEL (CONGEE)

★★

Cooking time: 35 minutes

Serves: 4-5

Cooking method: simmer

Easy to prepare

Serve on its own as a light meal

Illustrated on p.74

¼ *roast duck*

¼ *boiled chicken*

4 cups or bowls cooked rice gruel or congee (see page 69)

3 slices fresh root ginger

1 chicken stock cube

2 tbsp soya sauce

2 tbsp finely chopped spring onion

1 tbsp sesame oil

■ PREPARATION ■

Chop the duck and chicken into 12 equal pieces each.

■ COOKING ■

Pour the rice gruel or congee into a heavy pan or casserole. Add 2 cups or bowls of water, the ginger, duck and chicken pieces. Bring slowly to the boil. Sprinkle with the crumbled stock cube and stir in. Reduce the heat to very low and simmer gently for 30 minutes, stirring every 10 minutes.

■ SERVING ■

Ladle the rice mixture into 4 bowls, dividing the pieces of duck and chicken equally. Sprinkle the top of each bowl with about 1 teaspoon soya sauce, chopped spring onion and a drop or two of sesame oil.

| 2 cups long grain rice |
| 450g/1lb green cabbage or spring greens |
| 1½ tbsp dried shrimps |
| about 225g/8oz Chinese sausages |
| 2 tbsp vegetable oil |
| 20g/¾oz lard |
| 1½ tsp salt |

SHANGHAI VEGETABLE RICE

Surprisingly, this simple dish comes from Shanghai, the most populous and sophisticated of all Chinese cities. Without the sausage, it is a dish useful to serve with long-cooked meat dishes, such as Soy-Braised Pork (see page 196).

■ PREPARATION ■

Wash and measure the rice. Simmer in the same volume of water for 6 minutes. Remove from the heat and leave to stand, covered, for 7-8 minutes. Wash and dry the cabbage. Chop into 4 × 7.5 cm/1½ × 3 inch pieces, removing the tougher stalks. Soak the dried shrimps in hot water to cover for 7-8 minutes, then drain. Cut the sausages slantwise into 2.5 cm/ 1 inch sections.

■ COOKING ■

Heat the oil and lard in a deep saucepan. When hot, stir-fry the shrimps for 30 seconds. Add the cabbage and toss and turn for 1½ minutes until well coated with oil. Sprinkle the cabbage with the salt. Pack in the rice. Push pieces of sausages into the rice. Add 4-5 tablespoons water down the side of the pan. Cover and simmer very gently for about 15 minutes. Transfer to a heated serving dish.

★★★
Cooking time: about 15-18 minutes

Serves: 5-6

Cooking methods: stir-fry p.42 and simmer

Easy to prepare

Omitting sausages, a useful accompaniment to meat dishes

Illustrated on p.75

| 3 spring onions |
| 3 tbsp soya sauce |
| 3 tbsp wine vinegar |
| 450g/1lb wheat flour noodles, flat or Ho Fen noodles, or spaghetti |

Sauce:
| 3 tbsp peanut butter |
| 2 tbsp sesame paste |
| 3 tbsp sesame oil |

Garnish:
| radish rose |

BEGGARS' NOODLES

Although this is an extremely simple and inexpensive dish of noodles, it is surprising how appetizing and satisfying it can be.

■ PREPARATION ■

Coarsely chop or shred the onions. Mix the soya sauce and vinegar together. Mix the peanut butter, sesame paste and sesame oil together.

■ COOKING ■

Place the noodles in a saucepan of boiling water and simmer for 10 minutes, or spaghetti for about 10-12 minutes. Drain.

■ SERVING ■

Divide the hot noodles into 4-6 heated large rice bowls. Sprinkle evenly with the spring onion. Add a large spoonful of the peanut butter and sesame mixture to each bowl of noodles. Pour 1 tablespoon of soya sauce and vinegar mixture over contents of each bowl.

★
Cooking time: 10 minutes

Serves: 6

Cooking method: simmer

Easy to prepare

Inexpensive, tasty snack

Illustrated on p.78

FUKIEN CRAB RICE

▪ PREPARATION ▪

Place the bowl of glutinous rice in a saucepan with 1½ bowls of water. Bring to the boil and simmer very gently for 15 minutes. Add this rice to the cooked long grain rice and mix together. Clean and cut the leeks slantwise into 5 cm/2 inch sections. Shred the ginger. Coarsely chop the garlic. Chop each crab through the shell into 12 pieces, cracking the claws with the side of the chopper. Discard the dead men's fingers.

▪ COOKING ▪

Heat the oil in a wok or large frying pan. When very hot, add the crab pieces and turn them around in the hot oil for 3 minutes. Drain. Pour away the oil to use for other purposes, leaving 2 tablespoons. Add the lard and reheat the wok or pan. When hot, stir-fry the ginger and garlic over medium heat for 15 seconds. Add the leeks and salt and stir-fry for 1 minute. Pour in the stock and sprinkle in the crumbled stock cube, then add the tomato purée, paprika, soya sauce and sherry. Bring to the boil, stirring, and return the crab pieces to the pan. Cook over medium heat for 3 minutes. Add the blended cornflour, turn and stir a few times until thickened.

▪ SERVING ▪

Place the mixed rice into a medium 2 handled wok with a lid, or a large flameproof casserole. Pour the crab and leek mixture over the rice. Place the wok or casserole over a low heat, cover and cook gently for 5 minutes. Bring the container to the table for serving.

Ingredients
1 bowl cooked glutinous rice (see page 16)
2 bowls cooked long grain rice (see page 68)
225-350 g/8-12 oz young leeks
3 slices fresh root ginger
2 cloves garlic
2 medium crabs, about 1.5 kg/ 3 lb
150 ml/¼ pint vegetable oil
25 g/1 oz lard
1 tsp salt
200 ml/⅓ pint good stock (see page 56)
1 chicken stock cube
2 tbsp tomato purée
1 tsp paprika
1 tbsp light soya sauce
150 ml/¼ pint dry sherry
1 tbsp cornflour blended with 2 tbsp water

Gold and Silver Rice Gruel (Congee) (*above*), a substantial dish with roast duck and boiled chicken; recipe page 71.
Yangchow Fried Rice (*left*), most famous fried rice dish; recipe page 70.
Shanghai Vegetable Rice (*right*), can be cooked without the sausages; recipe page 72.

| 350-450g/12oz-1lb wheat flour or rice flour noodles |
| 225g/8oz lean pork |
| ½tsp salt |
| 4½tbsp vegetable oil |
| 50g/2oz drained, canned snow pickles |
| 225g/8oz bean sprouts |
| 2 spring onions |
| 20g/¾oz lard |
| 2tbsp soya sauce |
| 1tbsp sesame oil |

BASIC CHOW MEIN

'Chow' in Chinese means 'to stir-fry', and 'mein' means noodles, hence, 'stir-fried noodles'. Serve as a snack or add to a multi-course Chinese meal.

■ PREPARATION ■

Parboil the noodles in a saucepan of boiling water for 5 minutes, or 3 minutes for rice flour noodles. Drain. Cut the pork into matchstick-size shreds. Sprinkle with salt. Rub with 1 teaspoon of the oil. Coarsely chop the pickles. Wash and drain the bean sprouts. Cut the spring onions into 2.5cm/1 inch sections.

■ COOKING ■

Heat the vegetable oil in a wok or large frying pan. When hot, stir-fry the pork and pickles for 2½ minutes. Remove half the contents and put aside. Pour all the noodles into the pan to turn and stir for 2½ minutes. Transfer to a heated serving dish. Add the lard to the wok and return the reserved pork and pickles. Add the spring onions and stir-fry for 30 seconds over high heat. Add the bean sprouts, soya sauce and sesame oil. Continue to stir-fry for 1½ minutes.

■ SERVING ■

Spoon the stir-fried ingredients over the noodles. Toss before serving.

★★

Cooking time: about 10 minutes

Serves: 4-6

Cooking methods: parboil and stir-fry, p.42

Quick and easy to prepare

Good snack or adds bulk to a multi-course meal

| 350g/12oz packet wheat flour noodles or egg noodles |
| 350g/12oz steak, e.g. fillet, rump or sirloin |
| 2tbsp soya sauce |
| pepper to taste |
| 3 slices fresh root ginger |
| 2 spring onions |
| 4tbsp vegetable oil |
| 20g/¾oz lard |
| 1tbsp hoisin sauce |
| 2tbsp good stock (see page 56) |
| 1½tbsp dry sherry |
| 1tbsp cornflour blended with 2tbsp water |

BEEF CHOW MEIN

■ PREPARATION ■

Place the noodles in a saucepan of boiling water and simmer for 5 minutes. Drain. Cut the beef into 5 × 2.5cm/2 ×1 inch very thin slices. Rub with the soya sauce and pepper to taste. Shred the ginger. Cut the spring onions into 5cm/2 inch sections, separating the white from the green parts.

■ COOKING ■

Heat 3 tablespoons of the oil in a wok or frying pan. When hot, stir-fry the ginger and white parts of the spring onion for 30 seconds. Add the beef slices, spread them over the wok or pan, and stir-fry over high heat for 1½ minutes. Remove from the pan. Add the lard, hoisin sauce, remaining soya sauce and stock to the wok. Bring to the boil, stirring. Pour the noodles into the pan, toss and stir until heated through. Spread out on a heated serving dish. Add the remaining oil, green parts of the

★★★

Cooking time: about 10 minutes

Serves: 4-6

Cooking methods: simmer and stir-fry, p.42

Fairly quick and easy

Serve as a single snack or as part of a multi-dish meal

spring onions, sherry and beef to the wok or pan. When boiling, pour over the blended cornflour and turn the beef over a few times. Spoon the beef mixture evenly over the noodles.

SINGAPORE CHOW MEIN

★ ★ ★

Cooking time: about 10 minutes

Serves: 5-6

Cooking method: stir-fry, p.42

Fairly easy to prepare

Serve as Beef Chow Mein

Illustrated on p.79

■ PREPARATION ■

Soak the dried shrimps in hot water to cover for 8 minutes. Drain. Thinly slice the onions. Cut the bacon into matchstick size shreds. Cut the pork into 2.5 cm/1 inch lean and fat pieces. Chop the spring onions into 4 cm/1½ inch sections. Place the noodles in a saucepan of boiling water and blanch for 3 minutes. Drain.

■ COOKING ■

Heat the oil in a wok or large frying pan. When hot, stir-fry the dried shrimps, onion and bacon for 1 minute. Add the salt and curry powder and continue to stir-fry for 2 minutes. Stir in the stock. Add the noodles, turn and toss. Remove from heat. Heat the lard in a separate wok or frying pan. When hot, stir-fry the roast pork, cooked shrimps and spring onions over high heat for 1 minute. Sprinkle with soya sauce, and stir a few times. Add the bean sprouts, turn and stir for 1 minute.

■ SERVING ■

Add the freshly stir-fried ingredients to the noodles and return to a medium heat. Stir and turn the ingredients together for 1½ minutes. Sprinkle with sesame oil. Alternatively, pour the sauce over the noodles and beansprouts.

Ingredients
3 tbsp dried shrimps
2 medium onions
2 rashers bacon
225 g/8 oz Cha Siu roast pork (see page 274)
2 spring onions
350 g/12 oz packet rice flour noodles
4 tbsp vegetable oil
1½ tsp salt
1-1½ tbsp curry powder or to taste
4 tbsp good stock (see page 56)
20 g/¾ oz lard
100 g/4 oz shelled shrimps
1½ tbsp soya sauce
75 g/3 oz bean sprouts
1 tsp sesame oil

Beggars' Noodles (*left*), a
simple dish garnished with
a radish rose; recipe page
73.
Singapore Chow Mein
(above), a colourful dish
using Cha Siu roast pork;
recipe page 77.

2 tbsp dried shrimps

3 tbsp dry sherry

3 tbsp light soya sauce

2 tbsp wine vinegar

1½ tsp red chilli oil

2 spring onions

450 g/1 lb freshly-made noodles or 350 g/12 oz wheat flour noodles

2½ tbsp Sichuan hot Ja Chai pickles, coarsely chopped

2 tbsp snow pickles, coarsely chopped

1½ tbsp winter pickles, coarsely chopped

1½ tsp sesame oil

SHANGHAI COLD-TOSSED NOODLES

★★
Cooking time: about 3-6 minutes

Serves: 3-4

No cooking except for initial blanching or boiling of noodles

A good starter or summer snack

■ PREPARATION ■

Soak the dried shrimps in hot water to cover for 5 minutes. Drain and coarsely chop. Add the shrimps to the sherry and leave to soak for 15 minutes. Mix the soya sauce, vinegar and red chilli oil together. Cut the spring onions into 1 cm/½ inch shreds.

■ COOKING ■

Place the freshly-made noodles in a saucepan of boiling water and blanch for 3 minutes; if using wheat noodles, simmer for 5-6 minutes. Remove from heat and leave to soak in the hot water for a further 5-6 minutes. Drain and cool.

■ SERVING ■

Spread the noodles on a large serving dish. Sprinkle them evenly with the chopped pickles, shrimps and sherry, then the soya sauce mixture. Finally, add the spring onion shreds and sesame oil.

To serve the Chinese way, the diners mix and toss the noodles they require and transfer it to their bowls, adjusting any additional seasonings of soya sauce, red chilli oil or vinegar.

---

450 g/1 lb leg of lamb

2 slices fresh root ginger

1½ tbsp cornflour

4 tbsp vegetable oil

675 g/1½ lb mutton

3 medium onions

3 cloves garlic

350 g/12 oz young leeks

1 chicken stock cube

1 tsp salt

350 g/12 oz wheat flour noodles

15 g/½ oz lard

2 tbsp soya sauce

½ tbsp yellow bean paste

1 tbsp red chilli oil

1 tbsp prepared English mustard

MANCHURIAN BOILED AND BRAISED LAMB NOODLES

★★★
Cooking time: about 1½ hours

Serves: 6-8

Cooking methods: long simmer and stir-fry, p.42

Fairly easy to prepare

A substantial snack or useful addition to a multi-dish meal for hearty appetites

PREPARATION

Cut the lamb into 4 × 2.5 cm/1½ × 1 inch thin slices. Finely chop the ginger. Dust and rub the lamb with the ginger, cornflour and 1 tablespoon of the vegetable oil. Cut the mutton into 2.5 cm/1 inch cubes. Slice the onions. Coarsely chop the garlic. Clean and cut the leeks into 2.5 cm/1 inch sections

■ COOKING ■

Parboil the mutton in a saucepan of boiling water for 5 minutes. Drain. Place the mutton in a flameproof casserole and add 900 ml/1½ pt water, the crumbled stock cube, salt and onion. Bring to the boil and simmer gently for 1¼ hours or until the stock is reduced by a quarter. Place the noodles in a saucepan of boiling water and blanch for 3 minutes. Drain and add to the mutton. Cook for 10 minutes.

Meanwhile, heat the remaining oil in a wok or frying pan. When hot, stir-fry the leeks for 2 minutes, then push to the sides of the pan. Add the lard to the centre of the wok or pan. When hot, stir-fry the lamb and garlic over high for 1 minute. Add the soya sauce and yellow bean paste and stir-fry with the lamb for 1 minute. Mix the leeks with the lamb and stir-fry for 1 minute.

■ SERVING ■

Pour the noodles and mutton into a deep-sided heated serving dish. Pour the lamb and leeks over them. Trickle the red chilli oil and mustard in a criss-cross pattern over the dish.

SICHUAN DAN DAN NOODLES

★ ★ ★

Cooking time: about 15 minutes

Serves: 5-6

Cooking methods: simmer and stir-fry, p.42

Very versatile dish. Can be served as a starter, a final soup or just a spicy snack

■ PREPARATION ■

Place the noodles in a saucepan of boiling water and blanch for 3 minutes. Drain. Divide the noodles into 5-6 heated individual bowls. Heat the stock in a saucepan, add the salt and crumbled stock cube. Stir in the peanut butter, red chilli oil and sesame paste. Stir and slowly bring to the boil. Put aside. Cut the spring onions into 1 cm/½ inch shreds. Soak the dried mushrooms in hot water to cover for 25 minutes. Drain and discard the tough stalks. Coarsely chop the mushroom caps. Soak the dried shrimps in hot water to cover for 15 minutes. Drain and coarsely chop. Deseed and finely chop the chillies. Coarsely chop the onions and pickles.

■ COOKING ■

Heat the vegetable oil in a wok or frying pan. When hot, stir-fry the dried mushrooms, dried shrimps, chilli and onion over high heat for 1½ minutes. Add the pork and stir-fry for 2 minutes. Add the soya sauce, yellow bean paste and chilli sauce and continue to stir-fry for a further 1½ minutes. Add the blended cornflour and cook, stirring, for 1 minute until thickened.

■ SERVING ■

Reheat the flavoured stock. When boiling, pour an equal amount of stock into the 5-6 bowls of noodles. Sprinkle the bowls with the spring onion and sesame oil. Then pour an equal amount of sauce over the noodles.

Ingredients
225-350 g/8-12 oz packet rice flour noodles
750 ml/1¼ pt good stock (see page 56)
1 tsp salt
1 chicken stock cube
2 tbsp peanut butter
2 tsp red chilli oil
1 tbsp sesame paste
2 spring onions
2½ tbsp vegetable oil
Meat sauce:
6 medium dried Chinese mushrooms
2 tbsp dried shrimps
2 dried red chillies
2 medium onions
2 tbsp Sichuan hot Ja Chai pickles
225 g/8 oz minced pork
1½ tbsp soya sauce
1½ tbsp yellow bean paste
2 tsp chilli sauce
1 tbsp cornflour blended with 3 tbsp water
1 tbsp sesame oil

1 medium onion
2 slices fresh root ginger
2 cloves garlic
4 spring onions
15 cm/6 inch section cucumber
450 g/1 lb wheat flour noodles
    (like spaghetti)
4 tbsp vegetable oil
225 g/8 oz minced pork
½ tsp salt
1 tbsp yellow bean paste
1 tbsp soya sauce
4 tbsp good stock (see page 56)
1 tbsp cornflour blended with
    3 tbsp water

■ PEKING JA CHIANG ■ MEIN NOODLES

■ PREPARATION ■

Coarsely chop the onion, ginger and garlic. Cut the spring onions into 6 cm/2½ inch sections (dividing the larger stalks in half or a quarter). Cut the cucumber into matchstick-size shreds. Place the noodles in a saucepan of boiling water and simmer for 8-10 minutes. Drain. Rinse the noodles under running cold water to keep separate.

■ COOKING ■

Heat the oil in a wok or large frying pan. When hot, stir-fry the onion and ginger for 1 minute. Add the garlic and pork and stir-fry over medium heat for 3 minutes. Add the salt, yellow bean paste and soya sauce. Stir and cook for 3 minutes. Mix in the stock and continue to cook for a further 3 minutes. Pour in the blended cornflour, stirring until thickened.

■ SERVING ■

Reheat the noodles by dipping them in boiling water for 15 seconds, then drain thoroughly. Arrange them on a large heated serving dish. Pour the sauce into the centre of the noodles. Arrange the shredded cucumber and spring onion sections on either side of the sauce.

★★★
Cooking time: about 15 minutes
Serves: 4-6
Cooking methods: simmer and stir-fry, p.42
Fairly easy to prepare
Serve alone or as an accompaniment

5 large dried Chinese
    mushrooms
100 g/4 oz transparent pea-
    starched noodles
2 tsp dried shrimps
3 slices fresh root ginger
3 spring onions
100 g/4 oz lean pork
2 tbsp vegetable oil
300 ml/½ pt good stock (see
    page 56)
1 chicken stock cube
2 tbsp light soya sauce
1½ tbsp vinegar
½ tsp salt
¼ tsp pepper

BRAISED TRANSPARENT PEA-STARCHED NOODLES

■ PREPARATION ■

Soak the dried mushrooms in hot water to cover for 25 minutes. Drain and discard the tough stalks. Cut the mushroom caps into shreds. Soak the noodles in hot water to cover for 3 minutes, then drain. Soak the dried shrimps in hot water to cover for 5 minutes. Cut the ginger and spring onions into similar sized shreds as the mushrooms. Dice the pork.

■ COOKING ■

Heat the oil in a wok or frying pan. When hot, stir-fry the shrimps, ginger, pork and mushrooms over a medium heat for 1½ minutes. Add the spring onions, stock, crumbled stock cube and soya sauce. Bring to the boil and simmer gently for 4-5 minutes. Add the noodles, vinegar, salt and pepper. Stir and mix the contents evenly and continue to simmer for another 4-5 minutes.

★★★
Cooking time: 10-12 minutes
Serves: 4-6
Cooking method: stir-fry, p.42
Fairly easy to prepare
Good addition to meat or vegetable dish accompanied with rice
Illustrated on p.90

★★★

Cooking time:
about 15 minutes

Serves: 5-6

Cooking method:
stir-fry, p.42

Fairly easy to
prepare

Useful addition to
a main meal or
tasty snack

'TEN TREASURE' TAPESTRY NOODLES

This classical noodle dish, called in Chinese Shih Jing Chow Mein, is popular and widely cooked, partly because you can use odds and ends of ingredients already in the kitchen – well, at least in a Chinese kitchen. These 'bits and pieces' are the 'Ten Treasures'!

■ PREPARATION ■

Shred the bacon. Cut the pork, beef and chicken into similar matchstick-sized shreds. Rub the meats with the salt. Dust with the cornflour. Coat with the egg white. Cut the bamboo shoots and celery into similar matchstick-sized shreds. Cut the spring onions into 2.5 cm/1 inch sections, separating the white parts from the green. Top and tail the French beans and parboil in boiling water for 2 minutes. Drain. Soak the dried mushrooms in hot water to cover for 25 minutes. Drain and discard the tough stalks. Cut the mushroom caps into shreds. Blend the remainder of the cornflour with the stock and 1 tablespoon soya sauce. Place the noodles in a saucepan of boiling water and simmer for 4 minutes. Drain.

■ COOKING ■

Heat the oil in a wok or large frying pan. When hot, stir-fry the pork, chicken, beef, bacon and white parts of the spring onion over high heat for 2½ minutes. Remove two-thirds of the contents and put aside. Add all the vegetables and 15 g/½ oz of the lard to the wok or pan and stir-fry for 2 minutes. Stir in 2 tablespoons soya sauce and half the blended cornflour. Cook for 1 minute. Pour in the noodles, turn and mix for 1½ minutes until the noodles are heated through. Heat the remaining lard in a separate wok or pan. When hot, add the green parts of the spring onion and the reserved two-thirds meat mixture. Stir-fry over high heat for 1 minute. Pour in the remainder of the soya sauce and stir-fry for 30 seconds. Add the remainder of the blended cornflour, the sherry and sesame oil. Continue to stir and mix for 30 seconds.

■ SERVING ■

Spread the noodle mixture on to a large heated serving dish. Pour over the meat mixture from the second pan.

Ingredients
2 rashers of bacon
50-75 g/2-3 oz pork
50 g/2 oz beef or lamb
50 g/2 oz chicken
1 tsp salt
2 tbsp cornflour
1 egg white
50 g/2 oz canned bamboo shoots
2 sticks celery
2 spring onions
50-75 g/2-3 oz French beans
4 dried Chinese mushrooms
5 tbsp good stock (see page 56)
4 tbsp soya sauce
225-350 g/8-12 oz packet egg noodles or wheat flour noodles
4 tbsp vegetable oil
40 g/1½ oz lard
1 tbsp dry sherry
1 tsp sesame oil

VEGETABLES

The Chinese are at least partially vegetarian. The majority of Chinese families only eat meat about a couple of times a month, and most of these meat dishes are constituted of two-thirds vegetable. Quick stir-frying, which is one of the primary methods used in Chinese cooking, is particularly suitable for cooking vegetable dishes. Among the seasonings used there is likely to be some soya sauce and other soya bean derivatives, such as soya bean 'cheese', soya paste and hoisin sauce.

What the Chinese endeavour to do with their vegetables is to both inject and draw out flavour, by adding meat stock or gravy, oil and fat impregnated with the flavour of strong-tasting vegetables such as garlic, ginger, onion, various dried food and pickles. The aroma is then enhanced by adding some sesame oil and freshly cut spring onions at the last minute. Such treatment seems to have a beneficial effect on both short-cooked and long-cooked vegetable dishes. The latter are cooked over a very low heat and the vegetables sweated in their own juices to bring out their flavour.

1 kg/2 lb selected spring greens
1½ tbsp finely chopped dried shrimps
vegetable oil for deep-frying
6 tbsp blanched almonds
¾ tsp salt
1½ tsp caster sugar
¼ tsp MSG (optional)

CRISPY 'SEAWEED' WITH ALMONDS

■ PREPARATION ■
Remove the stalks from the spring greens and, with a sharp knife, cut the leaves into very fine shreds. Spread them out on absorbent kitchen paper to dry. Soak the dried shrimps in hot water to cover for 15 minutes. Drain and finely chop.

■ COOKING ■
Heat the oil in a wok or deep-fryer. When hot, fry the almonds until crisp, then drain well. Reheat the oil. When beginning to smoke, fry the spring greens for 3 minutes, turning and stirring occasionally. Remove with a long-handled metal sieve and drain well on absorbent kitchen paper.

■ SERVING ■
Pile the crispy 'seaweed' on to a heated serving plate. Sprinkle on the salt, sugar, monosodium glutamate, if using, and dried shrimps. Surprisingly, this 'seaweed' tastes like the real thing.

★★★

Cooking time: about 10 minutes

Serves: 4-6

Cooking method: deep-fry, p.45

A good starter dish

To shred greens, p.31

COLD TOSSED CUCUMBER SALAD

★
Preparation time:
about 40 minutes,
including
seasoning time

No cooking

Serves: 4-6

Quick and easy to
prepare

Complements rich
savoury dishes

Illustrated on p.90

1 medium cucumber
2 tsp salt
2 tbsp sugar
3 tbsp vinegar
1 tbsp vegetable oil
2¾ tbsp sesame oil
¼ tsp MSG (optional)

▓ PREPARATION ▓

Cut the cucumber slantwise into 3 mm/⅛ inch slices or cut into 5 cm/2 inch shreds. Place in a large bowl and sprinkle evenly with salt. Leave to season for 30 minutes. Pour away any water from the cucumber. Sprinkle the cucumber with sugar and vinegar, and toss together. Just before serving, add the oils and monosodium glutamate, if using. Toss well and sprinkle with presoaked, chopped dried shrimps, if liked.

QUICK FRIED MANGE TOUT

★
Cooking time:
about 8 minutes

Serves: 4-6

Cooking method:
stir-fry, p.42

Quick to prepare

Ideal
accompaniment to
meat dishes

450 g/1 lb mange tout
2 cloves garlic
150 ml/¼ pt vegetable oil for frying
¼ tsp MSG (optional)
1 tbsp light soya sauce
1 tbsp oyster sauce
2 tbsp good stock (see page 56)

This bright green vegetable dish is very attractive to serve with all meat dishes.

▓ PREPARATION ▓

Clean, trim, top and tail the mange tout. Crush the garlic.

▓ COOKING ▓

Heat the oil in a wok or frying pan. When hot, stir-fry the mange tout over high heat for 1 minute. Reduce the heat to low and continue to stir-fry for another minute. Drain off excess oil. Sprinkle the mange tout with the garlic, monosodium glutamate, if using, soya sauce, oyster sauce and stock. Simmer gently for 1½ minutes.

YANGTZE STIR-FRIED BROAD BEANS

★
Cooking time:
10 minutes

Serves: 4-6

Cooking methods:
stir-fry p.42 and
simmer

Easy to prepare

Complements
meat dishes

450 g/1 lb broad beans
2 spring onions
4 tbsp vegetable oil
2 tsp salt
3 tsp sugar
pinch of MSG (optional)
4 tbsp good stock (see page 56)
15 g/½ oz lard

▓ PREPARATION ▓

Blanch the beans in a pan of boiling water for 3 minutes, then drain. Cut the spring onions into 1 cm/½ inch shreds.

▓ COOKING ▓

Heat the oil in a wok or frying pan. When hot, stir-fry the spring onions and beans over medium heat for 1 minute. Add the salt, sugar, monosodium glutamate, if using, and stock. Stir and turn together a few times. Cover, reduce the heat to low and cook gently for 5 minutes. Add the lard and stir gently a few times.

| 1 medium Chinese white or Savoy cabbage, about 1.5 kg/3½ lb |
| 4 tbsp vegetable oil |
| 20 g/¾ oz lard |
| 4 tbsp soya sauce |
| 1 tbsp sugar |
| pepper to taste |
| 5 tbsp good stock (see page 56) |
| 1 chicken stock cube |

RED-COOKED CABBAGE

▓ PREPARATION ▓

Remove the cabbage stalk and any discoloured leaves. Cut the cabbage into 6 × 5 cm/2½ × 2 inch pieces.

▓ COOKING ▓

Heat the oil and lard in a wok or large saucepan. When hot, add all the cabbage and toss for 1 minute. Add the soya sauce, sugar, pepper, stock and crumbled stock cube and continue to stir and turn for another minute. Reduce the heat to low, cover and cook for 10 minutes, turning occasionally.

★
Cooking time: 15 minutes

Serves: 6-7

Cooking methods: stir-fry p.42 and simmer

Easy to prepare

Serve with savoury dishes and rice accompaniment

| 450 g/1 lb Chinese white cabbage |
| 6 dried Chinese mushrooms |
| 1 tbsp dried shrimps |
| 4 tbsp vegetable oil |
| 15 g/½ oz lard |
| 1 tsp salt |
| 1 tsp sugar |
| 2 tsp light soya sauce |
| 4 tbsp good stock (see page 56) |
| 1 tsp sesame oil |

STIR-FRIED CHINESE CABBAGE
WITH CHINESE MUSHROOMS AND DRIED SHRIMPS

▓ PREPARATION ▓

Cut the cabbage into 6 × 5 cm/2½ × 2 inch slices. Soak the dried mushrooms and shrimps separately in hot water to cover for 25 minutes. Drain and discard the tough mushroom stalks. Cut the mushroom caps into quarters.

▓ COOKING ▓

Heat the vegetable oil and lard in a wok or frying pan. When hot, stir-fry the dried mushrooms and shrimps for 30 seconds. Add the cabbage and stir-fry for 1 minute. Add the salt, sugar, soya sauce and stock and continue to stir-fry for another 1 minute. Reduce the heat to low, cover and cook for a further 1 minute. Sprinkle on the sesame oil and toss. Serve hot.

★
Cooking time: about 10 minutes

Serves: 4-6

Cooking method: stir-fry, p.42

Quick and easy to prepare

Complements meat and savoury dishes

| 2 bunches watercress |
| 10 medium drained, canned water chestnuts |
| ½ tsp salt |
| 2 tsp sugar |
| 1 tsp red chilli oil |
| 2 tsp vegetable oil |
| 2 tsp sesame oil |
| 1 tbsp light soya sauce |

WATERCRESS AND WATER CHESTNUT SALAD

▓ PREPARATION ▓

Cut away the tough stalks of the watercress. Clean thoroughly and blanch in a pan of boiling water for 1 minute. Drain and rinse in cold water. Dry thoroughly and chop finely. Place the watercress and water chestnuts in a bowl. Add the salt, sugar, oils and soya sauce. Toss well and serve.

★
Preparation time: 15 minutes

Serves: 4-6

Quick and easy to prepare

Serve with meat and savoury dishes

WHITE CABBAGE SALAD

★
Preparation time: about 10 minutes

Serves: 5-6

Quick to prepare

Ideal with rich and/or meaty dishes

½ Chinese white cabbage, about 1 kg/2 lb
½ tsp salt
2 tsp sugar
2 tbsp light soya sauce
1 tbsp vegetable oil
½ tbsp sesame oil

■ PREPARATION ■

Cut the cabbage into 7.5 × 1 cm/3 × ½ inch strips. Blanch in a pan of boiling water for 2 minutes, then drain. Dry well and place the cabbage in a large bowl. Add the salt, sugar, soya sauce and oils; toss well and serve.

CHINESE WHITE CHINESE CABBAGE WITH CHILLIES

★
Preparation time: 20 minutes plus 2-3 days seasoning

Serves: 5-6

Easy and quick to prepare except time required to season

Good accompaniment to rich and meaty dishes

Illustrated on p.91

1 Chinese white cabbage, about 1.5 kg/3½ lb
3 small fresh red chillies
2 dried red chillies
1½ tsp Sichuan peppercorns
2 tsp salt
½ tsp sesame oil
1 tbsp vegetable oil

■ PREPARATION ■

Chop the cabbage coarsely, discarding the tougher parts. Coarsely chop the chillies, discarding the seeds. Pound the peppercorns lightly. Place the cabbage in a large bowl, sprinkle evenly with the salt, chillies and peppercorns. Toss to mix. Refrigerate for 2-3 days before serving. Sprinkle the cabbage with the oils; toss well and serve.

WHITE-COOKED CABBAGE

★★
Cooking time: 15 minutes

Serves: 6-7

Cooking methods: stir-fry p.42 and simmer

Easy to prepare

Serve with meat and savoury dishes with rice

1½ tbsp dried shrimps
1 medium Chinese white or Savoy cabbage, about 1.5 kg/3½ lb
2 slices fresh root ginger
4 tbsp vegetable oil
20 g/¾ oz butter
½ tsp salt
pepper to taste
8 tbsp good stock (see page 56)
1½ chicken stock cubes
1 tsp sesame oil

■ PREPARATION ■

Soak the dried shrimps in hot water to cover for 15 minutes. Drain. Remove the cabbage stalk and any discoloured leaves. Cut the cabbage into 6 × 5 cm/2½ × 2 inch pieces Finely shred the ginger.

■ COOKING ■

Heat the vegetable oil and butter in a wok or large saucepan. When hot, stir-fry the ginger and shrimps for 15 seconds. Add the cabbage and sprinkle with the salt, pepper, stock and crumbled stock cubes. Bring to the boil. Toss a few times and reduce the heat to low. Cover and simmer gently for 10 minutes, turning occasionally. Sprinkle with sesame oil before serving.

50g/2oz 'hair' seaweed

6-8 dried Chinese mushrooms

150-175g/5-6oz Chinese white cabbage

50g/2oz bean curd skins, if available

vegetable oil for deep-frying

6 water chestnuts

50-75g/2-3oz canned bamboo shoots

2-3 tbsp pine nuts

300ml/½pt good stock (see page 56)

1 tsp salt

1½ tbsp light soya sauce

½ tsp MSG (optional)

2 tbsp vegetable oil

1 tsp sesame oil

1 tbsp cornflour blended with 3 tbsp water

THE BUDDHIST'S DELIGHT

This dish is eaten by all Chinese on the first day of the New Year. It is meant to cleanse the body. Among the older Chinese, meat is not eaten on New Year's Day.

■ PREPARATION ■

Soak the seaweed in warm water for 15 minutes. Drain. Soak the dried mushrooms in hot water to cover for 25 minutes. Drain and discard the tough stalks. Quarter the mushroom caps. Tear the cabbage into 5-7.5cm/2-3 inch pieces. Soak the bean curd skins in boiling water for 15 minutes. Drain. Deep-fry for 2 minutes. Cut each water chestnut into eighths. Cut the bamboo shoots the same size as the water chestnuts.

■ COOKING ■

Place the seaweed, mushrooms, cabbage, bean curd skins, water chestnuts, bamboo shoots and pine nuts in a wok or saucepan. Add the stock, salt, soya sauce, monosodium glutamate, if using, and the 2 tablespoons vegetable oil. Bring to the boil and simmer gently for 5 minutes. Add the sesame oil and blended cornflour, bring to the boil again and simmer for 2 minutes, stirring. Serve in a large bowl or deep-sided serving dish.

★★★
Cooking time: 12-15 minutes

Serves: 6-8

Cooking methods: deep-fry p.45 and simmer

Good accompaniment to meat dishes

450g/1lb young spinach

2 cloves garlic

4 tbsp vegetable oil

15g/½oz lard

1½ tsp bean curd cheese

15g/½oz bean curd cheese

½ tsp salt

¾ tsp sugar

¼ tsp MSG (optional)

QUICK-FRIED SPINACH WITH GARLIC AND BEAN CURD CHEESE

Unlike bean curd which is bland and somewhat tasteless, bean curd cheese, called Fu Yu in Chinese, comes in jars and small cans and is highly salty. Only a small quantity should be used at a time.

■ PREPARATION ■

Remove the tough stalks from the spinach. Cut the leaves into 7.5cm/3 inch slices. Wash thoroughly and drain well. Finely chop the garlic.

■ COOKING ■

Heat the oil and lard in a wok or frying pan. When hot, stir in the garlic and cheese until mixed. Add the spinach and stir-fry over high heat for about 1½ minutes. Sprinkle the spinach evenly with salt, sugar and monosodium glutamate, if using. Continue to stir-fry for another 30 seconds.

★
Cooking time: about 5 minutes

Serves: 4-6

Cooking method: stir-fry, p.42

Quick and easy to prepare

Serve as an accompaniment to meat and savoury dishes

MADAM FEI'S SPINACH AND RADISH SALAD

★ ★

Preparation time: 15 minutes

Serves: 4-6

Quite easy to prepare

Ideal starter or accompaniment to meat dishes

Illustrated on p.95

This dish makes an extremely effective starter.

■ PREPARATION ■

Clean and trim the radishes. Flatten with the side of a cleaver or with a meat tenderizer. Sprinkle with 1 teaspoon of the salt. Clean the spinach, remove all the tough stalks and discoloured leaves. Place the leaves into a saucepan and pour a kettleful of boiling water over the leaves. Strain immediately and rinse with cold water. Strain away all the water and dry thoroughly. Chop the spinach. Sprinkle the remaining salt, the soya sauce, sugar, oil, pepper and monosodium glutamate, if using, over the spinach. Mix the spinach well with the seasonings. Arrange on a large platter and place the salted radish on top.

1 bunch of large or medium-sized red radishes

2 tsp salt

900g/2lb young tender spinach, with small leaves

2 tsp light soya sauce

1½ tsp caster sugar

3 tsp sesame oil

pinch of pepper

¼ tsp MSG (optional)

Garnish:
radish roses

STIR-FRIED SPINACH IN SHRIMP SAUCE

★ ★

Cooking time: about 8 minutes

Serves: 5-7

Cooking method: stir-fry, p.42

Quick and easy to prepare

Good with meat and savoury dishes

WITH BEAN CURD CHEESE

■ PREPARATION ■

Soak the dried shrimps in hot water to cover for 25 minutes. Drain. Wash and trim the spinach. Finely chop the garlic.

■ COOKING ■

Heat the oil in a wok or frying pan. When hot, stir-fry the shrimps for 15 seconds. Add the spinach and turn around quickly for 1 minute until well coated with oil. Push the spinach to the side of the wok or pan. Add the garlic, bean curd cheese and stock to the centre of the wok or pan. Stir them around for a few seconds, then stir in the spinach. Sprinkle evenly with the shrimp sauce and salt. Turn and stir for 1 minute. Add the lard, continue to stir and turn. By this time the spinach will be glistening and full of flavour. Transfer the spinach mixture to a heated dish and serve.

1 tbsp dried shrimps

675g/1½lb spinach

3 cloves garlic

5 tbsp vegetable oil

½ tbsp bean curd cheese

1½ tbsp good stock (see page 56)

1½ tbsp shrimp sauce

½ tsp salt

20g/¾oz lard

Cold Tossed Cucumber Salad (*above left*), a simple vegetable accompaniment garnished with chopped dried shrimps; recipe page 85.
Quick Fried French Beans with Dried Shrimps and Pork (*centre left*), a substantial vegetable dish; recipe page 97.
Braised Pea-starched Noodles (*below left*), good accompaniment to meat or vegetable dish and boiled rice; recipe page 82.
Chinese White Cabbage with Chillies (*right*), an excellent accompaniment to rice gruel or congee; recipe page 86.

450g/1lb celery

Mustard dressing:

2tbsp prepared English
    mustard

1/2tsp salt

1tbsp warm water

6tbsp water

1tbsp light soya sauce

1/2tsp sugar

1/4tsp MSG (optional)

2tsp cornflour blended with
    2tbsp water

COLD TOSSED CELERY IN MUSTARD SAUCE

■ PREPARATION ■

To make the dressing, mix the mustard with the salt and warm water. Bring the 6 tablespoons water to the boil in a small pan and add the soya sauce, sugar, monosodium glutamate, if using, and blended cornflour. Stir until the liquid thickens, add the mustard mixture and leave to cool. Wash the celery well and chop off the leaves and tough ends. Cut the stalks into 5 × 2.5 cm/2 × 1 inch sections and place in a bowl. Pour the cooled sauce over the celery.

★
Preparation time: 30 minutes, including cooling time

Serves: 4-5

Easy to prepare

Complements meat dishes

450g/1lb broccoli

4tbsp vegetable oil

2tbsp oyster sauce

3tbsp crab meat

2tbsp dry sherry

3tbsp good stock (see page 56)

15g/1/2oz lard

2tsp cornflour blended with
    2tbsp water

QUICK-FRIED BROCCOLI IN OYSTER SAUCE WITH CRAB

■ PREPARATION ■

Break the broccoli into florets, removing any tough stalks.

■ COOKING ■

Heat the oil in a wok or frying pan. When hot, stir-fry the broccoli over high heat for 1 minute. Add the oyster sauce and stir-fry for another minute. Break up the crab meat and sprinkle with sherry, stock and chopped lard. Add to the pan and turn together for 30 seconds. Sprinkle with the blended cornflour and stir until the sauce thickens.

★
Cooking time: about 10 minutes

Serves: 4-6

Cooking method: stir-fry, p.42

Quick and easy to prepare

Serve as accompaniment to meat dishes

100g/4oz mange tout

75g/3oz drained, canned
    bamboo shoots

75g/3oz asparagus

75g/3oz carrot

75g/3oz ham

vegetable oil for deep-frying

3 slices fresh root ginger

1 1/2tbsp light soya sauce

1 1/2tbsp good stock (see page
    56)

1tbsp dry sherry

20g/3/4oz lard

1/2tsp sesame oil

SAUTE OF FOUR VEGETABLES

■ PREPARATION ■

Cut the mange tout, bamboo shoots, asparagus, carrot and ham into double-size matchstick shreds.

■ COOKING ■

Heat the vegetable oil in wok or deep-fryer. When hot, fry the vegetables for 2 1/2 minutes. Drain. Reserve the oil to use for other purposes, leaving 3 tablespoons. Reheat the wok or frying pan with the oil. When hot, stir-fry the ginger for 1 minute. Remove and discard. Add the ham, then the vegetables to the wok or pan and stir-fry for 1 minute. Stir in the soya sauce, stock and sherry. Sauté for 1 1/2 minutes. Add and melt the lard. Turn and toss the vegetables in the lard until glossy. Sprinkle over the sesame oil, turn once more and serve.

★★
Cooking time: about 5-10 minutes

Serves: 4

Cooking methods: deep-fry p.45 and stir-fry p.42

Illustrated on p.95

BEAN SPROUTS WITH GARLIC AND SPRING ONIONS

■ PREPARATION ■

Remove any discoloured bean sprouts, rinse under running cold water, drain and dry. Finely chop the garlic. Cut the spring onions into 2.5 cm/1 inch shreds.

■ COOKING ■

Heat the oil and lard in a wok or frying pan. When hot, stir-fry the garlic and pickles for 30 seconds. Add the spring onions, bean sprouts and sprinkle with the salt. Stir-fry over medium heat for 1½ minutes. Add the monosodium glutamate, if using, and stock and stir-fry quickly for 30 seconds. Stir in the blended cornflour to thicken the sauce.

450g/1 lb bean sprouts

3 cloves garlic

2 spring onions

4 tbsp vegetable oil

15g/½oz lard

2 tsp drained, canned finely chopped Sichuan Ja Chai hot pickles

1½ tsp salt

¼ tsp MSG (optional)

2 tbsp good stock (see page 56)

2 tsp cornflour blended with 2 tbsp water

DEEP-FRIED AUBERGINE CAKES

■ PREPARATION ■

Soak the dried shrimps in hot water to cover for 15 minutes. Drain and finely chop. Discard the aubergine stalks. Without peeling, cut the aubergine flesh diagonally into 0.5 cm/¼ inch slices, cutting one slice right through, but leaving every second slice connected at the base, which makes a pocket for stuffing. Finely chop the spring onions and ginger.

For the stuffing, mix together the pork, shrimps, salt, spring onions, soya sauce, ginger and sesame oil. Place equal amounts of filling in the space between each 2 hinged slices of aubergine. Mix the batter ingredients together and use to coat the stuffed aubergine slices.

■ COOKING ■

Heat the oil in wok or deep-fryer. When very hot, fry the coated aubergine slices for about 4 minutes. Drain. Meanwhile, make the dip. Fry the salt and pepper in a dry frying pan over low heat for about 30 seconds.

■ SERVING ■

Arrange the aubergine cakes on a heated plate. Surround the plate with a few saucers of the salt and pepper dip. Dip the aubergine cakes into the lightly aromatic dip before eating.

1½ tbsp dried shrimps

3 medium aubergines

2 spring onions

2 slices fresh root ginger

4 tbsp finely chopped belly pork

½ tsp salt

1 tbsp soya sauce

1 tbsp sesame oil

vegetable oil for deep-frying

Batter:

150g/5 oz plain flour

25g/1 oz cornflour

3 tbsp water

1 egg

Salt and pepper dip:

2 tbsp sea salt

2 tbsp pounded Sichuan peppercorns

Fu-Yung Cauliflower
(*left*), a light vegetable dish
with chicken; recipe page
97.
Madam Fei's Spinach and
Radish Salad (*above right*), a
good starter with attractive
radish garnish; recipe page
89.
Sauté of Four Vegetables
(*below left*), a colourful dish
garnished with carrot
flowers; recipe page 92.

350 g/12 oz Chinese white cabbage

40 g/1½ oz lard

salt and pepper to taste

5 tbsp good stock (see page 56)

3 tbsp vegetable oil

2 slices fresh root ginger

1 tbsp chopped white part of spring onion

150–175 g/5–6 oz crab meat

1 tbsp dry sherry or white wine

CRAB MEAT WITH CREAM OF CHINESE CABBAGE

■ PREPARATION ■

Cut the cabbage into 1–2.5 cm/½–1 inch sections.

■ COOKING ■

Heat the lard in a wok or frying pan. When hot, stir-fry the cabbage for 1 minute. Sprinkle with salt and pepper to taste and add 3 tablespoons of the stock. Stir-fry for 1½ minutes. Transfer to heated dish. Reheat the wok or frying pan with oil. When hot, stir-fry the ginger and white part of spring onion over medium heat for 30 seconds. Add the crab meat, stir and mix. Sprinkle with salt and pepper and add the remaining stock and sherry or white wine. Stir-fry over high heat for 30 seconds. Spoon over the cabbage in the dish.

★★

Cooking time: 5–6 minutes

Serves: 4–6

Cooking method: stir-fry, p.42

4 medium firm aubergines

3 slices fresh root ginger

3 cloves garlic

3 spring onions

6 tbsp vegetable oil

1½ tbsp Sichuan hot Tou Pan paste

2 tbsp soya sauce

1 tbsp sugar

½ tsp salt

8 tbsp good stock (see page 56)

¼ tsp MSG (optional)

1 tbsp vinegar

1 tsp sesame oil

SICHUAN BRAISED AUBERGINE

■ PREPARATION ■

Remove the aubergine stalks and, without peeling, cut aubergine flesh slantwise into approximately 6 × 4 cm/ 2½ × 1½ inch pieces. Finely chop the ginger and garlic. Cut the spring onions into fine shreds.

■ COOKING ■

Heat the vegetable oil in a wok or frying pan. When hot, add the aubergine pieces and stir and turn a few times. Reduce the heat to low and stir-fry for about 5 minutes until the aubergine pieces are soft. Press the aubergine to squeeze out any excess water or oil. Remove and set aside. Add the garlic, ginger and bean paste to the pan. Stir them a few times, then add the soya sauce, sugar, salt, stock and monosodium glutamate, if using. Bring to the boil, return the aubergines to the pan and cook until the sauce reduces to a glaze. Sprinkle the aubergine with the vinegar, sesame oil and spring onions. Turn the aubergines once more before serving.

★★

Cooking time: 12 minutes

Serves: 4–6

Cooking method: stir-fry p.42 and simmer

Easy to prepare

A rich dish, good with rice

QUICK-FRIED FRENCH BEANS WITH DRIED SHRIMPS AND PORK

★★
Cooking time: about 8-10 minutes

Serves: 4-6

Cooking methods: deep-fry p.45 and stir-fry p.42

Illustrated on p.90

675g/1½lb French beans
2 tbsp dried shrimps
1 tbsp chopped Sichuan Ja Chai hot pickle
vegetable oil for deep-frying
20g/¾oz lard
3 tsp chopped garlic
75g/3oz minced pork
3 tbsp good stock (see page 56)
1 tbsp soya sauce
½ tbsp sugar
2 tsp salt
3 tbsp water
1 tsp sesame oil
2 tsp vinegar
2 tbsp chopped spring onions (optional)

▓ PREPARATION ▓

Trim the French beans. Soak the dried shrimps in hot water to cover for 20 minutes. Drain and chop. Finely chop the pickle.

▓ COOKING ▓

Heat the oil in a wok or deep-fryer. When hot, fry the beans for 2 minutes. Remove and put aside. Pour away the oil to use for other purposes. Heat the lard in the wok or frying pan. When hot, add the garlic and stir a few times. Add the pork, shrimps, stock and pickle and stir-fry for 2 minutes. Stir in the soya sauce, sugar, salt and water. Add the French beans and turn and toss until the liquid in the pan has nearly all evaporated. Sprinkle with the sesame oil, vinegar and spring onions. Turn and stir once more, then serve.

FU-YUNG CAULIFLOWER

★★
Cooking time: about 11 minutes

Serves: 4-6

Cooking method: simmer

Illustrated on p.94

1 large cauliflower
2 egg whites
100g/4oz minced breast of chicken
4 tbsp good stock (see page 56)
1½ tbsp cornflour blended with 4 tbsp water
salt and pepper to taste
¼ tsp MSG (optional)
4 tbsp milk

▓ PREPARATION ▓

Remove the cauliflower stalk. Cut the cauliflower into florets. Beat the egg whites until nearly stiff. Mix in all the remaining ingredients thoroughly. Lightly beat together.

▓ COOKING ▓

Place the cauliflower florets in a saucepan of boiling water and simmer for 7-8 minutes. Drain. Put the cauliflower in a wok or pan. Add the egg white and chicken mixture. Bring to the boil, reduce the heat and gently simmer for 3 minutes, stirring and turning gently.

▓ SERVING ▓

Transfer the cauliflower to a heated dish and pour the sauce over. If liked, sprinkle with chopped spring onion and finely chopped ham or presoaked, chopped dried shrimps.

BEAN CURD AND EGGS

A simple bean curd stir-fry (*left*).
A selection of Chinese eggs (*above*); see page 27.

豆腐和蛋

BEAN CURD
One of the most widely eaten foods in China, bean curd may seem bland to the average Westerner, whose palate may not readily appreciate the subtle yet, to attuned taste buds, nutty flavour to be experienced when eating this unusual food. Bean curd is made from a thick, soya bean milk, derived from soya bean purée which has been boiled with water and then filtered for the milk. The milk is then induced to set through overnight cooling and the addition of a small amount of plaster of Paris. Once set the bean curd can be cut into various shapes and sizes, but it is usually sold in 7.5 × 7.5 cm/3 × 3 inch cakes, about 2.5 cm/1 inch thick.

Bean curd is reputed to be highly nutritious and easily digestible, and is rapidly gaining in popularity among health-conscious Westerners. A very attractive yet useful vegetarian food – one that can be cooked into innumerable dishes with all kinds of vegetables – bean curd can also be mixed and married successfully with almost any meat, fish, seafood and poultry. So, not only does this seemingly non-descript food possess great culinary versatility but, nutritionally, it is one of the pillars of the Chinese diet.

5 tbsp dried shrimps
2 tbsp dry sherry or rice wine
1½ tbsp drained, canned Sichuan hot Ja Chai pickles
1½ tbsp drained, canned snow pickles
2 cloves garlic
2½ tbsp vegetable oil
2½ tbsp sesame oil
2 tbsp dark soya sauce
3 tbsp lemon juice or vinegar
2 tsp sugar
¼ tsp MSG (optional)
3 cakes bean curd

COLD TOSSED BEAN CURD

Because bean curd has already been cooked (boiled) during its preparation, it usually requires very little cooking and heating when incorporated into a dish; or it may not need any cooking at all, as shown in the following recipe.

PREPARATION
Soak the dried shrimps in hot water to cover for 15 minutes. Add the sherry or wine and leave for a further 15 minutes. Drain the shrimps and finely chop. Finely chop both types of pickle. Crush the garlic. Place the shrimps, pickle and garlic in a bowl with the oils, soya sauce, lemon juice, sugar and monosodium glutamate, if using; mix well.

SERVING
Cut the bean curd into large sugar lump sized cubes and pile on to a serving dish. Spoon the sauce mixture over the bean curd and toss lightly. Serve with plain boiled rice.

★
Preparation time: about 10 minutes, plus soaking

Serves: 5-6

Quick to prepare

Useful starter for vegetarian or meat meal

BEAN CURD WITH CRAB MEAT AND PEAS

★★
Cooking time:
about 6 minutes

Serves: 4-6

Cooking method:
stir-fry, p.42

Quick to prepare

Illustrated on
p.103

■ PREPARATION ■

Cut the bean curd into 0.5 cm/¼ inch slices, then quarter each slice. Shred the spring onions. Flake the crab meat.

■ COOKING ■

Heat the oil in a wok or frying pan. When hot, stir-fry the ginger for 10-15 seconds. Stir in the crab meat and peas and stir-fry for 45 seconds. Add the bean curd pieces, spring onions, salt and pepper to taste, soya sauce and sherry, and turn and toss for 1½ minutes. Sprinkle with the blended cornflour, then toss for a further 45 seconds.

Ingredients
2 cakes bean curd
2 spring onions
150-175 g/5-6 oz crab meat
2½ tbsp vegetable oil
1 tbsp finely chopped fresh root ginger
1 tbsp peas
salt and pepper to taste
2 tsp light soya sauce
1 tbsp dry sherry
3 tsp cornflour blended with 3 tbsp good stock (see page 56)

STIR-FRIED BEAN CURD WITH SHRIMPS

★★
Cooking time:
4-5 minutes

Serves: 4-6

Cooking method:
stir-fry, p.42

Quick to prepare

Suitable for
family meal

■ PREPARATION ■

Soak the dried shrimps in hot water to cover for about 5 minutes, then drain. Cut the bean curd into sugar cube sized pieces. Cut the spring onions into 1 cm/½ inch sections.

■ COOKING ■

Heat the oil in a wok or frying pan. When hot, stir-fry the ginger and dried shrimps over medium heat for about 30 seconds. Add the white parts of the spring onions, fresh or frozen shrimps, salt, pepper and stock. Bring to the boil and add the bean curd, soya sauce, oyster sauce and green parts of the spring onions. Turn and stir the contents around gently. Simmer for 2 minutes.

Ingredients
2 tsp dried shrimps
3 cakes bean curd
3 spring onions
3 tsp vegetable oil
3 slices fresh root ginger
4-5 tbsp fresh or frozen shrimps
½ tsp salt
pepper to taste
4 tbsp good stock (see page 56)
1½ tbsp light soya sauce
1 tbsp oyster sauce

Sichuan Ma Po Tofu
(*above left*), sprinkle with
chopped spring onion and
serve with chilli dip; recipe
page 106.
Stir-fried Chinese Omelette
with Tomatoes (*below left*),
a simple, light yet colourful
dish; recipe page 109.
Bean Curd with Crab
Meat and Peas (*right*), a
quick to prepare dish;
recipe page 101.

2 cakes bean curd

50 g/2 oz button mushrooms

50 g/2 oz chicken breast meat

50 g/2 oz chicken livers

50 g/2 oz lamb's kidney

50 g/2 oz drained, canned
  bamboo shoots

2 cloves garlic

2 spring onions

1 tbsp cornflour

vegetable oil for deep-frying,
  about 300 ml/½ pt

¾ tsp salt

pepper to taste

3 tbsp vegetable oil

15 g/½ oz lard

½ tbsp finely chopped fresh
  root ginger

50 g/2 oz shrimps

2 tbsp white wine

1½ tbsp light soya sauce

3 tbsp good stock (see page 56)

¼ tsp MSG (optional)

½ tsp sesame oil

BEAN CURD WITH EIGHT PRECIOUS INGREDIENTS

The appeal of this dish lies in the savouriness of the sauce coating all the ingredients and in the different textures of the foods.

■ PREPARATION ■

Cut the bean curd into large sugar lump-sized pieces. Quarter the mushrooms. Cut the chicken breast meat and livers into bite-sized pieces. Score the kidney in a criss-cross pattern on the surface and then cut into bite-sized pieces. Cut the bamboo shoots into small wedges. Finely chop the garlic and spring onions. Blend the cornflour with 3 tablespoons water. Heat the oil in a wok or deep-fryer. When hot, gently fry the bean curd for about 1 minute. Drain thoroughly, pour away the oil for other uses. Sprinkle the chicken breast meat, chicken livers and kidney with the salt and pepper and 1 tablespoon of oil.

■ COOKING ■

Heat the 3 tablespoons oil in a wok or frying pan until hot, then add the lard. Add the ginger, garlic and half of the spring onions and stir together briefly over the high heat. Add the chicken meat, shrimps, chicken livers and kidney and stir-fry over medium heat for about 1½ minutes. Stir in the vegetables and toss together for a further 1½ minutes. Mix in the bean curd, then pour in the wine, soya sauce and stock. Bring to the boil then simmer gently for 3–4 minutes. Finally sprinkle on the monosodium glutamate, if using, blended cornflour and sesame oil. Turn them over a few times and serve.

■ SERVING ■

Serve in a very large plate or bowl. This dish is served in China as an accompaniment for rice and as a snack for nibbling when sipping wine. Part of its attraction lies in the fact that there are so many different ingredients to choose from.

★ ★ ★

Cooking time:
about 10 minutes

Serves: 6-8

Cooking method:
stir-fry, p.42

Needs time to
prepare

Serve as part of a
multi-dish meal

Scoring kidney
p.39

BRAISED BEAN CURD FAMILY-STYLE

★★★

Cooking time: about 15 minutes

Serves: 4-6

Cooking methods: stir-fry p.42, deep-fry p.45 and simmer

Good family dish

Family-style simply means bean curd which has been braised with whatever bits and pieces are available in the family kitchen; in a typical Chinese kitchen, this includes cooked pork (usually Soya Braised Pork), ginger, bamboo shoots, spring onions, soya sauce and oyster sauce.

■ PREPARATION ■

Cut the bean curd into 10-12 pieces per cake. Heat the oil in a wok or deep-fryer. When hot, fry the bean curd for about 2 minutes. Drain, pour away oil to use for other purposes. Cut the spring onions into 2.5 cm/1 inch sections. Cut the pork into bite-sized pieces. Cut the bamboo shoots into 4 cm/1½ inch wedges. Blend the cornflour with 3 tablespoons water.

■ COOKING ■

Heat 3-4 tablespoons oil in a wok or frying pan. When hot, stir-fry the ginger and half of the spring onions for about 1 minute. Add the bamboo shoots, pork and bean curd pieces. Turn them over high heat for about 1½ minutes. Stir in the stock, soya sauce, hoisin sauce, oyster sauce, sugar and monosodium glutamate, if using. Bring to the boil and stir gently. Reduce the heat and simmer gently for a further 10 minutes. Finally add the blended cornflour and wine and stir until thickened. Sprinkle over the remaining spring onions.

3 cakes bean curd

vegetable oil for deep-frying, about 300 ml/½ pt

3 spring onions

100 g/4 oz Soya Braised Pork (see page 196)

75 g/3 oz drained, canned bamboo shoots

1 tbsp cornflour

3 slices fresh root ginger

150 ml/¼ pt good stock (see page 56)

3 tbsp soya sauce

1 tbsp hoisin sauce

1 tbsp oyster sauce

1 tbsp sugar

¼ tsp MSG (optional)

3 tbsp rice wine

3 cakes bean curd
2 tbsp salted black beans
3 spring onions
2 slices fresh root ginger
2 chillies, dried or fresh
3 slices drained, canned Sichuan hot Ja Chai pickle
1½ tbsp cornflour
4 tbsp vegetable oil
225 g/8 oz minced pork
½ tsp salt
4 tbsp good stock (see page 56)
2 tbsp white wine
2 tbsp light soya sauce
¼ tsp pepper
2 tsp chilli sauce
2 tsp sesame oil

SICHUAN MA PO TOFU
(HOT BEAN CURD WITH MINCED PORK)

This dish, which has always been popular in Japan, is now gaining in popularity in the West.

■ PREPARATION ■

Cut the bean curd into sugar lump-sized pieces. Place in a pan of boiling water and simmer for 3 minutes, then drain. Soak the black beans in hot water for 5 minutes, then drain and crush. Coarsely chop the spring onions. Finely chop the ginger, chillies, discarding seeds, and pickle. Blend the cornflour with 4 tablespoons water.

■ COOKING ■

Heat the vegetable oil in a wok or frying pan. When hot, stir-fry the ginger, chilli, pickle and black beans for about 1 minute. Add the pork, spring onion and salt and continue to stir-fry for another 4 minutes. Pour in the stock, wine and soya sauce and simmer for a further 2 minutes. Add the bean curd to the pan and toss gently to coat. Bring to the boil and sprinkle on the pepper, chilli sauce and blended cornflour. Stir gently for another 30 seconds. Finally, sprinkle on the sesame oil and serve immediately.

★★★
Cooking time: 8-10 minutes

Serves: 5-6

Cooking method: stir-fry, p.42

Fairly quick to prepare

Serve this spicy dish with plenty of rice for hungry appetites

Illustrated on p.102

2 cakes bean curd
225 g/8 oz button mushrooms
6 medium dried Chinese mushrooms
1 tbsp dried shrimps
1 tbsp cornflour
3 tbsp vegetable oil
15 g/½ oz lard
½ tbsp bean curd cheese (optional)
2 tbsp light soya sauce
2 tbsp white wine
7 tbsp good stock (see page 56)
¼ tsp pepper
1½ tsp sesame oil

BRAISED BEAN CURD WITH MUSHROOMS

■ PREPARATION ■

Cut the bean curd into sugar lump-sized pieces. Halve the fresh mushrooms. Soak the dried mushrooms and dried shrimps separately in hot water to cover for 25 minutes. Drain, retaining the shrimp soaking liquid. Discard the tough mushroom stalks then cut the caps into quarters. Blanch the bean curd in boiling water for 2 minutes. Drain thoroughly. Blend the cornflour with 3 tablespoons water.

■ COOKING ■

Heat the vegetable oil and lard in a wok or frying pan. When hot, stir-fry the dried mushrooms for about 30 seconds. Add the shrimps and stir-fry for 30 seconds before adding the bean curd cheese, bean curd, soya sauce and wine. Blend together and put in the fresh mushrooms, shrimp soaking water and stock. Bring to the boil, stir gently and simmer for 2 minutes. Sprinkle on the blended cornflour and turn over once more to combine. Finally sprinkle on the pepper and sesame oil. By this time the bean curd will have absorbed the mushroom flavour.

★★
Cooking time: about 6 minutes

Serves: 4-6

Cooking methods: stir-fry p.42 and simmer

Quick to prepare

A light dish that goes well with any combination

★ ★ ★ ★

Cooking time:
20 minutes

Serves: 6-8

Cooking method:
steam, p.49

Requires time and
care in preparation

Serve as part of a
multi-dish party
dinner

STEAMED STUFFED BEAN CURD

Bean curd is also often steamed in China. Stuffed bean curd is a little more difficult to prepare than diced bean curd dishes, as the cakes must be cut with more care. These are often served at party meals.

PREPARATION

Cut each cake of bean curd into 4 pieces. Scoop out a deep hollow in the centre of each piece, about half-way through. Soak the dried shrimps in hot water to cover for 5 minutes, then drain and finely chop. Crush the garlic. Mix the pork, garlic, shrimps, salt, pepper, half of the oil and the egg white together in a bowl. Spoon this mixture into the bean curd and place a whole prawn or shrimp firmly on top.

COOKING

Arrange the 12 pieces of stuffed bean curd on a heatproof dish, place in a steamer and cook for 20 minutes. Meanwhile, heat the oil for the sauce in a small pan. When hot, add the ginger, spring onion, stock, oyster sauce and soya sauce. Bring to the boil and stir well. When the bean curd is ready, add the sesame oil to the sauce and pour it evenly over the bean curd.

3 cakes bean curd

1 tbsp dried shrimps

1 clove garlic

100g/4oz minced pork

1/4 tsp salt

pepper to taste

1/2 tbsp vegetable oil

1 egg white

12 medium fresh or frozen
    prawns or shrimps

Sauce:

1 1/2 tbsp vegetable oil

1 1/2 tsp finely chopped fresh
    root ginger

2 tbsp coarsely chopped spring
    onions

3 tbsp good stock (see page 56)

1 tbsp oyster sauce

1/2 tbsp light soya sauce

1 tsp sesame oil

107

EGGS

There is poultry in abundance in China, so it follows that eggs should be one of the most popular foods eaten there. Eggs in China are usually eaten either boiled, scrambled, stir-fried or steamed in the form of savoury custards. They are often hard-boiled and seasoned; for example, as soya eggs, marbled tea eggs, salted eggs or preserved and pickled 'hundred-year-old' eggs.

These latter are buried in a mixture of mud and lime, and the heat generated by the small amount of water added to the lime cooks the eggs. They are usually stored in stone jars with pine-ash and salt added – ingredients which seem to pickle the eggs. During their two months of maturation the eggs become encrusted in dried mud and lime and are covered with straw to separate them. When these layers have been removed and the eggs shelled, the whites of the eggs will be green in colour and the yolks a dark yellowish-green. These eggs have a very pungent and cheesey flavour. They are often eaten at breakfast with congee (rice gruel) or cut into slices and used as an hors d'oeuvres.

The majority of eggs consumed at mealtimes in China are usually stir-fried or scrambled. Chinese scrambled eggs bear little similarity to Western scrambled eggs, being only lightly stirred. There are innumerable ingredients that can be mixed and cooked with beaten eggs, enabling a large variety of stir-fried egg dishes. The most popular ingredients used for this purpose are ham, bacon, tomatoes, mushrooms, shrimps, peas, spring onions, shredded meats and chicken. Invariably, a large pinch of finely chopped spring onions and a little soya sauce or sherry are sprinkled over the top shortly before the dish is served. To any hungry Chinese, such a dish eaten with plain boiled rice is as appetizing as any other in the entire Chinese culinary repertoire.

CHINESE STIR-FRIED 'OMELETTES'

Chinese 'omelettes' are not strictly omelettes in the Western sense. In China, the eggs are stirred during the frying rather than being allowed to set before they are folded over. In Chinese cooking, the stirring should be done just as half of the eggs have set. The final product should be 85-90 per cent set. Since almost any kind of food, suitably chopped or shredded, can be combined and cooked in this manner with the eggs, there is almost an unlimited number of variations of these stir-fried omelettes. The following are just a few examples. The two indispensable requisites for the success of such a dish are finely chopped spring onion and a spoonful or two of good quality soya sauce, which are sprinkled over the omelettes just before serving.

BASIC PLAIN STIR-FRIED OMELETTE

4-5 eggs
¹/₂tsp salt
pepper to taste
4-5 tbsp vegetable oil
1¹/₂ tbsp finely chopped spring onion
1¹/₂ tbsp good quality dark soya sauce

▣ PREPARATION ▣

Break the eggs into a bowl with the salt and pepper and beat lightly with a fork.

▣ COOKING ▣

Heat the oil in a wok or frying pan. When hot, pour in the eggs. When the edges of the egg begin to set, continue to cook over medium heat for a further 15 seconds. Stir and turn the mixture over several times until it is almost all set and then arrange on a heated dish. Sprinkle the omelette evenly with chopped spring onion and soya sauce.

STIR-FRIED CHINESE OMELETTE WITH TOMATOES

4-5 eggs
¹/₂tsp salt
pepper to taste
1 medium onion
3 medium tomatoes
4-5 tbsp vegetable oil
1 tsp sesame oil
1¹/₂ tbsp finely chopped spring onion
1¹/₂ tbsp good quality dark soya sauce

▣ PREPARATION ▣

Break the eggs into a bowl with the salt and pepper and beat lightly with a fork. Peel and finely slice the onion. Cut each tomato into 8 segments.

▣ COOKING ▣

Heat the vegetable oil in a wok or frying pan. When hot, gently stir-fry the onion for about 30 seconds, then add the tomatoes. Spread evenly over the bottom of the pan. Pour over the beaten egg and allow to flow over the base of the pan. When the edges of the egg have begun to set, gently turn and stir several times, allowing any uncooked liquid to come in contact with the surface of the pan. Sprinkle on the sesame oil and arrange the omelette on a heated dish. Sprinkle over the chopped spring onion, with extra spring onion shreds if liked, and soya sauce and serve.

4-5 eggs

½ tsp salt

pepper to taste

1 medium onion

2 rashers bacon

4-5 tbsp vegetable oil

1½ tbsp finely chopped spring onion

1½ tbsp good quality dark soya sauce

STIR-FRIED CHINESE OMELETTE WITH ONION AND BACON

■ PREPARATION ■

Break the eggs into a bowl with the salt and pepper and beat lightly with a fork. Peel and finely slice the onion. Derind and finely slice the bacon.

■ COOKING ■

Heat the oil in a wok or frying pan. When hot, stir-fry the onion and bacon for about 1½ minutes. Spread evenly over the bottom of the pan. Pour over the beaten egg and allow to flow over the base of the pan. When the edges of the egg have begun to set, gently turn and stir several times, allowing any uncooked liquid to come in contact with the surface of the pan. Arrange on a heated dish, sprinkle over the spring onion and soya sauce and serve.

★★

Cooking time: about 5 minutes

Serves: 4-6

Cooking method: stir-fry, p.42

Quick to prepare

Serve as a snack or part of a multi-dish meal.

---

225 g/8 oz King prawns, fresh or frozen, shelled

1 tsp salt

pepper to taste

5 tbsp vegetable oil

2 tsp cornflour

2 cloves garlic

3 spring onions

4 eggs

1 tbsp dry sherry

STIR-FRIED PRAWN 'SOUFFLÉ'

■ PREPARATION ■

Sprinkle the prawns with the salt, pepper, ½ tablespoon of the oil and dust with the cornflour. Crush the garlic. Cut the spring onions into 2.5 cm/1 inch sections. Beat the eggs in a bowl.

■ COOKING ■

Heat the remaining oil in a wok or frying pan. When hot, stir-fry the garlic and prawns for 1½ minutes. Pour in the beaten egg and let the egg flow over the surface of the pan. Reduce the heat to low, sprinkle on the spring onions and cook for 1½ minutes. When the eggs are almost set, toss with a metal spoon. Sprinkle on the sherry and place on a heated serving plate.

★★

Cooking time: about 5-7 minutes

Serves: 4-6

Cooking method: stir-fry, p.42

Easy to prepare

A light dish to serve as part of a multi-dish meal

★★★

Cooking time: about 10 minutes

Serves: 4-6

Cooking method: stir-fry, p.42

An attractive stacked pancake dish to serve as a light meal or part of a multi-dish meal

HUANG-PU BOATMEN'S EGG OMELETTE

This is a favourite dish invented by the boatmen of Huang-Pu, which is a stretch of the Pearl River just below Canton. The contrast in colours between the dark soya sauce and the different coloured pancakes make the dish visually attractive as well as appealing in flavour.

■ PREPARATION ■

Break the eggs into a bowl with the salt and pepper and beat lightly with a fork.

■ COOKING ■

Heat 3 tablespoons of the oil in a wok or frying pan. When hot, stir-fry the onion for a few seconds. Add the crab meat and spread evenly over the bottom of the pan. Pour in one third of the eggs and cook until almost set. With the aid of a fish slice, transfer to a heated dish. Reheat the wok or pan with about 2 tablespoons oil and, when hot, add the shrimps. Spread over the bottom of the pan and then pour on another third of the eggs. Cook until almost set, then stack on top of the first 'pancake'. Reheat the wok or pan with about 2 tablespoons oil and, when hot, add the peas and spring onions. Stir-fry for a few seconds, then spread evenly over the bottom of the pan. Pour in the remaining egg and cook until almost set, then stack on top of the other 2 pancakes.

■ SERVING ■

Cut the 'triple pancake' into 8 segments. Sprinkle with soya sauce.

Ingredients
7 eggs
1 tsp salt
pepper to taste
8 tbsp vegetable oil
1 tbsp finely chopped onion
3 tbsp cooked crab meat
3 tbsp fresh, shelled shrimps
3 tbsp peas
2 tbsp finely chopped spring onion
1½ tbsp soya sauce

2 eggs

300 ml/½ pt good stock (see page 56) or water

salt and pepper to taste

1 tbsp soya sauce

1 tbsp finely chopped spring onion

Optional extras:

2-3 tbsp shredded crab meat or prawns

pinch of MSG (optional)

1-2 tbsp chopped ham

1-2 tbsp petits pois

BASIC STEAMED EGG AND FANCY STEAMED EGGS

Chinese steamed egg would be called egg custard in Western cuisine, except that in the West they are usually sweet; in China they are invariably savoury.

■ PREPARATION AND COOKING ■

The most basic Chinese steamed egg dish consists of no more than 2 eggs mixed with 300 ml/½ pt stock or water in a dish with seasoning added and cooked in a steamer for about 15 minutes, or until the custard has set. It is then topped with a spoonful of soya sauce and a scattering of chopped spring onions.

A more elaborate version consists of using the best grade stock, perhaps with a little shredded crab meat or prawns added, and a pinch of monosodium glutamate stirred into the stock to help enhance the flavours, if liked. After steaming, the top of the custard should be set and firm enough so that more prawns or crab meat can be arranged on top, together with some chopped ham and petits pois. The dish is then returned to the steamer for a further 3-4 minutes. After the second steaming, a large pinch of chopped spring onion is sprinkled over the top. When cooking this dish, never use too many eggs, as this will cause the custard to become too firm and hard after steaming. The dish is meant to be very light, for this is the appeal of the dish.

★★

Cooking time: about 15 minutes

Serves: 4-6

Cooking method: steam, p.49

Easy to prepare

Excellent with rice

Illustrated opposite

豆
腐
和
蛋

6 eggs
½ tsp salt
pepper to taste
4-5 tbsp vegetable oil

EGG POUCHES (OR SMALL OMELETTES)

★★

Cooking time: about 2½ minutes per pouch (plus time for making filling)

Serves: 4-6

Cooking method: shallow-fry

These pouches can be filled with any kind of filling. The most common ones are minced pork, beef, ham, shrimps and fish, which have been stir-fried with shredded spring onions, seasonings, salt and pepper and a small amount of finely chopped ginger. The pouches themselves are made as follows:

■ PREPARATION ■

Break the eggs into a bowl with the salt and pepper and beat lightly with a fork.

■ COOKING ■

Heat a small wok or frying pan and add 2 tablespoons of the oil. Ensure the oil coats the entire base of the pan. When hot, add 1 tablespoon of the egg mixture and tilt the pan so it too coats most of the base. Cook quickly over high heat until the underneath is cooked but the top surface is still moist. At this point, spoon about 1½ teaspoons chosen filling on to the centre of the omelette. Fold the omelette in half to form a half circle, press the edges together and then cook for a further 30 seconds. Remove and keep warm on a plate on top of a double boiler.

■ SERVING ■

These egg 'pouches' can be served on a bed of shredded lettuce with a dash of soya sauce and tomato sauce spooned over.

3 salt eggs
3 'hundred year old' eggs
2 fresh eggs
1 tsp salt
pepper to taste
½ tbsp cornflour
10 tbsp good stock (see page 56)
½ tsp MSG (optional)
1½ tbsp chopped spring onion

STEAMED EGGS IN THREE COLOURS

★

Cooking time: 15-18 minutes

Serves: 4-6

Cooking method: steam, p.49

Easy to prepare

■ PREPARATION ■

Shell the salt eggs and 'hundred year old' eggs. Cut them into 6 segments each. Arrange in a pattern in the bottom of a flat ovenproof dish. Beat the fresh eggs, salt, pepper, cornflour, stock, and monosodium glutamate, if using, together in a bowl. Pour the mixture into the ovenproof dish, nearly covering the eggs already in the dish.

■ COOKING ■

Place the dish in a steamer and steam vigorously for 15-18 minutes or until set. Sprinkle with the spring onion and serve with rice.

STIR-FRIED EGGS WITH OYSTERS

★★
Cooking time:
about 5 minutes

Serves: 4-6

Cooking method:
stir-fry, p.42

Easy to prepare

5-6 eggs
1/2 tsp salt
2 tsp chopped fresh root ginger
100-150g/4-5oz fresh or
  canned oysters
2 spring onions
3 tbsp vegetable oil
25g/1oz lard
1 tbsp rice wine or dry sherry

This is a somewhat unusual dish by Western standards, but it is quite common along the coastal provinces of China.

■ PREPARATION ■

Break the eggs into a bowl with half the salt and beat lightly with a fork. Mix the ginger and remaining salt with the oysters and marinate for 15 minutes, then drain. Coarsely chop the spring onions.

■ COOKING ■

Heat the oil and lard in a wok or frying pan. When hot, stir-fry the ginger, oysters and spring onions for 1 minute. Pour in the eggs and, when they are almost set, stir a few times and sprinkle on the wine or sherry. Cook for a further 30 seconds and serve.

YELLOW FLOWING EGG – LUI HUANG DAN

★★
Cooking time:
about 3 minutes

Serves: 4-6

Cooking method:
shallow-fry

Quick to prepare

3 egg yolks
2 eggs
1 1/2 tsp salt
2 1/2 tbsp melted lard
2 tbsp cornflour
300ml/1/2 pt good stock (see
  page 56)
1/2 tsp MSG (optional)
3 tbsp vegetable oil
3 tbsp finely chopped ham

Like Mu Shu Rou (see page 250), this is a popular dish in Peking and the north of China.

■ PREPARATION ■

Mix the egg yolks, eggs, salt, lard, cornflour, stock and monosodium glutamate, if using, together in a bowl.

■ COOKING ■

Heat the oil in a wok or frying pan. When hot, pour in the egg mixture. Stir quickly over the high heat for about 2 1/2 minutes or until the mixture is steaming and beginning to set.

■ SERVING ■

Pour the mixture into a heated dish and sprinkle the top with the ham. Ladle spoonfuls of the egg mixture into rice bowls and mix with boiled rice.

FISH AND SEAFOOD

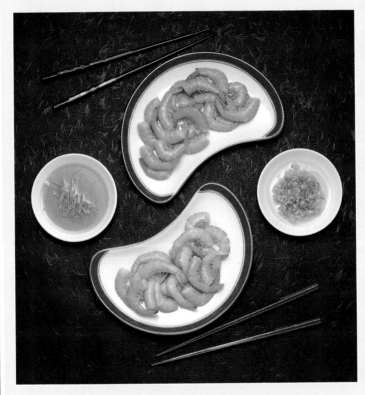

Cantonese Poached Prawns with Two Dips *(above)*;
recipe page 137.

魚類和海鮮

FISH
It seems strange but nevertheless is true that the Chinese enjoy fresh fish more than do the residents of an island such as Britain. Although a continental country, China has countless rivers, streams, canals, lakes and ponds, not to mention tens of thousands of miles of coastline. China has fish in abundance, not only from these natural sources but from her cultivation of fish farming which has been widely practised in China for centuries. And, until the recent advent of refrigeration in China, fish was eaten fresh and kept alive in water.

Whenever I become nostalgic about meals I have had in China, invariably it is fish dishes which come to mind, for Chinese culinary practice has been particularly successful with fish. The reason for this success lies in the Chinese chef's ability to preserve the freshness of the fish by careful heat control.

The Chinese practice of marrying the spicy and seasoned with the sweet and fresh in all dishes is particularly effective with fish; of using quantities of ginger, garlic and onions, and seasoned oil into which the flavour of these strong-tasting vegetables have been impregnated. The fish is then briefly cooked in the ingredients with the result that the sweet freshness of the fish and seafood is enhanced. When strong-tasting ingredients are not cooked with the fish or seafood, they are invariably used as dip sauces or 'mixes' (aromatic mixed condiments) to accompany the dish.

I have chosen some typical Chinese fish dishes (ranging from basic dishes to classical and regional) to illustrate the characteristics of methods and ingredients used.

450g/1 lb sole or plaice fillets
1½ tsp salt
pepper to taste
1½ tsp sesame oil
3 spring onions
3 cloves garlic
5 eggs
6 tbsp vegetable oil
Sauce:
6 tbsp good stock (see page 56)
1½ tbsp light soya sauce
1½ tbsp dry sherry

PEKING SLICED FISH OMELETTE

▰ PREPARATION ▰
Cut each fillet into 3 equal-sized pieces. Sprinkle with the salt, pepper and sesame oil. Cut the spring onions into 4 cm/1½ inch shreds. Crush the garlic. Beat the eggs lightly in a bowl. Mix the sauce ingredients together in a separate bowl.

▰ COOKING ▰
Heat the vegetable oil in a wok or frying pan. When hot, gently fry the fish slices for about 45 seconds. Pour over the beaten eggs; these should completely immerse the fish. Cook for 2½ minutes and, when quite set, turn the fish over. Fry over medium heat for another 2½ minutes. Add the spring onions and garlic. Pour over half the sauce mixture which will begin to boil immediately. Cover and simmer very gently for about 3 minutes. Remove the egg-covered fish slices and arrange on a heated serving dish. Heat the remaining sauce in the wok or pan and pour over the fish.

★★★
Cooking time: 12 minutes

Serves: 4-6

Cooking method: shallow-fry

Care required in cooking

Goes well with rice to complement meat and vegetable dishes

FISH FU-YUNG

350g/12oz white fish
2 slices fresh root ginger
1½tsp salt
pepper to taste
pinch of MSG (optional)
6 egg whites
50g/2oz ham
2 spring onions
vegetable oil for deep-frying
3tbsp peas
1tbsp light soya sauce
3tbsp good stock (see page 56)
2tbsp vinegar

★★★

Cooking time: about 12 minutes

Serves: 6-7

Cooking methods: deep-fry p.45 and stir-fry p.42

Quite easy to prepare

Good with most combinations, particularly red-cooked meat dishes and vegetables

■ PREPARATION ■

Coarsely chop the fish. Finely chop the ginger. Mix the fish, ginger, salt, pepper, monosodium glutamate, if using, and egg whites in a bowl and beat for 20 seconds with a fork. Coarsely chop the ham and spring onions.

■ COOKING ■

Heat the oil in a wok or deep-fryer. When hot, add the minced fish and egg white mixture, stirring all the time with a pair of chopsticks. Cook over medium heat for 1½ minutes. Pour the contents through a strainer to remove the oil and transfer the mixture to a heated plate. Reheat the wok with 2 tablespoons oil. When hot, stir-fry the ham and peas over medium heat for 1 minute. Add the soya sauce, stock, vinegar and spring onions and stir-fry for a further 30 seconds.

■ SERVING ■

Pour the ham, peas and spring onion mixture over the fish fu-yung.

POACHED FISH BALLS WITH PRAWNS AND MUSHROOMS

450g/1lb white fish
2½tsp salt
pepper to taste
2½tbsp cornflour
1 egg white
5-6 medium button mushrooms
2 spring onions
2 cloves garlic
2 slices fresh root ginger
3tbsp vegetable oil
75-100g/3-4oz peeled prawns
1½tbsp dry sherry
2tbsp good stock (see page 56)
2tbsp light soya sauce
1tsp sesame oil

★★★★

Cooking time: about 12-15 minutes

Serves: 4-6

Cooking methods: poach and stir-fry, p.42

Quite easy to prepare

Serve with meat and vegetable dishes

■ PREPARATION ■

Mince the fish finely. Add 1½ teaspoons of the salt, pepper, the cornflour and egg white and beat thoroughly until smooth. Form the fish paste into balls, half the size of a medium egg. Cut the mushrooms into quarters. Cut the spring onions into 2.5cm/1 inch sections. Coarsely chop the garlic and ginger.

■ COOKING ■

Poach the fish balls in a pan of boiling water for 3½ minutes, then drain. Heat the vegetable oil in a wok or frying pan. When hot, add the garlic, ginger, spring onions, mushrooms and prawns, sprinkle with the remaining salt and stir-fry quickly for 1½ minutes. Add the sherry, stock and soya sauce. Turn the ingredients over a few times, then add the fish balls. Turn and toss together for 1 minute. Reduce the heat to low and continue to cook for a further 1½ minutes. Sprinkle with the sesame oil.

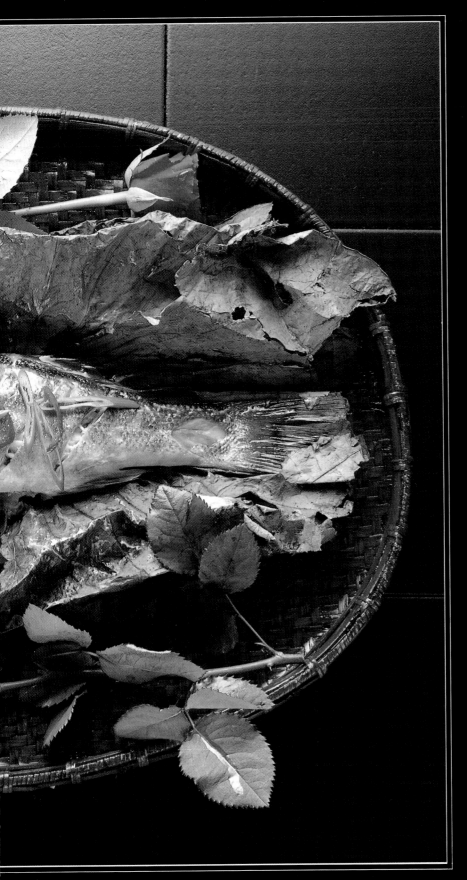

Steamed Whole Fish
Wrapped in Lotus Leaves,
an unusual presentation;
recipe page 122.

1 sea bass, about 1 kg/2 lb
2 tbsp dark soya sauce
3 cloves garlic
3 slices fresh root ginger
2 spring onions
2 dried chillies
vegetable oil for deep-frying
1½ tsp salt
pepper to taste
100 g/4 oz minced pork

Sauce:
2 tbsp light soya sauce
2 tbsp red wine
300 ml/½ pt good stock (see page 56)
1½ tbsp cornflour blended with 4 tbsp water
2 tsp sesame oil

DEEP-FRIED AND BRAISED SEA BASS

■ PREPARATION ■

Clean the fish and dry well. Rub inside and out with the dark soya sauce. Coarsely chop the garlic, ginger, spring onions and chillies.

■ COOKING ■

Heat the oil in a wok or deep-fryer. When hot, fry the fish for 5 minutes. Drain. Pour away the oil to use for other purposes, reserving 3 tablespoons. Heat the oil in the wok or frying pan. When hot, stir-fry the spring onions, garlic, ginger, chillies, salt, pepper and minced pork for 4 minutes. Add the light soya sauce, wine and stock and bring to the boil. Place the fish on top of the mixture in the wok or pan, cover and simmer gently for about 6 minutes. Lift out the fish and place on a heated serving plate. Add the blended cornflour and sesame oil to the wok. Stir until the sauce comes back to the boil and thickens. Pour over the fish.

★★★★
Cooking time: about 15-18 minutes

Serves: 4-6

Cooking methods: deep-fry p.45 and braise

Goes well with lightly cooked meat and vegetable dishes

1 whole fish, about 1 kg/2 lb
1½ tbsp dark soya sauce
2 lotus leaves
3 tbsp vegetable oil

Garnish and sauce:
75-100 g/3-4 oz canned snow pickles
3 slices fresh root ginger
2 spring onions
2 fresh chillies
2 tbsp light soya sauce
2 tbsp dry sherry
6 tbsp good stock (see page 56)
2 tsp sugar

■ STEAMED WHOLE FISH WRAPPED IN LOTUS LEAVES

■ PREPARATION ■

Clean the fish and dry well. Rub inside and out with the dark soya sauce. Shred the pickles, ginger, spring onions and fresh chillies, discarding seeds. Soak the lotus leaves in warm water for 10 minutes to soften. Drain.

■ COOKING ■

Heat the oil in a wok or frying pan. When hot, stir-fry the pickles, spring onions, ginger and chillies over medium heat for 1 minute. Add the soya sauce, sherry, stock and sugar, bring to the boil and stir for 30 seconds. Place the fish on the lotus leaves. Pour half the contents of the wok or pan over the length of the fish. Turn the fish over and pour over the remainder. Wrap the fish completely in the lotus leaves. Secure by tying with string. Place in a steamer and steam for 25 minutes.

★★★★
Cooking time: about 30 minutes

Serves: 4-6

Cooking methods: stir-fry p.42 and steam p.49

An interesting addition to a multi-course meal

Illustrated on p.120-121

*Cooking time:
about 12 minutes*

Serves: 4-6

*Cooking methods:
shallow-fry and
stir-fry, p.42*

*Fairly simple to
prepare*

*Serve to
complement meat
and vegetable
dishes*

SAUTEED FISH STEAKS WITH GARNISH

■ PREPARATION ■

Clean and dry the fish steaks. Rub with the salt, pepper and 1 tablespoon of the oil. Soak the dried mushrooms in hot water to cover for 25 minutes. Drain and discard the tough stalks. Cut the mushroom caps into matchstick-size shreds. Cut the spring onions into 2.5 cm/1 inch sections.

■ COOKING ■

Heat the remaining oil in a wok or frying pan. When hot, add the ginger slices and spread out evenly to flavour the oil. Lay the fish steaks in the hot flavoured oil and shallow fry or sauté for 2 minutes on each side. Pour away any excess oil and remove from the heat. Heat the lard in a separate pan. When hot, stir-fry the chopped onion, ginger and mushrooms for 1 minute. Add the minced pork and stir over high heat for 3 minutes. Mix in the soya sauce, stock, sherry and spring onion. Bring to the boil and continue to stir-fry for 1 minute. Meanwhile, reheat the first pan and return the fish steaks to it. Heat through, then pour the sauce and garnish over the fish. Transfer contents to a heated serving plate.

675-900 g/1½-2 lb fish, cut into 4-6 steaks
2 tsp salt
pepper to taste
6 tbsp vegetable oil
5 slices fresh root ginger
Garnish and sauce:
4 medium dried Chinese mushrooms
2 spring onions
35 g/1¼ oz lard
2 tbsp coarsely chopped onion
1½ tbsp chopped fresh root ginger
100 g/4 oz minced pork
3 tbsp soya sauce
4 tbsp good stock (see page 56)
2 tbsp dry sherry

*Cooking time:
10 minutes*

Serves: 4-6

*Cooking method:
shallow-fry and
simmer*

*Quite easy to
prepare*

*Serve with rice to
complement meat
and vegetable
dishes*

SOYA-BRAISED SLICED FISH

■ PREPARATION ■

Cut the fish into 6 × 4 × 2.5 cm/2½ × 1½ × 1 inch pieces. Toss in the salt, pepper and 2 teaspoons of the oil. Dust in the cornflour. Cut the spring onions into 2.5 cm/1 inch sections, separating the green from the white parts. Combine the soya sauce, stock, sherry and sugar into a sauce.

■ COOKING ■

Heat the oil in a wok or frying pan. When hot, stir-fry the ginger and white parts of the spring onions for about 15 seconds, to flavour the oil. Add the fish pieces, one by one, spacing them in the pan. Fry for 1½ minutes on either side. Drain off the excess oil. Pour the sauce over the fish pieces. Sprinkle with the green parts of the spring onions and bring to the boil. Baste the fish with the boiling sauce, turning the fish after 1½ minutes. Simmer for another 2 minutes and then transfer to a heated plate. Pour the sauce and spring onions over the fish.

675 g/1½ lb fish steak, eg cod, haddock, halibut, mullet, etc.
1½ tsp salt
pepper to taste
6½ tbsp vegetable oil
1½ tbsp cornflour
3 spring onions
4 slices fresh root ginger
3 tbsp soya sauce
3 tbsp good stock (see page 56)
1½ tbsp dry sherry
2 tsp sugar

Steamed Fish with Garnish
(*above*), serve the garnished
fish with lemon slices;
recipe page 126.
Braised Whole Fish in Hot
Vinegar Sauce (*right*), a
colourful dish for a multi-
course meal; recipe page
127.

450g/1lb fish fillets, eg cod, haddock, sole, turbot
1½ tsp salt
1 egg
50g/2oz cornflour
3 slices fresh root ginger
3 stalks celery
3 spring onions
100g/4oz bean sprouts
vegetable oil for deep-frying
2 tbsp light soya sauce
1½ tbsp wine vinegar
1 tbsp chilli sauce
1 tbsp sesame oil

YANGTZE 'FISH SALAD'

Ideal dish for those vegetarians who eat fish. In the way it is prepared, this dish can justifiably be called a salad. An excellent dish for a light meal. The contrast between the crunchiness of the vegetables and the crispy fish makes for an interesting variation in texture.

■ PREPARATION ■

Cut the fish into thin slices, then cut the slices into matchstick-size strips. Rub in the salt, coat with the beaten egg and dust with the cornflour. Cut the ginger into thin shreds. Cut the celery into thick matchstick-size strips. Blanch the celery in a pan of boiling water for 1½ minutes, then drain. Cut the spring onions into 5 cm/2 inch sections. Wash the bean sprouts and drain thoroughly.

■ COOKING ■

Heat the oil in a wok or deep-fryer. When hot, fry the fish in 2 batches for about 2 minutes. Drain.

■ SERVING ■

Place the celery and bean sprouts in the base of a deep sided dish. Arrange the strips of fish, like French fries, in one layer on top. Sprinkle with the ginger, spring onions, soya sauce, vinegar, chilli sauce and sesame oil. Toss the salad before eating.

★★★

Cooking time: about 5 minutes

Serves: 5-8

Cooking method: deep-fry, p.45

Excellent starter for a multi-dish meal

---

1 whole fish, about 675-900g/1½-2lb
2 tsp salt
pepper to taste
1½ tbsp finely chopped fresh ginger
Garnish and sauce:
2-3 spring onions
3 slices fresh root ginger
3 large fresh or Chinese dried mushrooms (optional)
1 tbsp dry sherry
2½ tbsp soya sauce
4 tbsp vegetable oil

STEAMED FISH WITH GARNISH

As often as not, the Chinese steam their fish, since steam is widely available in the Chinese kitchen. When fish is steamed, there is a tendency to undercook it; hence, a characteristic process to complete the cooking of the fish is to pour a few tablespoons of very hot oil over the length of the fish and its garnish. The oil and the fish are impregnated with the flavour of the garnish, usually spring onions and ginger. Alternatively, after the fish has been steamed or poached, lay it on the serving dish. Fry the garnish and sauce, usually consisting of a little spring onion, ginger, mushrooms, shredded pork, with a sprinkling of dried shrimps and soya sauce, for a minute or two. When very hot, pour over the length of the fish or pieces of fish.

■ PREPARATION ■

Clean the fish and dry well. Rub inside and out with the salt, pepper and finely chopped ginger. Leave to season for 30 minutes. Shred the spring onions and ginger. Slice the mushroom caps; if using dried, soak first in hot water for 25 minutes.

★★★

Cooking time: about 15 minutes, plus seasoning time

Serves: 4-5

Cooking method: steam, p.49

Fairly simple to prepare

Serve with meat and vegetable dishes

Illustrated on p.124

■ COOKING ■

Place the fish on a heatproof dish and put into a steamer. Steam vigorously for 10 minutes. Remove the dish from the steamer and pour away any excess water which has collected. Pour the sherry and soya sauce down the length of the fish and garnish the fish with the spring onions, mushrooms and ginger. Heat the oil in a small pan and, when smoking hot, pour it in a thin stream down the length of the fish over the spring onions, mushrooms and ginger. The fish is brought to the table on the dish in which it was cooked.

★ ★ ★

Cooking time: about 10 minutes, plus seasoning time

Serves: 4-6

Cooking methods: shallow-fry and braise

Fairly simple to prepare

Serve with meat and vegetable dishes

Illustrated on p.125

■ BRAISED WHOLE FISH IN HOT VINEGAR SAUCE ■

■ PREPARATION ■

Finely chop the 2 slices of ginger. Clean the fish and dry well. Rub evenly inside and out with salt, pepper, chopped ginger and 1 tablespoon of the oil. Leave to season for 30 minutes. Shred the 3 slices of ginger, bamboo shoots, red pepper, carrot, chillies, discarding seeds, and spring onions.

■ COOKING ■

Heat the remaining oil in a wok or frying pan. When hot, fry the fish for 2½ minutes on each side. Remove and drain. Add the shredded ginger, bamboo shoots, red pepper, carrot, chillies and spring onions to the remaining oil and stir-fry over medium heat for 1 minute. Add the lard, soya sauce, stock and half the vinegar and cook for another minute. Lay the fish back in the wok or pan and cook gently for 2 minutes on both sides, basting. Transfer the fish to a serving dish. Stir the remaining vinegar into the wok, then add the blended cornflour, stirring over high heat until the sauce thickens.

■ SERVING ■

Pour the sauce from the wok over the length of the fish and garnish with the shredded vegetables.

2 slices fresh root ginger

1 whole fish, 675-900g/1½-2lb

1 tsp salt

pepper to taste

4 tbsp vegetable oil

Sauce:

3 slices fresh root ginger

40g/1½oz drained, canned bamboo shoots

½ red pepper

1 small carrot

1 green chilli

2 dried chillies

2 spring onions

25g/1oz lard

2 tbsp light soya sauce

3 tbsp good stock (see page 56)

6 tbsp vinegar

½ tbsp cornflour blended with 2 tbsp water

Cantonese Ginger and
Onion Crab (*left*), makes a
spectacular starter; recipe
page 140.
Peking 'Pomegranate'
Snow Flake Prawn Balls
(*above*), an attractive party
dish; recipe page 135.

1 whole fish, about 675-900g/1½-2lb
2tsp salt
pepper to taste
4 slices fresh root ginger
Garnish and sauce:
3 slices fresh root ginger
3 spring onions
2 rashers bacon
3tbsp vegetable oil
15g/½oz lard
1tbsp vinegar
3tbsp soya sauce
2tbsp dry sherry
2tbsp good stock (see page 56)
1½tsp chilli sauce

POACHED FISH WITH GARNISH

■ PREPARATION ■

Clean the fish and dry well. Rub inside and out with the salt and pepper. Leave to season for 30 minutes. Heat the 4 ginger slices in water in a pan until boiling. For the garnish, shred the ginger, spring onions and bacon.

■ COOKING ■

Immerse the fish in the ginger water, making sure the fish is completely covered. Simmer gently for 8 minutes. Remove, drain and place on a heated serving dish. Meanwhile, heat the oil and lard in a small pan. When hot, fry the bacon over high heat for 1½ minutes. Add the ginger and spring onion and continue to stir-fry for another 30 seconds. Pour in the vinegar, soya sauce, sherry, stock and chilli sauce. The mixture will boil almost immediately. Stir once more and then pour the boiling sauce and garnish over the fish. Spread the garnish out evenly to serve.

★★
Cooking time: about 12 minutes, plus seasoning time
Serves: 4-5
Cooking methods: simmer and stir-fry, p.42
Fairly simple to prepare
Complements meat and vegetable dishes

1 whole fish, 675-900g/1½-2lb
3 slices fresh root ginger
1½tsp salt
pepper to taste
3-4tbsp cornflour
vegetable oil for deep-frying
Sauce:
2tbsp wood ears
6 medium dried Chinese mushrooms
2 spring onions
25g/1oz lard
25g/1oz drained, canned bamboo shoots
3tbsp soya sauce
1tbsp sugar
4tbsp good stock (see page 56)
2tbsp wine vinegar
2tbsp dry sherry

'SQUIRREL' FISH

This dish derives its name from the fact that, when cooked and served, the fish's tail curves up like a squirrel; also, when the hot sauce is poured over the hot freshly cooked fish, it 'chatters'!

■ PREPARATION ■

Clean the fish and slit open from head to tail on the underside so that it lays flat. Cut 7-8 deep slashes on one side of the fish and only 2 on the other side. Finely chop the ginger. Rub the fish inside and out with the salt, pepper and ginger, then coat in the cornflour. Soak the wood ears and mushrooms separately in hot water to cover for 25 minutes. Drain and discard the tough stalks. Cut the mushroom caps into shreds. Finely slice the wood ears. Cut the spring onions into 5cm/2 inch sections.

■ COOKING ■

Heat the oil in a wok or deep-fryer. When hot, gently fry the fish over medium heat for 4 minutes, then reduce the heat to low. Meanwhile, melt the lard in a smaller wok or pan. When hot, stir-fry the wood ears, mushrooms, spring onions and bamboo shoots over medium heat for 1½ minutes. Add the soya sauce, sugar, stock, vinegar and sherry. Stir the ingredients over low heat for about 2 minutes. Raise the heat under the wok containing the fish and fry for another 2 minutes. The tail should have curled by now due to the uneven amount of cuts on the fish. Lift out the fish, drain and place on a heated dish.

★★★★
Cooking time: about 8 minutes
Serves: 4-6
Cooking methods: deep-fry p.45 and stir-fry p.42
Serve as part of a multi-course meal

SERVING

During the last minute of the fish cooking, raise the heat under the smaller wok and boil the sauce rapidly. Pour it over the hot fish as soon as it has come out of the oil – the fish will sizzle and 'chatter'. The noise should draw the attention of the diners, reminding them that it is a dish to be eaten quickly while the fish is still freshly cooked and crisp.

★ ★ ★

Cooking time: about 12 minutes

Serves: 4-6

Cooking method: shallow-fry

Care required in cooking

Goes well with red-cooked meat dishes and vegetables

SOFT-FRIED PEKING SLICED FISH IN WINE

The white of the fish contrasts well with the black of the wood ears. Being only quickly cooked, the taste of the wine and spirit in the sauce is very pronounced.

PREPARATION

Cut the fish into 4 × 2.5 cm/1½ × 1 inch slices. Rub evenly with the salt, dust with the cornflour and coat with the egg white. Soak the wood ears in hot water to cover for 10 minutes. Drain. Shred the ginger.

COOKING

Heat the oil in a wok or frying pan. When hot, lay out the fish slices evenly on the bottom of the wok and turn after 30 seconds. Cook for a further 1 minute, then remove the wok from the heat. Carefully remove the fish and arrange on a heated serving dish. Pour away the oil except about 2 tablespoons and reheat the wok. When hot, cook the ginger for 30 seconds to flavour the oil, then remove from the wok. Add the wood ears and fry for 30 seconds, then push to the side of the wok. Mix together the stock, white wine, vodka, sugar and blended cornflour in a bowl. Add to the wok and stir until thickened. Return the fish slices to the wok and reheat.

SERVING

Transfer the fish and wood ears to a heated serving dish, then pour over the sauce.

---

450 g/1 lb fish fillets, eg sole or plaice

1½ tsp salt

2 tbsp cornflour

1 egg white

50 g/2 oz wood ears

300 ml/½ pt vegetable oil

Sauce:

2 slices fresh root ginger

5 tbsp good chicken stock (see page 56)

4 tbsp white wine

2 tsp vodka or wine-lee if available

1½ tsp sugar

2½ tsp cornflour blended with 1½ tbsp water

Quick-fried Crystal
Prawns *(above left)*, a
simple yet delicious dish;
recipe page 143.
Steamed Scallops with
Black Bean Sauce *(below
left)*, a popular starter
served in their shells with
parsley and radish garnish;
recipe page 138.
Braised Mussels with Bean
Curd and Mushrooms
(right), served with rice to
mop up the juices; recipe
page 142.

SEAFOOD AND CRUSTACEANS

Fresh-water crustaceans abound in many areas of China and, indeed, a sizeable proportion of all Chinese crustaceans are found in fresh water. I have many happy, childhood memories of fishing for crabs and shrimps or digging them up from muddy river banks and along the sides of canals, ponds and lakes. These crustaceans are found in profusion during certain seasons and a celebration of their coming is made.

The east coast of China is another rich source of both crustaceans and other seafood, stretching as it does from the frozen wastes of Manchuria to the tropical waters of Vietnam. Many dishes have been created from the enormous harvest yielded annually by these waters and fresh-water sites. Here are some of the better known, many of which can be cooked as readily in the West as in the East.

Ingredients
450g/1lb peeled prawns, fresh or frozen
75g/3oz pork fat
4 water chestnuts
1 tsp salt
1 tbsp dry sherry
2 spring onions
5 slices fresh root ginger
2 egg whites
2½ tbsp cornflour
vegetable oil for deep-frying
1½ tbsp salt and pepper dip (see page 93)

DEEP-FRIED CRISPY PRAWN BALLS

PREPARATION

Mince or finely chop the prawns, pork fat and water chestnuts. Place in a bowl and add the salt and sherry. Mix together thoroughly. Cut the spring onions into shreds. Finely chop the ginger. Place the spring onions and ginger in a small saucepan with 150ml/¼pt water and bring to the boil. Simmer until the liquid has reduced by half, about 2 tablespoons. Leave to cool, then add to the prawn mixture, straining out the spring onion and ginger. Beat the egg whites until stiff and fold into the prawn mixture with the cornflour. Fold together until the mixture is smooth. Form into 24 even-sized balls.

COOKING

Heat the oil in a wok or deep-fryer. When hot, add the prawn balls one at a time and fry in about 2 batches over medium heat for about 3 minutes until golden brown. Remove with a perforated spoon and drain on absorbent kitchen paper.

SERVING

Transfer the prawn balls to a heated serving dish. Serve with a small bowl of salt and pepper dip. Another dip which could be used is the Peking duck sauce (see page 178).

★★★★
Cooking time: about 6-8 minutes

Serves: 5-7

Cooking method: deep-fry, p.45

Requires some time to prepare

Ideal starter for a party meal

海
鮮
和
貝
殻
類

VARIATION

PEKING 'POMEGRANATE' SNOW FLAKE PRAWN BALLS

★★

Cooking time:
about 10 minutes

Serves: 5-7

Cooking method:
deep-fry, p.45

Requires some
time to prepare

Excellent starter
for a dinner party

Illustrated on
p.129

This is a popular version of Deep-Fried Crispy Prawn Balls, often served during parties in Peking.

This is very similar to the previous recipe but only half of the egg white is beaten stiffly and the other half if beaten only lightly. The stiff egg white is added first, then the lightly beaten egg white, making the mixture much wetter. After forming into balls, they are rolled evenly and firmly in croûtons.
To make the croûtons, cut 4-5 slices of white bread into small cubes, then dry in a preheated moderate oven at 180°C, 350°F, Gas Mark 4 for about 3 minutes.
These coated prawn balls are then deep fried as in the previous recipe and served in the same way. They are, however, crisper as the croûton coating crisps up well during frying.

★★★★

Cooking time:
about 6 minutes

Serves: 5-6

Cooking method:
deep-fry, p.45

A little fiddly to
make

An excellent
starter

DEEP-FRIED CRAB CLAWS

This dish makes a popular starter.

10 large frozen crab claws

2 slices fresh root ginger

3 eggs

1 tsp salt

225g/8oz peeled prawns

3 tbsp cornflour

225g/8oz dry breadcrumbs

vegetable oil for deep-frying

■ PREPARATION ■

Defrost the claws and chop into half lengthwise. Finely chop the ginger. Beat the eggs. Add the salt and ginger to the prawns and finely chop, mixing well. Divide the prawn mixture into 10 portions, and press each portion on to the meat of the crab claws. Sprinkle the prawn mixture with cornflour, dip each meat side of the claw into beaten egg, and coat with breadcrumbs. Place the prawn-filled claws on a plate and chill for 1 hour.

■ COOKING ■

Heat the oil in a wok or deep-fryer. When hot, fry the claws in about 2 batches for 3 minutes. Drain.

■ SERVING ■

Serve hot on a heated dish, garnished with wedges of lemon and sprigs of parsley.

CANTONESE FRESH POACHED PRAWNS WITH TWO DIPS

575g/1¼lb fresh unshelled prawns
1½tsp salt

Dip 1:
2 spring onions
3 slices fresh root ginger
2 green chillies
3tbsp vegetable oil
3tbsp light soya sauce
1tbsp wine vinegar
½tbsp sesame oil

Dip 2:
1tbsp shredded fresh root ginger
3tbsp vinegar

■ PREPARATION ■

Wash the prawns thoroughly under running water. Finely chop the spring onions, ginger and chillies, discarding the seeds, together. Place them in a small heatproof bowl.

■ COOKING ■

Bring 1.2lt/2pt water to the boil in a saucepan and add the salt. Simmer the prawns for 2 minutes, then leave to stand in the water, off the heat, for a further minute. Drain.

■ SERVING ■

Place the prawns in a medium bowl. Heat the vegetable oil in a pan. When smoking hot, pour over the ginger, spring onions and chillies. Leave for 30 seconds then add the soya sauce, vinegar and sesame oil, stir well. For the other dip, place the shredded ginger in a small bowl and spoon over the vinegar. To eat, peel each prawn up to the tail and then, holding the tail, dip into the dip sauces.

DEEP-FRIED CRISPY KING PRAWNS

1 slice fresh root ginger
2 eggs
75g/3oz plain flour
2tbsp self-raising flour
1½tsp salt
4tbsp water
675g/1½lb King prawns, fresh or frozen, unshelled
vegetable oil for deep-frying

■ PREPARATION ■

Finely chop the ginger. Beat the eggs for 15 seconds, then fold in both types of flour, salt, ginger and water. Beat for 1 minute until a light batter. Shell the prawns, leaving the tail shells on. Clean, scraping away any dark or gritty bits.

■ COOKING ■

Heat the oil in a wok or deep-fryer. When hot, hold each prawn by the tail and dip the flesh into the batter. Lower into the oil, frying 6 prawns at a time for 3 minutes. Remove with a perforated spoon and drain. When the first batch has been fried, keep hot and crispy in the oven while frying the remaining prawns.

■ SERVING ■

Serve with lemon slices and salt and pepper dip (see page 93).

12 fresh scallops, with shells

Sauce:

1½ tbsp salted black beans

4 tbsp vegetable oil

1 tbsp finely chopped fresh root
    ginger

½ tbsp finely chopped red
    chilli

½ tbsp crushed garlic

1 tsp pounded Sichuan
    peppercorns

1 tbsp finely chopped spring
    onion

2 tbsp soya sauce

1 tbsp dry sherry

2 tbsp good stock (see page 56)

1 tsp sesame oil

STEAMED SCALLOPS WITH BLACK BEAN SAUCE

■ PREPARATION ■

Scrub the scallops under running cold water, then remove the flat shell. Soak the black beans in hot water for 5 minutes, then drain and crush.

■ COOKING ■

Put the scallops on a large heatproof dish, place in a steamer and steam for 8-9 minutes. Meanwhile, heat the vegetable oil in a small wok or saucepan. When hot, stir-fry the ginger, chilli, garlic, peppercorns, spring onion and black beans for 30 seconds. Add the soya sauce, sherry and stock and continue to stir-fry for another 15 seconds. Sprinkle on the sesame oil.

■ SERVING ■

Drip about 2 teaspoons of the sauce over each scallop and serve them in the shells. The diners should be able to remove the scallops from their shells with a pair of chopsticks or a fork, then drink the remaining sauce from the shells.

★ ★ ★

Cooking time:
1-2 minutes

Serves: 6-8

Cooking methods:
steam p.49 and
stir-fry p.42

Easy if you have
a large steamer

Excellent starter

Illustrated on
p.132

450g/1lb King prawns

8 tbsp vegetable oil

2 spring onions

2 cloves garlic

2 dried chillies

1½ tsp Sichuan peppercorns

1½ tsp salt

SALT AND PEPPER PRAWNS

The impact of the heat on the salt and pepper coating on the prawns makes this a very aromatic dish. A very suitable dish as an hors d'oeuvre for nibbling with wine.

■ PREPARATION ■

Wash and shell the prawns. Sprinkle on 1½ teaspoons of the oil. Cut the spring onions into 2.5 cm/1 inch sections. Thinly slice the garlic. Shred the chillies. Lightly pound the peppercorns and mix with the salt.

■ COOKING ■

Heat the remaining oil in a wok or frying pan. When hot, stir-fry the prawns over high heat for 1 minute. Remove the prawns and pour away the oil to use for other purposes, except for 1 tablespoon. Reheat the oil in the wok or pan. When hot, quickly stir-fry the chilli, garlic and spring onion. Spread out the spring onion and chilli and return the prawns. Sprinkle on the salt and pepper mixture and stir-fry for another 45 seconds.

★ ★ ★

Cooking time:
about 6 minutes

Serves: 6-7

Cooking method:
stir-fry, p.42

Quite easy to
prepare

A good starter dish

★★★★

Cooking time: about 10 minutes

Serves: 2-3

Cooking method: steam, p.49

Easy, except for killing and preparing lobster

Serve with grated ginger and vinegar dip

STEAMED LOBSTER

1 live lobster, about 450-675g/1-1½lb
2 spring onions
2 slices fresh root ginger
1 tbsp dry sherry
Dip sauce:
2 spring onions
2 slices fresh root ginger
2 dried red chillies
2½ tbsp vegetable oil
3 tbsp soya sauce
1 tbsp vinegar
½ tsp sesame oil

■ PREPARATION ■

Kill the lobster (see recipe for Cantonese Ginger and Onion Crab, page 140). Cut in half lengthwise, discarding stomach sac and dark intestinal vein, then cut into 5 cm/2 inch sections. Place in a heatproof dish. Finely chop the spring onions and ginger. Mix with the sherry. Sprinkle this mixture on to the lobster.

■ COOKING ■

Place the lobster in the steamer and steam for about 10 minutes.

■ SERVING ■

To prepare the dip sauce, finely chop the spring onions, ginger and chilli. Place in a small heatproof bowl. Heat the vegetable oil in a pan until smoking hot. Pour into the bowl. Stir a few times, then add the soya sauce, vinegar and sesame oil, mixing well. Serve with the freshly steamed lobster.

★★

Cooking time: about 5 minutes

Serves: 4-6

Cooking method: stir-fry, p.42

Quick and easy to prepare

Goes well with meat and vegetable dishes

PRAWN FU-YUNG

2 spring onions
2 slices fresh root ginger
150g/5oz peeled prawns
2 tsp cornflour
5 egg whites
1 tsp salt
5 tbsp vegetable oil
1 tbsp dry sherry
15g/½oz lard

The pink of the prawns, the whiteness of the egg white and the green of the spring onions makes an attractive colour combination.

■ PREPARATION ■

Finely chop the spring onions. Finely shred the ginger. Place the prawns in a bowl with the ginger and cornflour. Beat the egg whites in a bowl, with the salt and half of the chopped spring onion for 15 seconds with a fork.

■ COOKING ■

Heat 2 tablespoons of the oil in a wok or frying pan. When hot, stir-fry the prawns with the sherry over medium heat for 1½ minutes. Remove the prawns from the wok and place in the bowl with the egg whites. Mix together well. Heat the remaining oil in the wok or pan. When hot, pour in the egg white and prawn mixture. Stir quickly for 1 minute, then add the lard. Sprinkle on the remaining spring onion. Turn and scramble for a further minute. When the mixture has just set, transfer to a heated serving dish.

| 20-25 medium oysters |
| 1 tsp salt |
| pepper to taste |
| 2 tsp finely chopped fresh ginger |
| vegetable oil for deep-frying |
| 1½ tbsp finely chopped spring onion |

| Batter: |
| 1 egg |
| 5 tbsp plain flour |
| 1 tbsp cornflour |
| 5 tbsp water |
| ½ tsp baking powder |

DEEP-FRIED OYSTERS

■ PREPARATION ■

Shell and drain the oysters. Sprinkle with salt, pepper and ginger. Combine the ingredients for the batter until smooth.

■ COOKING ■

Heat the oil in a wok or deep-fryer. When very hot, dip the oysters individually into the batter, then fry in batches for about 2½-3 minutes until golden brown. Drain.

■ SERVING ■

Transfer the crispy-fried oysters to a heated serving dish and sprinkle with the spring onion.

★★★

Cooking time: 2½-3 minutes per batch

Serves: 4-6

Cooking method: deep-fry, p.45

Serve as a starter with grated ginger and vinegar or salt and pepper dips

| 1.5 kg/3 lb crab or 1 kg/2 lb live lobster |
| 5 slices fresh root ginger |
| 4 spring onions |
| 1 medium pepper |
| vegetable oil for deep-frying |
| ½ tsp salt |
| 150 ml/¼ pt good stock (see page 56) |
| 2 tbsp light soya sauce |
| 3 tbsp dry sherry |
| 1 tsp sesame oil |

CANTONESE GINGER AND ONION CRAB OR LOBSTER

Crab or lobster cooked this way is an outstanding dish by any standards. The Chinese chop up their lobsters while still alive! If you prefer to kill the lobster first, tie the pincers up firmly and cover the tail with a cloth. Holding the tail firmly, plunge the pointed end of a sharp knife into the place where the head and body meet, to cut the nerve cord. This kills the lobster instantly.

■ PREPARATION ■

Scrub the crab thoroughly under running water. Chop the crab into 4 pieces, discarding the grey dead men's fingers. Alternatively, scrub the lobster under running cold water and chop into bite sized pieces, discarding the hard stomach sac behind the head and the black intestinal vein. Crack the claws with the back of a chopper. Cut the ginger and spring onions into matchstick-size shreds. Thinly slice the red pepper.

■ COOKING ■

Heat the oil in a wok or deep-fryer. When very hot, add the crab or lobster pieces one by one to the oil. Fry over high heat for 2½ minutes. Remove and drain. Pour away the oil to use for other purposes, reserving about 2 tablespoons. Reheat the wok or a frying pan. When hot, stir-fry the ginger, spring onion, red pepper and salt over medium heat for 1 minute. Pour in the stock, soya sauce and sherry. Bring to the boil and return the crab or lobster to the wok or pan. Toss a few times, then cover and cook for 3-4 minutes until the sauce is reduced by half. Sprinkle on the sesame oil, toss and transfer to a heated serving dish.

★★★★

Cooking time: 15 minutes

Serves: 5-6

Cooking methods: deep-fry p.45 and stir-fry p.42

Best eaten by itself, perhaps as a starter to a multi-dish meal

Illustrated on p.128

Cooking methods:
stir-fry p.42 and
deep-fry p.45

★★★★

*Cooking time:
12-15 minutes*

Serves: 5-6

*Cooking methods:
stir-fry p.42 and
deep-fry p.45*

*Needs a little time
to prepare*

*Excellent as part
of a multi-dish
meal*

QUICK-FRIED PRAWNS IN SAUCE ON CRISPY RICE

In China, the scrapings of rice from the bottom of the rice cooking pan are often dried and fried to form a crispy sizzling bed for a saucy mixture of food.

■ PREPARATION ■

Rub the prawns with the salt. Dust with the cornflour and coat with the egg white. Cut the spring onions into 1 cm/½ inch shreds. Cube the bamboo shoots.

■ COOKING ■

Heat 8 tablespoons vegetable oil in a wok or frying pan. When hot, stir-fry the prawns for about 1½ minutes. Remove and drain. Pour away the oil to use for other purposes, leaving only about 1 tablespoon. Reheat the wok or pan. When hot, stir-fry the peas, mushrooms, spring onions and bamboo shoots over medium heat for 30 seconds. Add the stock, sugar, monosodium glutamate, if using, soya sauce, sherry, tomato purée and blended cornflour. Bring to the boil, stirring gently, until the sauce thickens, then return the prawns to the wok or pan. Continue to simmer very gently over low heat for a further 1 minute. Meanwhile, heat the oil in a wok or deep-fryer. When smoking hot, place the rice scrapings into a wire basket and fry for about 2 minutes. The rice will puff up immediately. Drain and place in a heated deep-sided serving dish.

■ SERVING ■

Place the dish of crispy rice scrapings in the centre of the table and pour over the prawn sauce. Serve immediately while the rice is still crisp.

225 g/8 oz peeled prawns
½ tsp salt
1 tbsp cornflour
1 egg white
2 spring onions
75 g/3 oz drained, canned bamboo shoots
vegetable oil for deep-frying
75 g/3 oz peas
75 g/3 oz drained, canned straw mushrooms
450 ml/¾ pt good stock (see page 56)
3 tsp sugar
pinch of MSG (optional)
1½ tbsp light soya sauce
1½ tbsp dry sherry
1½ tbsp tomato purée
1 tbsp cornflour blended with 2 tbsp water
100 g/4 oz rice scrapings (see above)

141

1 lt/2½ pt mussels

4 slices fresh root ginger

6 medium dried Chinese
mushrooms

2 cakes bean curd

3 cloves garlic

3 spring onions

450 ml/¾ pt good stock (see
page 56)

4-5 tbsp dry sherry

½ tsp salt

pepper to taste

1 chicken stock cube

1 tbsp cornflour blended with
2 tbsp water

1 tsp sesame oil

BRAISED MUSSELS WITH BEAN CURD AND MUSHROOMS

■ PREPARATION ■

Scrub the mussels thoroughly. Poach in a large saucepan of simmering water with the ginger for 1½ minutes, then drain. Discard any unopened ones. Transfer the mussels to a large pan or flameproof casserole. Soak the dried mushrooms in hot water to cover for 25 minutes. Drain and discard the tough stalks. Cut the mushroom caps into quarters. Cut the bean curd into cubes or rectangles. Finely chop the garlic. Shred the spring onions.

■ COOKING ■

Place the pan of mussels over medium-high heat. Pour in the stock and sherry or wine, then add the bean curd, mushrooms, garlic, half the spring onion, salt and pepper. Bring to the boil and sprinkle in the crumbled stock cube. Stir, then simmer gently for 10 minutes. Stir in the blended cornflour. Sprinkle with the remaining spring onion and the sesame oil.

★★★

Cooking time:
15 minutes

Serves: 5-6

Cooking methods:
poach and simmer

Fairly easy to
prepare

A useful starter to
eat by itself

Illustrated on
p.133

---

450 g/1 lb fresh squid

1 tsp salt

1 medium red pepper

1 medium green pepper

3 tbsp vegetable oil

3 slices fresh root ginger

Sauce:

20 g/¾ oz lard

2 tsp finely chopped garlic

2½ tbsp yellow bean paste

2 tsp sugar

1 tbsp soya sauce

1 tbsp tomato purée

1 tsp red chilli oil

2 tsp chilli sauce

1 tbsp dry sherry or white
wine

2 tsp cornflour blended with
1½ tbsp water

HUNAN CHILLI SQUID

■ PREPARATION ■

Clean the squid under running cold water. Cut into 2.5 × 1 cm/1 × ½ inch pieces. Sprinkle and rub with salt. Cut the peppers into similar-size pieces.

■ COOKING ■

Heat the oil in a wok or frying pan. When hot, stir-fry the ginger over medium heat for 30 seconds. Add the squid and stir-fry for 1½ minutes. Remove and drain. Add the lard to the wok or pan. When hot, add the garlic, yellow bean paste, sugar, soya sauce, tomato purée, red chilli oil and chilli sauce, and stir together over medium heat for 30 seconds. Add the sherry and blended cornflour. Stir and mix for 15 seconds. Return the squid to the pan, stirring and coating with the sauce. Stir in the peppers, turn and stir in the sauce for 1 minute.

★★★

Cooking time:
about 8 minutes

Serves: 4-6

Cooking method:
stir-fry, p.42

Quite easy to
prepare

Goes well with
most lightly
flavoured dishes

海鮮和貝殼類

QUICK-FRIED CRYSTAL PRAWNS

★★★

Cooking time:
about 6 minutes

Serves: 4-5

Cooking methods:
shallow-fry and
stir-fry, p.42

Quick to do

A nice light dish
that combines well
with other dishes

Illustrated on
p.132

Shell prawns,
p.40

PREPARATION

Shell the prawns. Wash in salted water, then rinse under running cold water. Drain well. Place in a bowl. Add salt, cornflour, egg white, sugar, pepper and ½ teaspoon vegetable oil. Mix well. Finely chop the spring onions and ginger.

COOKING

Heat the oil in a wok or deep frying pan. When hot, add the prawns, stir around and fry over medium heat for 1¾ minutes. Remove and drain. Pour away the oil to use for other purposes leaving only 1-1½ tablespoons. Reheat the wok or pan. When hot, stir-fry the ginger, spring onion and peas over high heat for 15 seconds. Add the stock and sherry or wine. As the sauce boils, return the prawns and adjust the seasoning. Fry for 1 minute.

350g/12oz King prawns, fresh or frozen, unshelled

1 tsp salt

1½ tbsp cornflour

1 egg white

½ tsp sugar

pepper to taste

150ml/¼pt vegetable oil

2 spring onions

2 slices fresh root ginger

3-4 tbsp green peas (optional)

2½ tbsp good stock (see page 56)

1½ tbsp dry sherry or white wine

QUICK-FRIED CHILLI PRAWNS

★★★

Cooking time:
about 6-8 minutes

Serves: 5-6

Cooking methods:
shallow-fry and
stir-fry, p.42

Quick to make

Will accompany
most other
Chinese dishes

Shell prawns,
p.40

PREPARATION

Shell the prawns. Wash in salted water, then rinse under cold running water. Drain well. Finely chop the chillies, discarding the seeds. Coarsely chop the ginger and spring onions. Place the prawns in a bowl. Add 1 teaspoon of the salt, the cornflour, egg white and wine or sherry and mix well.

COOKING

Heat the oil in a wok or frying pan. When hot, add the prawns, stir around and fry for 2 minutes. Remove and drain. Pour away the oil to use for other purposes leaving only 2 tablespoons. Reheat the wok or pan. When hot, stir-fry the chillies and ginger over medium heat for 30 seconds. Add the sugar, yellow bean paste, tomato purée, stock, remaining salt, vinegar and spring onions. Toss and stir for 15 seconds. Return the prawns to the pan. Stir and turn for 30 seconds. Pour in the blended cornflour. Sprinkle over the sesame oil. Stir and turn once more.

450g/1lb King prawns

1 small fresh green chilli

2 small dried red chillies

2 slices fresh root ginger

2 spring onions

1½ tsp salt

1½ tbsp cornflour

1 egg white

1 tbsp dry sherry or white wine

150ml/¼pt vegetable oil

1½ tsp sugar

1 tbsp yellow bean paste

1 tbsp tomato purée

2½ tbsp good stock (see page 56)

1 tbsp wine vinegar

2 tsp cornflour blended with 2 tbsp water

1 tsp sesame oil

900g/2lb (2 crabs)
5-6 spring onions
5-6 slices fresh root ginger
3 tbsp dry sherry
1½ tsp salt
5 tbsp vegetable oil
2 eggs
Sauce:
1 red chilli
3 cloves garlic
2 tbsp salted black beans
2 tbsp good stock (see page 56)
2 tbsp vinegar
1 tbsp sugar
2 tsp cornflour blended with 2 tbsp water
1½ tsp sesame oil

QUICK-FRIED CRAB IN HOT BLACK BEAN SAUCE

■ PREPARATION ■

Scrub the crabs under running cold water. Break each crab into 6 pieces, discarding the grey dead men's fingers. Crack the claws and legs with the back of a chopper. Cut the spring onions in 1 cm/½ inch shreds. Finely chop the ginger and chilli, discarding the seeds. Crush the garlic. Soak the black beans in hot water for 5 minutes, then drain and crush. Place the crab pieces in a bowl with half of the spring onion and the ginger, sherry and salt. Mix together and leave to marinate for 15 minutes.

■ COOKING ■

Heat the vegetable oil in a wok or frying pan. When very hot, stir-fry the crab pieces over high heat for 2½ minutes. Remove and drain. Pour away the oil to use for other purposes leaving about 1 tablespoon. Reheat the wok or pan. When hot, stir-fry the remaining spring onion, the garlic, chilli and black beans over medium heat for 30 seconds. Add the stock, vinegar and sugar. Continue to stir-fry quickly, then return the crab pieces to the wok or pan. Turn and stir for 1 minute, then add the beaten egg and cook for 30 seconds, stirring. Add the blended cornflour and sesame oil. Turn and stir until thickened.

★★★
Cooking time: about 10 minutes

Serves: 5-6

Cooking method: stir-fry, p.42

A dish that is good by itself, perhaps as an hors d'oeuvre

2 spring onions
2 eggs
3 tbsp vegetable oil
225g/8oz fresh shelled scallops
1 tsp salt
½ tsp sugar
1½ tbsp dry sherry
pepper to taste
20g/¾oz lard
1½ tbsp finely chopped ham

STIR-FRIED SCALLOPS WITH EGG

■ PREPARATION ■

Coarsely chop the spring onions, dividing the white and green parts. Lightly beat the eggs.

■ COOKING ■

Heat the oil in a wok or frying pan. When hot, stir-fry the scallops and white parts of the spring onions over medium heat for 1 minute. Add the salt, sugar, sherry and pepper. Continue to stir-fry for 1 minute. Remove from the pan. Add the lard to the wok or pan. When hot, pour in the beaten eggs. Stir them around a couple of times and, before they have set, return the scallops to the pan. Turn and stir with the egg for 30 seconds. Sprinkle with the green parts of the spring onion. Stir once more, then transfer to a heated serving dish. Sprinkle with chopped ham.

★★
Cooking time: 6-8 minutes

Serves: 4-6

Cooking method: stir-fry, p.42

Quick and easy to prepare

Goes well with most Chinese dishes. Serve with good quality soy sauce or grated ginger and vinegar dip sauce

★★

Cooking time:
10 minutes

Serves: 5-6

Cooking method:
stir-fry, p.42

Quick and easy to
prepare

Versatile dish for
any part of a
Chinese meal

STIR-FRIED PRAWNS IN GARLIC AND TOMATO SAUCE

■ PREPARATION ■

Toss the prawns in the salt, dust with the cornflour and coat in the egg white. Crush the garlic. Cut the spring onions into shreds. Skin the tomatoes and cut into eighths.

■ COOKING ■

Heat the oil in a wok or frying pan. When hot, stir-fry the prawns over high heat for 1½ minutes. Remove from the wok or pan. Pour away the excess oil and reheat the wok or pan. When hot, stir-fry the garlic, half the spring onions and tomatoes over high heat for 30 seconds. Add the tomato purée, salt, sugar, monosodium glutamate, if using, and stock and continue stir-frying for another 30 seconds. Stir in the blended cornflour until the sauce thickens. Sprinkle on the sesame oil and remaining spring onions. Return the prawns to the wok or pan, stir once more and serve.

350g/12oz peeled prawns, fresh or frozen

1 tsp salt

¾ tbsp cornflour

1 egg white

2 cloves garlic

2 spring onions

2 small firm tomatoes

6 tbsp vegetable oil

Sauce:

2 tbsp tomato sauce or purée

¼ tsp salt

1 tbsp sugar

pinch of MSG (optional)

6 tbsp good stock (see page 56)

1½ tbsp cornflour blended with 3 tbsp water

1 tsp sesame oil

★★★

Cooking time:
20 minutes

Serves: 4-5

Cooking method:
poach

A good starter

FUKIEN CLAM SOUP

■ PREPARATION ■

Wash and clean the clams well with a stiff brush under running water. Bring 1.2lt/2pt water to the boil in a saucepan and add the salt. Simmer the clams for 2 minutes, then leave to stand in the water, off the heat, for a further minute. Drain. Discard any clams which are unopened. Soak the dried shrimps in hot water to cover for 5 minutes, then drain. Finely shred the ginger and spring onions. Crush the garlic.

■ COOKING ■

Place the poached clams in a saucepan. Add the dried shrimps, ginger, garlic, salt, pepper and crumbled stock cubes. Pour in the stock and bring to the boil. Reduce the heat and simmer for 10 minutes. Add the spring onions, soya sauce and vinegar, and continue to simmer for another 5 minutes.

■ SERVING ■

Place the clams and soup in a heated large serving bowl and sprinkle on the sesame oil. Serve in individual bowls and eat like 'Moules Marinière' or the dish can be eaten from a large central bowl in the normal Chinese way.

1.5kg/3lb clams

2 tbsp salt

1½ tbsp dried shrimps

2 slices fresh root ginger

3 spring onions

2 cloves garlic

2 tsp salt

pepper to taste

1½ chicken stock cubes

900ml/1½pt good stock (see page 56)

1½ tbsp light soya sauce

1 tbsp vinegar

½ tsp sesame oil

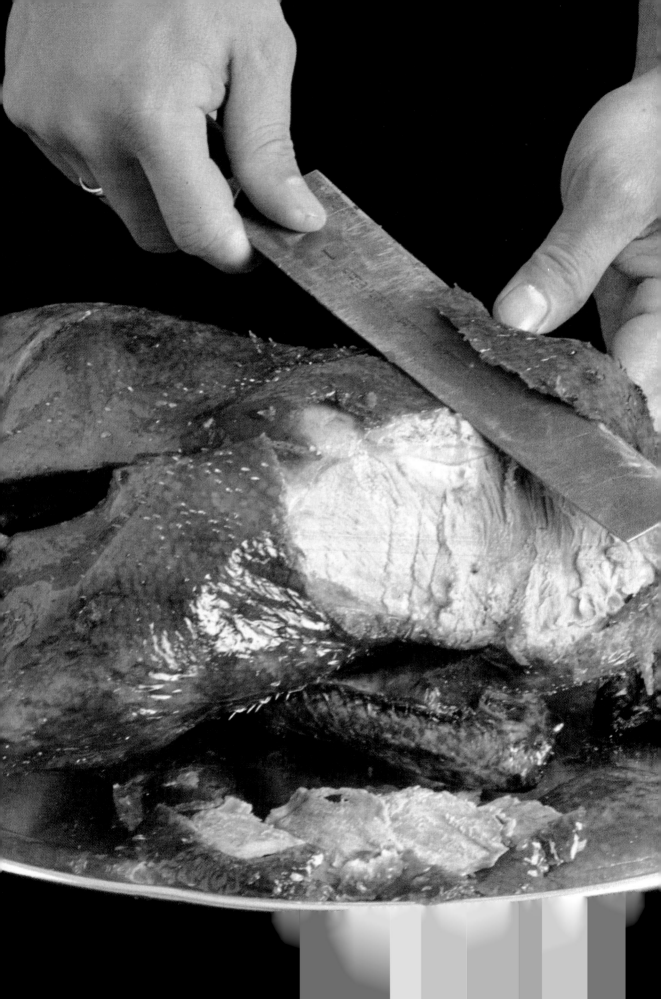

POULTRY

Carving Peking Duck (*left*); recipe page 178.
Crispy 'Five Spiced' Chicken Legs (*above*); recipe page 166.

家禽類

CHICKEN
Chicken is regarded as a greater delicacy than pork on the Chinese menu and is nearly as widely used, mainly because of its convenient unit size. It is a relatively simple matter for a Chinese family to kill a chicken in order to provide an extra large dish for visiting guests or relatives. This is especially true of peasant families, who make up over 90 per cent of the Chinese population.

Visitors to China often find the free-range chickens produced there tough but full of flavour. This natural flavour is heightened by the unique Chinese treatment of chicken as a dish. Indeed, the Chinese knack of incorporating a wide range of ingredients in their dishes is an example that many Western cooks would do well to follow. The flavour blending and flavour development techniques used can compensate for the reduction in flavour of the mass-produced chicken mainly produced in the West.

Chinese chicken, like pork, has a neutral savouriness which enables it to combine easily with other foods and ingredients, a characteristic which has allowed almost unlimited potential for the development of new dishes. The cooking and flavouring techniques used for many of these dishes are similar, as you will see.

1.5-1.75 kg/3-4 lb chicken
300 ml/½ pt good stock (see page 56)
1 chicken stock cube
4 slices fresh root ginger
¼ tsp salt
1½ tbsp sugar
pepper to taste
5-6 tbsp light soya sauce
2 pieces star anise

RED-COOKED CHICKEN

'Red-cooked' means that the chicken is cooked with soya sauce instead of in stock and water with seasonings added. Red-cooked chicken is about the most common chicken dish in China.

■ PREPARATION ■
Bring a large pan of water to the boil, add the chicken and simmer for about 8 minutes. Remove and drain thoroughly. Place the bird in a flameproof casserole, add the stock, crumbled stock cube, ginger, salt, sugar, pepper, soya sauce and star anise. Bring to the boil.

■ COOKING ■
Cover and place the casserole in a preheated oven at 200°C, 400°F, Gas Mark 6, and cook for 30 minutes. Turn the bird over, reduce the oven temperature to 180°C, 350°F, Gas Mark 4, and cook for a further 25 minutes, turn the bird over again and continue to cook for a final 25 minutes.

★★

Cooking time:
1 hour 20 minutes

Serves: 6-8

Cooking method: casserole

Easy and straightforward

A main meal to accompany most vegetable and savoury dishes

WHITE-CUT CHICKEN

★★

Cooking time:
15 minutes, plus
cooling time

Serves: 4

Cooking method:
simmer

Easy to prepare

■ PREPARATION ■

Wash the chicken thoroughly. Cut the spring onions into 5 cm/2 inch sections.

■ COOKING ■

Bring about 1.75 lt/3 pt water to the boil in a saucepan. Add the ginger, salt, spring onions and sherry. Place the chicken in the water, bring to the boil and simmer for about 15 minutes. Remove from the heat and allow the bird to cool in the water. To make the dip sauce, heat the oil in a small saucepan. Add the garlic, then the soya sauce and mustard. Stir together well. Take out the chicken and drain. Cut into large bite sized pieces. Arrange the chicken on a large platter and serve with the dip sauce.

Ingredients
1.25 kg/2½ lb young chicken
3 spring onions
4-5 slices fresh root ginger
3 tsp salt
3 tbsp dry sherry
Dip sauce:
2 tbsp peanut oil
2 cloves garlic, crushed
4 tbsp soya sauce
1 tbsp prepared English mustard

STIR-FRIED CHICKEN
WITH GARLIC AND CUCUMBER CUBES

★★★

Cooking time:
about 5-6 minutes

Serves: 5-6

Cooking method:
stir-fry, p.42

Fairly quick and
easy to make

A light dish.
Serve as a starter
or with vegetables
and red-cooked
dishes

Illustrated on
p.154

■ PREPARATION ■

Cut the chicken into 1 cm/½ inch cubes. Cut the cucumber into similar-size cubes. Sprinkle and rub the chicken evenly with the 1 teaspoon salt, pepper and half the cornflour, then wet with egg white. Crush the garlic. Chop the lard. Blend the remaining cornflour with the 2 tablespoons stock. Cut the spring onions into 4 cm/1½ inch sections.

■ COOKING ■

Heat the vegetable oil in a wok or frying pan. When hot, stir in ginger slices for 15 seconds to flavour the oil. Remove and discard the ginger. Add the chicken cubes to the pan and stir-fry over medium to high heat for 45 seconds. Remove and drain. Add the lard and garlic to the wok or pan and stir over medium heat for 15 seconds. Add the cucumber cubes and sprinkle with the ½ teaspoon salt, pepper and monosodium glutamate, if using. Stir-fry for 1 minute. Add the sherry, soya sauce and spring onion. Return the chicken to the pan and stir-fry for 1 minute. Add the blended cornflour and sesame oil and stir-fry for 10 seconds.

■ SERVING ■

Serve this light coloured dish as a starter to a multi-course Chinese meal.

Ingredients
about ½ chicken breast
1 medium cucumber
1 tsp salt
pepper to taste
4 tsp cornflour
½ egg white
2 cloves garlic
15 g/½ oz lard
2 tbsp good stock (see page 56)
2 spring onions
3 tbsp vegetable oil
2 slices fresh root ginger
½ tsp salt
¼ tsp MSG (optional)
1½ tbsp dry sherry
1 tbsp light soya sauce
½ tsp sesame oil

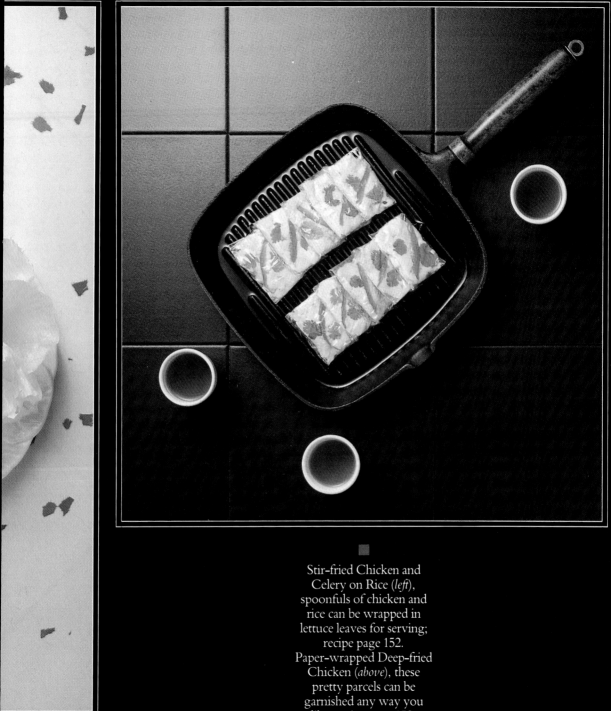

Stir-fried Chicken and
Celery on Rice (*left*),
spoonfuls of chicken and
rice can be wrapped in
lettuce leaves for serving;
recipe page 152.
Paper-wrapped Deep-fried
Chicken (*above*), these
pretty parcels can be
garnished any way you
like; recipe page 152.

Ingredients
2-3 medium dried Chinese mushrooms
1 chicken breast
1 stalk celery
50g/2oz drained, canned bamboo shoots
2 slices fresh root ginger
2 spring onions
3tbsp vegetable oil
salt and pepper to taste
2tbsp good stock (see page 56)
2tbsp dry sherry
1tbsp light soya sauce
225g/8oz boiled rice or 100-150g/4-5oz crispy rice (see pages 68 or 141)

STIR-FRIED CHICKEN AND CELERY ON RICE

★★ Cooking time: about 5 minutes. Serves: 4. Cooking method: stir-fry, p.42. Quick to prepare. Illustrated on p.150

PREPARATION

Soak the dried mushrooms in hot water to cover for 25 minutes. Drain and discard the tough stalks. Cut the mushroom caps into small cubes. Dice the chicken into small cubes. Dice the celery and bamboo shoots into similar sized cubes. Finely chop the ginger. Chop the spring onions.

COOKING

Heat the oil in a wok or frying pan. When hot, stir-fry the ginger, spring onion, mushrooms, celery and bamboo shoots over high heat for 1 minute. Add the chicken and stir-fry for 1 minute. Sprinkle with salt and pepper to taste. Add the stock, sherry and soya sauce, turn and toss for further minute.

SERVING

Serve on boiled or crispy rice. If liked, wrap spoonfuls of chicken and rice in lettuce leaves to eat with the fingers.

Ingredients
450g/1lb chicken breasts
5 dried Chinese mushrooms
2 slices ham
2 spring onions
2 bunches parsley
15 sheets cellophane paper – not plastic or cling film
2tbsp sesame oil
vegetable oil for deep-frying
Marinade:
3tbsp light soya sauce
½tsp salt
1½tbsp dry sherry
½tsp sugar
¼tsp pepper
2tsp sesame oil
2tsp cornflour

PAPER-WRAPPED DEEP-FRIED CHICKEN

★★★★ Cooking time: about 5 minutes. Serves: 5-6. Cooking method: deep-fry, p.45. Takes time to prepare. An attractive hot starter. Illustrated on p.151

Serve these savoury parcels as part of an hors d'oeuvres selection. The parcels can be garnished in many different ways.

PREPARATION

Cut the chicken into 5 × 1cm/2 × ½ inch strips. Place in a bowl and add all the ingredients for the marinade. Mix well and leave to marinate for 20 minutes. Soak the dried mushrooms in hot water to cover for 25 minutes. Drain and discard the tough stalks. Cut the mushroom caps into about 6 pieces each. Cut the ham into 5cm/2inch strips. Cut the spring onions into 5cm/2 inch sections. Cut and divide the parsley into about 15 portions. Brush 1 sheet of cellophane paper with sesame oil and place a spray of parsley in the middle. Divide and place a little mushroom and ham on either side, lay some sliced chicken on top and a spring onion on top of that. Fold the cellophane to completely enclose the filling.

COOKING

Heat the oil in a wok or deep-fryer. When hot, fry the envelopes for about 2 minutes. Remove. Reheat the oil and fry again for 2 minutes. Drain. Serve the envelopes arranged on a large heated plate.

SIMULATED BEGGARS' CHICKEN

★ ★ ★ ★ ★

Cooking time: 2 hours 15 minutes

Serves: 6-8

Cooking method: bake

Takes time to prepare and cook

An interesting party dish

I recommend this Simulated Beggars' Chicken in preference to the original recipe which requires encasing the whole chicken in a layer of mud. Since suitable mud is difficult to find in the West, this recipe is much easier.

■ PREPARATION ■

Bring a large pan of water to the boil. Add the chicken and simmer for about 5 minutes. Remove, drain and dry very thoroughly. Finely chop the ginger. Mix together the salt, hoisin sauce, oyster sauce, sherry, soya sauce, sugar and ginger. Rub about three-quarters of this mixture both inside and outside the chicken. Leave the chicken to season for 30 minutes.

For the stuffing, soak the dried mushrooms in hot water to cover for 25 minutes. Drain and discard the tough stalks. Finely slice the mushroom caps. Cut the pork, bamboo shoots and pickles into similar-size shreds. Place the pork into the remaining marinade and leave to marinate. Heat the oil in a small frying pan. When hot, stir-fry the mushrooms and pork for about 2 minutes. Add the pickle and bamboo shoots and stir-fry for 1 minute. Stuff all these ingredients into the chicken cavity. Soak the lotus leaves in water for 10 minutes until soft. Wrap the chicken in the suet, then the lotus leaves. Mix together the flour and water to form a thick dough and wrap the chicken in the dough. Finally cover the chicken completely in foil.

■ COOKING ■

Place the foil parcel in a preheated oven at 200°C, 400°F, Gas Mark 6, and cook for 45 minutes. Reduce the oven temperature to 190°C, 375°F, Gas Mark 5, and cook for a further 45 minutes. Reduce the heat again to 180°C, 350°F, Gas Mark 4, and cook for a final 45 minutes.

■ SERVING ■

Remove the foil and crack the tough casing with a hammer. Lift out the lotus-wrapped chicken and serve on a heated platter straight from the leaves.

1.5-1.75kg/3½-4lb chicken
2 slices fresh root ginger
2 tsp salt
1 tbsp hoisin sauce
1½ tbsp oyster sauce
3½ tbsp dry sherry
2½ tbsp soya sauce
2 tsp sugar

Stuffing:
6 medium dried Chinese mushrooms
450g/1lb pork
275g/10oz drained, canned bamboo shoots
100g/4oz drained, canned Sichuan hot Ja Chai pickles
2 tbsp vegetable oil

Wrapping:
2 large lotus leaves
1 large sheet of suet
575g/1¼lb plain flour
450ml/¾pt water

153

Chicken Fu–Yung (*above left*), a light chicken dish with egg garnished with chopped dried shrimps; recipe page 167.
Stir-fried Chicken with Garlic and Cucumber (*below left*), a quick stir-fried dish; recipe page 149.
Shanghai Quick-braised Chicken on the Bone (*above*), garnished with spring onion tassels and served with extra soya sauce; recipe page 164.

1 tbsp salt

2 tsp crushed Sichuan
  peppercorns

1½ tsp ground ginger

1½ tsp sugar

1.5 kg/3-3½ lb chicken

Cooking stock:

1.2 lt/2 pt good stock (see page
  56)

2 tsp salt

2 tsp crushed Sichuan
  peppercorns

½ tsp five spice powder

6 spring onions

6 slices fresh root ginger

Fuel for smoking:

4-5 tbsp damp tealeaves

2 tbsp five spice powder or in
  pieces

2 tbsp brown sugar

8 tbsp sawdust, pine, oak etc.

Garnish:

2 tbsp sesame oil

2½ tbsp chopped coriander
  leaves

SIMPLE SICHUAN SMOKED CHICKEN

■ PREPARATION AND COOKING ■

Mix together the salt, peppercorns, ground ginger and sugar. Wash the chicken and dry thoroughly. Rub the chicken inside and out with this mixture and leave to marinate overnight. Bring a large pan of water to the boil, add the chicken, making sure it is covered with water, and simmer for about 5 minutes. Mix the stock ingredients together. Pour away the water and replace with the cooking stock. Bring to the boil and simmer gently for 25 minutes. Drain.

■ SMOKING ■

Use an old pot, pan or wok large enough to suspend the chicken in. Mix the fuel together and place in the bottom of the pan. Arrange a wire rack about 5-7.5 cm-2-3 inches above the fuel. Place the pan over high heat and, when smoke rises, put the chicken on the rack. Cover with a large lid or another pan. Smoke the chicken for 10 minutes, then turn it over, cover and smoke again for 10 minutes.

■ SERVING ■

Rub the chicken evenly with sesame oil, then chop it into about 24 bite-sized pieces. Reassemble the chicken on a large heated platter and sprinkle on the coriander leaves.

★★★★★

Cooking time: 30 minutes, plus 20 minutes smoking time

Serves: 8-10 (at a party)

Cooking methods: simmer and smoke

Takes time and a lot of preparation

An unusual dish to serve as a change from stir-fried

1.5-1.75 kg/3½-4 lb chicken

vegetable oil for deep-frying

2 tbsp soya sauce

1 tbsp oyster sauce

3 medium onions

4 slices fresh root ginger

3 cloves garlic

100 g/4 oz button mushrooms

225 g/8 oz belly pork

2 tsp salt

300 ml/½ pt good stock (see
  page 56)

1 chicken stock cube

300 ml/½ pt dry white wine

450 ml/¾ pt dry sherry

ROYAL CONCUBINE CHICKEN

This dish is said to date from Yan Kwie-Fei, a royal concubine who was drunk more often than not; it might also be called 'Chinese Coq au Vin'.

■ PREPARATION ■

Wash the chicken and dry thoroughly. Heat the oil in a wok or deep-fryer. When hot, gently fry the chicken for about 7 minutes. Drain. Plunge the chicken momentarily into a pan of boiling water to remove any fat. Dry, then rub the bird inside and out with the soya and oyster sauces. Place the chicken in a casserole and leave to season. Peel and thinly slice the onions. Crush the ginger and garlic. Cut the mushrooms in half. Cut the pork into 4 × 7.5 cm/1½ × 3 inch slices.

■ COOKING ■

Heat 3 tablespoons oil in a wok or frying pan. When hot, stir-fry the pork over high heat for about 2 minutes. Add the ginger, onion, garlic and salt and continue to stir-fry for 2

★★★★★

Cooking time: about 1½ hours

Serves: 6-8

Cooking methods: deep-fry p.45, stir-fry p.42 and casserole

A rich dish to serve with vegetables and stir-fried dishes

minutes. Pour in the stock and add the crumbled stock cube and white wine. Bring to the boil and pour over the chicken in the casserole. Cover the casserole and place in a preheated oven at 200°C, 400°F, Gas Mark 6, for 30 minutes. Reduce the oven temperature to 190°C, 375°F, Gas Mark 5, and turn the bird over. Continue to cook for another 30 minutes. Turn the bird over again, add the sherry and mushrooms and cook for an additional 30 minutes.

■ SERVING ■

Serve this dish straight from the casserole at the table. Spoon the soup into individual bowls to serve as a soup.

★ ★

Cooking time: about 5 minutes

Serves: 5-6

Cooking method: stir-fry, p.42

Quick and easy

Serve alone or accompany with other stir-fried dishes

PEKING DICED CHICKEN STIR-FRIED IN CAPITAL SAUCE

Capital Sauce is used and served more frequently in Peking than anywhere else in China. It consists of a mixture of yellow bean paste, soya sauce, sugar, ginger or ginger water, sesame oil, a small amount of sherry and cornflour all blended together over high heat.

■ PREPARATION ■

Cut the chicken into cubes, then toss them in salt and cornflour and wet with egg white. To make ginger water, boil 3 slices of fresh root ginger in 6 tablespoons water until reduced by half.

■ SMOKING ■

Heat the vegetable oil in a wok or frying pan. When hot, add the chicken and separate the cubes. Stir-fry over high heat for about 30 seconds, then remove and keep warm. Pour away the excess oil. Reheat the wok or pan and add the yellow bean paste and ginger water. Add the sherry, sugar and soya sauce, then stir in the blended cornflour over high heat. Add the chicken and stir in the thickened sauce. Add the sesame oil and stir together.

■ SERVING ■

Serve hot on its own to nibble while sipping wine; or eat as a dish with rice as part of a meal.

450g/1lb chicken breasts

3/4 tsp salt

1 tbsp cornflour

1 egg white

6 tbsp vegetable oil

Sauce:

1 3/4 tbsp yellow bean paste

1 1/2 tbsp ginger water (see Preparation)

1 tbsp dry sherry

2 tsp sugar

2 tsp soya sauce

2 tsp cornflour blended with 1 1/2 tbsp water

1 tsp sesame oil

1.5 kg/3-3½ lb chicken
sea salt

SALT BURIED BAKED CHICKEN

★★★
Cooking time:
1 hour 25 minutes

Serves: 4-6

Cooking method:
bake

Illustrated
opposite

This is a favourite Cantonese dish, producing a chicken with crispy dry skin. As long as the salt and the chicken are both dry, the chicken will not be over-salty when cooked.

PREPARATION

Wash the chicken and dry very carefully. Hang up overnight in a well ventilated place to ensure it is perfectly dry. Heat the salt in a saucepan to ensure it too is dry.

COOKING

Spoon a layer of salt in the bottom of a flameproof casserole. Put the chicken in the casserole and cover with the salt. Place a heavy lid on the casserole and cook over a low heat for about 15 minutes. Place in a preheated oven at 190°C, 375°F, Gas Mark 5, and cook for 30 minutes. Reduce the oven temperature to 180°C, 350°F, Gas Mark 4, and continue to cook for another 40 minutes without lifting the lid.

SERVING

Remove the chicken from the salt and chop it into small bite-size pieces. Arrange on a heated platter. If liked, a mixture of 3 chopped spring onions fried in 3 tablespoons vegetable oil can be poured over the chicken.

½ medium chicken
1 medium onion
3 tsp salt
3 slices fresh root ginger
1 medium cucumber

Sauce:
1½ tbsp chilli sauce or red chilli oil
1 tbsp chopped garlic
1 tbsp chopped fresh root ginger
1 tbsp peanut butter
1 tbsp chopped spring onion
2 tsp sesame oil
1½ tbsp vegetable oil
4 tbsp good stock (see page 56)
½ tsp salt
¼ tsp MSG (optional)

HOT TOSSED SHREDDED CHICKEN IN RED CHILLI OIL

★★
Cooking time:
45 minutes, plus
cooling time

Serves: 4-6

Cooking method:
simmer

Easy to prepare

Usually served as
a starter

This dish is usually eaten cold or as a starter. It can be a useful dish to serve while waiting for stir-fried dishes to appear.

PREPARATION AND COOKING

Bring about 1.2 lt/2 pt water to the boil in a pan. Add the chicken and simmer for about 10 minutes. Peel and slice the onion. Pour away a quarter of the water and add the salt, ginger and onion. Cook for another 35 minutes. Cut the cucumber into shreds, leaving the skin on. Remove the chicken and cool. Shred the meat into pieces of similar size to cucumber shreds.

SERVING

Place all the sauce ingredients in a bowl and mix well. Arrange the cucumber on a plate and pile the chicken on top. Pour over the sauce.

家禽類

1.5-1.75 kg/3½-4 lb chicken
1½ tsp salt
6 tbsp vegetable oil
6 slices fresh root ginger
300 ml/½ pt good stock (see page 56)
2 tbsp light soya sauce
2 tbsp dark soya sauce
2 tbsp yellow bean paste
1½ tbsp sugar
4 tbsp dry sherry or rice wine
5 tbsp honey

QUICK BRAISED CHICKEN WITH HONEY

The sweetness of the honey contrasts well with the savoury soya chicken.

■ PREPARATION ■

Chop the chicken through the bone into 28–30 bite-size pieces. Sprinkle and rub with salt.

■ COOKING ■

Heat the oil in a wok or flameproof casserole. When hot, add the ginger and stir over high heat for 30 seconds. Add the chicken, stir and turn in the flavoured oil over high heat for 5 minutes. Drain away any excess oil. Pour the stock, soya sauces, yellow bean paste, sugar and sherry or wine evenly over the chicken. When the contents begin to boil, turn and stir the chicken in the sauce for 2 minutes over high heat. Cover the wok or casserole and continue to boil for a further 10 minutes. Remove the lid and turn the chicken so that all the pieces are coated in the sauce. Continue to boil rapidly until the sauce is reduced to less than 10 per cent of its original volume, stirring now and then. The consistency will be very sticky and rich. Stir the chicken pieces to coat in the thickened sauce. Pour the honey evenly over the chicken. Turn the contents once more, then serve.

★★
Cooking time: about 20 minutes

Serves: 6-8

Cooking method: stir-fry p.42 and quick-braise

Easy to prepare

A main item in a multi-dish meal

450 g/1 lb chicken breasts
salt and pepper to taste
2 eggs
2 spring onions
2 cloves garlic
4-5 tbsp vegetable oil
5 tbsp good stock (see page 56)
2 tsp wine vinegar
1½ tbsp dry sherry
¼ tsp MSG (optional)

PEKING SLICED EGG–BATTERED CHICKEN
IN GARLIC AND ONION SAUCE

■ PREPARATION ■

Cut chicken meat into approximately 5 × 10 × 0.5 cm/ 2 × 4 × ¼ inch thick slices. Sprinkle and rub with salt and pepper. Break the eggs in a bowl, add the chicken slices and coat thoroughly. Finely chop the spring onions and garlic.

■ COOKING ■

Heat the oil in a wok or frying pan over medium heat. Add the battered chicken slices, one by one, and spread them out evenly over the surface of the wok or pan. Shake the pan and reduce the heat to low. Cook the chicken pieces for 1½ minutes. Once the egg has set, turn the chicken slices over to cook for 30 seconds. Sprinkle the chicken with garlic and onion. Mix the stock with 1½ teaspoons salt, vinegar and sherry in a bowl. Pour half this mixture evenly over the chicken pieces. Simmer gently for 1¾ minutes.

★★
Cooking time: about 8 minutes

Serves: 4-6

Cooking method: shallow-fry

Easy to prepare

Serve as part of a multi-dish meal

■ SERVING ■

Remove the chicken slices with perforated spoon and place them on a chopping board. Cut into 0.5 cm/¼ inch wide strips. Arrange them on a heated serving dish. Add ¼ teaspoon salt, the monosodium glutamate, if using, and remaining stock to the pan. Bring to the boil and pour it evenly over the chicken pieces.

■ DRUNKEN CHICKEN ■

★ ★ ★

Cooking time: 15 minutes, plus cooling and soaking time

Serves: 8-10 (as a starter)

Cooking method: simmer

Quite easy to prepare, but time needed for soaking

A good starter

1.5 kg/3-3½ lb chicken
2 medium onions
6 slices fresh root ginger
1½ tbsp salt
1.2 lt/2 pt water
600 ml/1 pt rice wine or dry sherry

This is a dish which is often used as part of a multi-dish hors d'oeuvres. Although it takes time to make, the process is comparatively straightforward. If liked, the remaining wine or sherry may be reused in cooking.

■ PREPARATION ■

Wash, dry and cut the chicken in half. Peel and thinly slice the onions. Cut the ginger into shreds. Place the onion and ginger in a saucepan, add the salt and pour in the water. Bring to the boil and simmer for 10 minutes.

■ COOKING ■

Add the chicken halves to the pan, making sure they are totally immersed. Bring slowly to the boil and simmer gently for 15 minutes. Turn off the heat and allow the chicken to cool in the water for 1 hour.

■ SOAKING ■

Remove the chicken pieces from the pan and drain. Transfer to a bowl. Pour the wine or sherry over the chicken. Turn the halves over a few times, making sure they are completely covered. Place the bowl in the refrigerator overnight (or longer), again turning the chicken over a couple of times during this time.

■ SERVING ■

When required, lift the chicken pieces out of the wine or sherry and place them on a chopping board. Chop each half of the chicken through the bones into 10-12 pieces. Arrange them attractively on a serving dish or as an item on a much larger platter.

1.5-2kg/3½-4½lb chicken
1 medium Chinese white cabbage
6 slices fresh root ginger
1.2lt/2pt good stock (see page 56) or water
2½tsp salt
2 chicken stock cubes
pepper to taste
½tsp MSG (optional)

WHITE-COOKED OR CLEAR-SIMMERED CHICKEN
WITH CHINESE WHITE CABBAGE

★★
Cooking time: about 2 hours

Serves: 6-8

Cooking method: simmer

Easy to prepare

Unlike red-cooked chicken, the aim of which is to produce a very rich meaty dish with a highly savoury gravy or sauce suitable for consuming with rice, the aim of white-cooked chicken is to produce a dish where the richness of the chicken combines with the sweet freshness of the cabbage. As a whole chicken is cooked, there is likely to be more than 900ml/1½pt of liquid, therefore, the Chinese call this recipe a semi-soup dish.

■ PREPARATION ■

Bring a large pan of water to the boil, add the chicken and boil for about 7 minutes. Remove and drain thoroughly. Cut the cabbage into about 5 even sections and wash carefully.

■ COOKING ■

Arrange the slices of ginger in the bottom of a large flameproof casserole and place the chicken on top. Add the stock or water and salt and bring to the boil. Simmer gently for 30 minutes and then turn the bird over. Add the crumbled stock cubes, pepper and monosodium glutamate, if using, and simmer for another 30 minutes, then turn the bird over once more. After 1½ hours, remove the bird from the casserole and place the cabbage in the bottom of the casserole. Put the chicken back on top to submerge all the cabbage. Simmer again for another 30 minutes.

■ SERVING ■

Serve the dish straight from the casserole at the table with the help of a small ladle. The chicken will be tender enough to serve with the chopsticks and can be dipped into good quality soya sauce.

Note: The above recipe can be made into a more elaborate party meal by adding 50-75g/2-3oz smoked ham, slices, and 6-8 medium Chinese dried mushrooms (soaked for 25 minutes, stalks removed). These should be added at the beginning of the cooking. At the party, serve the dish as a soup or semi-soup, divide the chicken and cabbage and ladle into the individual bowls with a tablespoon of Chinese rice wine.

★★★

Cooking time:
about 5-7 minutes

Serves: 5-6

Cooking method:
stir-fry, p.42

Quick to prepare

A spicy dish, best
served with
vegetables and
lighter tasting
dishes

CHICKEN WITH CHILLIES AND RED PEPPER

■ PREPARATION ■

Skin the chicken and cut into cubes. Add the salt, cornflour, wine and egg white. Mix together thoroughly. Finely chop the ginger, garlic and fresh and dried chillies, discarding the seeds, together. Shred the spring onions. Cut the red pepper into cubes.

■ COOKING ■

Heat the oil in a wok or frying pan. When hot, stir-fry the chicken cubes over high heat for about 45 seconds. Drain and pour away the oil to use for other purposes. Reheat the wok or pan. Stir-fry the chillies, ginger and garlic over high heat for a few seconds until the fragrance begins to rise. Add the spring onion and red pepper and stir-fry for 30 seconds. Return the chicken to the wok or pan and add the stock, sugar, soya sauce and vinegar. Turn all the ingredients together for 15 seconds.

450g/1lb chicken breasts
1 tsp salt
1½ tbsp cornflour
1½ tbsp rice wine
1 egg white
2 slices fresh root ginger
1 clove garlic
1 fresh chilli
1 dried chilli
2 spring onions
1 red pepper
150ml/¼pt vegetable oil
2 tbsp good stock (see page 56)
1 tsp sugar
1 tbsp light soya sauce
1¼ tbsp wine vinegar

★★★

Cooking time:
1 hour

Serves: 6-8

Cooking method:
steam, p.49

Excellent as
variety to stir-fried
dishes

STEAMED CHICKEN IN AROMATIC GROUND RICE

Ground rice, which has coarser grains than rice flour, can be made aromatic either by roasting or frying in a dry frying pan until slightly browned. It is then used much as breadcrumbs are used in English cooking, for coating meats and fish.

■ PREPARATION ■

Chop the ginger. Chop the chicken into 20 bite-size pieces. Sprinkle with salt, pepper and ginger and leave to season for 10 minutes. Dip in the egg white and coat with the ground rice.

■ COOKING ■

Place the coated pieces of chicken on to a heatproof dish, place in a steamer and steam for 1 hour. Drain off the liquid which has collected in the dish into a small pan. Add the chicken fat and bring to the boil. Add the rest of the sauce ingredients and stir together for about 15 seconds. Arrange the chicken pieces on a heated plate and pour over the sauce.

2 slices fresh root ginger
1.5-1.75kg/3½-4lb chicken
2 tsp salt
pepper to taste
1 egg white
6 tbsp roasted ground rice

Sauce:
1 tbsp chicken fat
2 tbsp light soya sauce
½ tsp salt
3 tbsp good stock (see page 56)
1 tbsp malt vinegar
1½ tbsp dry sherry
1 tbsp chopped spring onion
2 cloves garlic, crushed

350g/12oz chicken breasts
3 medium courgettes
1 tsp salt
2½ tsp cornflour
1 egg white
6½ tbsp vegetable oil
3 slices fresh root ginger
2 tbsp good stock (see page 56)
1 tbsp dry sherry
1 tbsp soya sauce
1 tbsp chilli sauce
pepper to taste
¼ tsp MSG (optional)
1½ tsp cornflour blended with 2 tbsp water

STIR-FRIED SLICED CHICKEN WITH COURGETTES

■ PREPARATION ■

Cut the chicken into flat sheets. Cut the courgettes into 0.5cm/¼ inch slices. Place the chicken into a bowl and mix with the salt, 2½ teaspoons cornflour and the egg white.

■ COOKING ■

Heat 5 tablespoons of the oil in a wok or frying pan. When hot, add the ginger and heat until the oil begins to smoke. Remove the ginger and discard. Add the chicken slices and stir-fry for about 1½ minutes. Remove with a perforated spoon and place in a bowl. Add the remaining 1½ tablespoons oil and heat. When hot, stir-fry the courgettes for about 1½ minutes. Add the stock, sherry, soya sauce, chilli sauce, pepper and monosodium glutamate, if using. Remove the courgettes and arrange on a heated plate in a circle. Return the chicken pieces to the pan and stir over high heat for 1 minute to reheat. Add the blended cornflour, stirring until the sauce thickens. Spoon into the middle of the courgette circle.

★★★
Cooking time: about 8 minutes

Serves: 6-7

Cooking method: stir-fry, p.42

Quick to prepare

Goes well with most dishes

1.5-1.75kg/3-4lb chicken
1 tbsp cornflour
4 tbsp vegetable oil
5 slices fresh root ginger
2 tbsp sugar
3 tbsp light soya sauce
3 tbsp dark soya sauce
1 tbsp hoisin sauce
1 tbsp oyster sauce
½ tsp MSG (optional)
4 tbsp rice wine
450ml/¾pt good stock (see page 56)
Garnish:
spring onions

SHANGHAI QUICK-BRAISED CHICKEN ON THE BONE

This dish can only be successfully made if cooked over very high heat.

■ PREPARATION ■

Chop the chicken through the bone into about 30 bite-size pieces. Bring a large pan of water to the boil, add the chicken and simmer for about 5 minutes. Remove and drain thoroughly. Blend the cornflour with 3 tablespoons water.

■ COOKING ■

Heat the oil in a wok or pan. When hot, stir in the ginger for about 1½ minutes. Add the chicken pieces and stir-fry for about 3 minutes. Put in the sugar, soya sauces, hoisin sauce, oyster sauce, monosodium glutamate, if using, wine and stock. Bring to the boil and continue to stir over the highest heat until the sauce begins to thicken and reduce. Add the blended cornflour and stir until the sauce is thick and coats the chicken pieces.

★★★
Cooking time: about 25 minutes

Serves: 6-8

Cooking methods: stir-fry p.42 and boiling

Quite easy to prepare

A main item for a multi-course meal

Illustrated on p.155

MELON CHICKEN

Melon chicken is simply chicken cooked and served in a melon. It is one of the favourite ways of serving chicken at a Chinese dinner party.

■ PREPARATION ■

Soak the dried mushrooms and dried shrimps separately in hot water to cover for 25 minutes. Slice the top of the melon off and reserve for a lid. Scrape out most of the flesh and reserve about a quarter for cooking with the chicken. Drain and discard the tough mushroom stalks. Cut the mushroom caps in quarters. Cut the ham and bamboo shoot into cubes.

■ COOKING ■

Place the chicken in a steamer and steam for about 1 hour. Leave to cool. When cool enough to handle, remove the meat from the bones and cut into cubes. Heat the oil in a wok or large frying pan. When hot, stir-fry the ginger, dried shrimps and dried mushrooms over high heat for about 2 minutes. Add the ham, half of the chicken, the bamboo shoots, reserved melon, fresh mushrooms, salt and pepper. Stir-fry for a further 3 minutes. Pack all the stir fried ingredients into the melon. Add any excess to the remaining chicken. Mix the crumbled stock cube with the stock and sherry and pour on to the melon until it fills to the brim. Replace the melon lid and fasten it with a few wooden cocktail sticks. Place on a heatproof plate and steam for 30 minutes.

■ SERVING ■

Bring the whole melon to the table to serve. This is a pretty dish and the different savoury flavours in the chicken-ham-mushroom stuffing and the sweetness of the melon gives it a unique appeal. At a banquet in Canton, I have had a similar dish where frogs' legs were used instead of chicken. Accompany the dish with the remaining chicken and stir-fried ingredients.

★ ★ ★ ★ ★

Cooking time: 1 hour 35 minutes

Serves: 6-8

Cooking methods: steam p.49 and stir-fry p.42

Takes time and care in preparation

An attractive item for a multi-dish dinner party

Illustrated on p.172

---

3 large dried Chinese mushrooms

25 g/1 oz dried shrimps

1 large melon, approximately 20 cm/8 inches in diameter

75 g/3 oz ham

75 g/3 oz drained, canned bamboo shoots

1.25-1.5 kg/2½-3 lb chicken

2 tbsp vegetable oil

2 slices fresh root ginger

75 g/3 oz button mushrooms

1 tsp salt

pepper to taste

300 ml/½ pt good stock (see page 56)

2 tbsp dry sherry

3 tbsp rice

3 pieces lotus leaf

1.5-1.75 kg/3½-4 lb chicken

2 tbsp dark soya sauce

vegetable oil for deep-frying

2 medium onions

2 spring onions

2 tbsp drained, canned chopped winter pickles

LONG-STEAMED LOTUS LEAF-WRAPPED CHICKEN

■ PREPARATION ■

Soak the rice in cold water to cover for 20 minutes. Drain. Soak the lotus leaves in warm water for 15 minutes. Drain. Bring a large pan of water to the boil, add the chicken and simmer for 5 minutes. Drain thoroughly. Brush the chicken with soya sauce. Heat the oil in a wok or deep-fryer. When hot, fry the chicken until brown all over. Drain. Chop the onions and mix with the pickles, salt, rice and sherry. Stuff this mixture into the chicken cavity. Wrap the chicken in the lotus leaves to form a neat parcel.

■ COOKING ■

Place the wrapped chicken in a steamer and steam for about 2½ hours.

■ SERVING ■

Bring the chicken to the table still wrapped in the lotus leaves. Open the parcel and serve the chicken with the stuffing.

★ ★ ★ ★ ★

Cooking time: 2½ hours

Serves: 6-8

Cooking methods: simmer, deep-fry p.45 and steam p.49

Takes time to prepare

A main item for a multi-dish meal

---

8 chicken drumsticks

2½ tsp salt

pepper to taste

1 tsp ground ginger

vegetable oil for deep-frying

Cooking sauce:

300 ml/½ pt good stock (see page 56)

1½ tbsp hoisin sauce

1½ tbsp yellow bean paste

¾ tsp pepper

1½ tbsp mixed five spice pieces

CRISPY 'FIVE SPICED' CHICKEN LEGS

■ PREPARATION ■

Rub the chicken drumsticks with a mixture of the salt, pepper and ground ginger. Leave to season for 30 minutes. Bring a pan of water to the boil, add the drumsticks and cook for 3 minutes. Drain and cool.

■ COOKING ■

Place the cooking sauce ingredients in a wok or pan and bring to the boil. Add the drumsticks and simmer for about 15 minutes. Leave the drumsticks to cool in the sauce for 15 minutes, then remove and drain thoroughly. Heat the oil in a wok or deep-fryer. When hot, gently fry the chicken for about 5 minutes until golden brown.

■ SERVING ■

Remove the knuckle from the drumstick and put a cutlet frill on the exposed bone. Arrange on a heated plate and serve with Peking Duck Sauce (see page 178).

★ ★ ★

Cooking time: about 25 minutes, plus seasoning and cooling time

Serves: 4-6

Cooking methods: simmer and deep-fry, p.45

Useful dish for a party buffet

Illustrated on p.147

CHICKEN FU YUNG

▓ PREPARATION ▓

Cut chicken meat into 4 × 6.5 cm/1½ × 2½ inch thin slices. Place them in a bowl. Add the 1½ tablespoons cornflour and coat the chicken pieces evenly. Beat the egg whites lightly in another bowl. Blend the 2½ teaspoons cornflour with 2 tablespoons water.

▓ COOKING ▓

Heat the oil in a wok or deep-fryer. When hot, gently fry the chicken pieces over low to medium heat for 1½ minutes. Pour in the egg white slowly and evenly over the contents in the pan. When the egg white rises, turn them around once with the chicken pieces. Transfer with a perforated spoon to a bowl. Pour away the oil to use for other purposes. Return the wok or pan to the heat. Add the stock, salt, peas and monosodium glutamate, if using. Bring to the boil and stir in the blended cornflour until thickened. Return the chicken and egg white pieces to the pan. Bring back to the boil and serve. If liked, sprinkle with presoaked, chopped dried shrimps.

Ingredients
350g/12oz chicken breasts
1½ tbsp cornflour
8 egg whites
2½ tsp cornflour
300ml/½pt vegetable oil for deep-frying
150ml/¼pt good stock (see page 56)
1 tsp salt
3 tbsp peas
¼tsp MSG (optional)

STRANGE FLAVOUR CHICKEN

I am not certain why the people in Sichuan have come to call this dish 'Strange Flavour' since the hot nutty flavour is quite commonplace in the Province. But the presence of both sugar and vinegar in the sauce does make the final taste somewhat unusual.

▓ PREPARATION AND COOKING ▓

Place the salt and ginger in a saucepan with 900 ml/1½ pt water. Bring to the boil, add the drumsticks and simmer gently for 25 minutes. Drain. Remove the bone from the drumstick with a sharp knife, making as small a cut as possible. Thinly slice the onions and arrange them in a serving dish. Place the sesame seeds and peppercorns in a wok or small frying pan. Stir them over a low heat for 2½ minutes, until seeds have browned. Reserve half of this mixture and add the remainder to a bowl. Mix in the remaining sauce ingredients.

▓ SERVING ▓

Cut the meat from the boned drumsticks slantwise into thin circular slices. Sprinkle them with the reserved roasted sesame seeds. Arrange the chicken over the bed of onion on the serving dish. Pour over the sauce evenly.

Ingredients
1 tbsp salt
3 slices fresh root ginger
8 chicken drumsticks
1 large or 2 medium onions
Sauce:
4 tbsp sesame seeds
1 tsp pounded Sichuan peppercorns
2 tbsp sesame paste or peanut butter
1 tbsp sugar
1 tbsp chilli sauce
3 tbsp vinegar
1½ tbsp dry sherry
3 tbsp soya sauce

DUCK

In China, ducks are reared with much greater care and produced in larger concentrations than chickens. Around Nanking, which is situated just south of the Yangtze river, over 40 million ducks are produced annually for a dish called Nanking Pressed Duck, and vast quantities of duck are raised for probably one of the most famous Chinese dishes, Peking Duck.

Duck is not commonly found on the average Chinese dining table and for every duck dish served there are probably as many as ten chicken dishes. In my father's household, which was considered well-to-do, I don't recollect eating duck more than three or four times a year. Chicken was consumed at least once a week.

What has made Peking Duck famous is not the quality of the bird, but the way it is cooked. A typical restaurant specializing in this dish in Peking will cook several thousand duck each day. The bird is roasted in a room-size oven, the heat source for which is a large bed of glowing, red embers. Dozens of ducks are hung on sticks and suspended from just below the ceiling of the oven. The cooking of each bird can be conveniently checked at any time and the stick removed from the heat. The sticks can also be moved around to hotter or cooler parts of the oven; whatever is required. For a chef to make a success of this dish, he needs a thorough knowledge of the heat distribution of his particular oven and of the particular fuel he is using.

1.75-2.25 kg/4-5 lb duck

75-100 g/3-4 oz lotus seeds

8 medium dried Chinese mushrooms

100-150 g/4-5 oz drained, canned bamboo shoots

4 slices fresh root ginger

2 tsp salt

1 chicken stock cube

100-150 g/4-5 oz smoked ham (in one piece)

4-5 tbsp dry sherry

2 tbsp finely chopped spring onions

BASIC WHITE-SIMMERED DUCK

In China, when poultry is not cooked with soya sauce, it is called white cooked or white simmered. A variety of ingredients can be added to the poultry to vary the flavour as well as adding substance to the dish. So duck cooked this way is enjoyed as much as the popular red cooked duck in soya sauce. Although appearing less rich, it is just as flavoursome, and the soup is excellent served during the course of a long meal.

■ PREPARATION ■

Place the duck and lotus seeds in a large pan of water. Bring to the boil and simmer for 7-8 minutes. Drain and transfer to a flameproof casserole or pan. Soak the dried mushrooms in hot water to cover for 25 minutes. Drain and discard the tough stalks. Cut the bamboo shoots into 5 × 6 cm/2 × 2½ inch slices.

■ COOKING ■

Add the mushrooms, ginger and bamboo shoots to the casserole. Pour in 1.5 lt/2½ pt water and bring to the boil. Reduce the heat to very low and simmer for 2 hours, turning the bird every 30 minutes. Add the salt, crumbled stock cube, ham and sherry and continue to simmer for another 30 minutes.

★★

Cooking time: 2½ hours

Serves: 6-8

Cooking method: long simmer

Easy to make

A main item for a multi-dish meal

■ SERVING ■

Remove the ham, place on a chopping board and cut into 4 × 6.5 cm/1½ × 2½ inch thin slices and use them to garnish the bird in the casserole. Sprinkle the duck with the spring onions and serve directly from the casserole at the table.

BASIC RED-COOKED DUCK

★★

Cooking time: about 2 hours

Serves: 6-8

Cooking method: long simmer

A good centrepiece for a family meal, surrounded by smaller vegetable and savoury dishes

1.75-2.25 kg/4-5 lb duck
3 spring onions
4 slices fresh root ginger

Sauce:
½ tsp salt
6 tbsp soya sauce
2 tbsp yellow bean paste
2½ tsp sugar
4 tbsp dry sherry

■ PREPARATION ■

Wipe the duck inside and out with a damp cloth. Place breast side up in a flameproof casserole and cover with water. Bring to the boil for 10 minutes, then pour out about a quarter of the water. Cut the spring onions into 4 cm/1½ inch sections.

■ COOKING ■

Add the ginger, spring onions, salt, soya sauce, yellow bean paste to the casserole. Bring to the boil, cover and simmer for about 1 hour, turning the duck over a couple of times during the cooking. Add the sugar and sherry and continue to cook, covered, for another 45 minutes.

■ SERVING ■

Serve the duck whole, or chopped through the bone into bite-sized pieces. The remaining sauce can be reduced over high heat and thickened with a small amount of cornflour mixed with a little water, if liked. Two teaspoons sesame oil can also be added. Pour the sauce over the whole duck or pieces of duck arranged on a large heated plate.

VARIATION
RED COOKED DUCK WITH CHESTNUTS AND CHINESE MUSHROOMS

★★

Cooking time: 2¾ hours

Serves: 6-8

Cooking method: long simmer

Serve as Basic Red-cooked Duck

Two traditional ingredients used for stuffing poultry are often added to the Red-cooked Duck; namely chestnuts and dried Chinese mushrooms.

Soak about 8-10 medium dried Chinese mushrooms in hot water to cover for 25 minutes. Drain and discard the tough stalks. Cut the mushroom caps in half. Place about 350 g/12 oz chestnuts in a pan of boiling water and simmer for about 15 minutes. Peel. Both of these ingredients can withstand lengthy cooking, so add to the casserole at the beginning of cooking. They add to the flavour of the dish and complement the duck meat. Serve with rice and steamed buns (see page 240), the staple food of the North.

2 tbsp soya sauce
1½ tbsp yellow bean paste
1½ tbsp oyster sauce
1.75-2 kg/4-4½ lb duck
2-3 large sheets lotus leaf
Stuffing:
100 g/4 oz glutinous rice
2 medium onions
6 medium dried Chinese mushrooms
2 tbsp dried shrimps
3 slices fresh root ginger
2 cloves garlic
4 tbsp vegetable oil
3-4 tbsp diced ham
7-8 fresh chestnuts
4 tbsp drained, canned diced bamboo shoots
1 tsp salt
2 tbsp good stock (see page 56)
1½ tbsp hoisin sauce

LOTUS LEAF-WRAPPED LONG-STEAMED DUCK

■ PREPARATION ■

Mix the soya sauce, yellow bean paste and oyster sauce together. Use to rub the inside and outside of the duck. Leave to marinate for 30 minutes. Soak the lotus leaves in warm water for about 3 minutes, then drain. Soak the glutinous rice in cold water to cover for 30 minutes, then drain. Peel and finely dice the onions. Soak the dried mushrooms and dried shrimps separately in hot water to cover for 25 minutes. Drain and discard the tough mushroom stalks. Cut the caps into quarters. Coarsely chop the shrimps and ginger. Crush the garlic.

■ COOKING ■

Heat the oil in a wok or frying pan. When hot, stir-fry the onions, ginger, garlic, shrimps and mushrooms over a medium heat for 3-4 minutes. Add the ham, chestnuts and bamboo shoots and stir-fry for another 2 minutes. Finally add the rice, salt, stock and hoisin sauce and stir-fry for another 2 minutes. Leave to cool. Stuff all the stir-fried ingredients into the cavity of the duck and sew up to secure. Wrap the bird in the lotus leaves, then wrap in a large sheet of foil. Place the foil parcel in a steamer and steam for about 3 hours.

■ SERVING ■

Unwrap the duck at the table – the meat will be tender enough to be taken apart with a pair of chopsticks. Spoon out the stuffing and serve with the duck.

★★★★★
Cooking time: about 3 hours

Serves: 6-8

Cooking methods: stir-fry p.42 and long steam

A principal dish for a multi-dish dinner party

1.75-2.25 kg/4-5 lb duck
1½ tbsp soya sauce
1½ tbsp vegetable oil
2 medium onions
3 pieces star anise
2 pieces dried tangerine peel
4 slices fresh root ginger
Sauce:
1½ tbsp cornflour blended with 3 tbsp water
1 tsp salt
1½ tbsp soya sauce
1½ tbsp oyster sauce
lettuce leaves

■ WHITE-SIMMERED DOUBLE-COOKED TANGERINE DUCK ■

■ PREPARATION ■

Dry the duck both inside and out and rub evenly with 1½ tablespoons soya sauce and the oil. Peel and thinly slice the onions. Place in the cavity of the duck with the star anise. Soak the tangerine peel in warm water for about 15 minutes, then break into small pieces.

■ COOKING ■

Put the duck on a wire rack over a roasting dish. Place in a preheated oven at 200°C, 400°F, Gas Mark 6, and roast for 30

★★★★
Cooking time: about 2 hours

Serves: 6-8

Cooking methods: roast and simmer

A main item for a multi-dish meal

minutes, turning over once. Heat 1.2lt/2pt water in a large casserole or pan and, when boiling, add the duck, together with the tangerine peel and ginger. Bring to the boil and simmer gently for 1½ hours. Turn the duck over every 30 minutes. Remove the duck from the casserole and leave to cool. Cut into large bite-sized pieces. Strain the liquid from the pan and reduce to half the volume over high heat. Stir in the blended cornflour, salt, soya sauce and oyster sauce. When the liquid has thickened, pour it into 2 small bowls.

■ SERVING ■

Arrange the duck pieces on top of lettuce leaves. Use the 2 bowls of liquid as dipping sauce for the duck.

KOU SHOA DEEP-FRIED BONELESS DUCK

★ ★ ★ ★

Cooking time: about 50 minutes

Serves: 6-8

Cooking methods: simmer and deep-fry, p.45

Interesting to eat between stir-fried dishes

1.75-2.25kg/4-5lb duck

1.5lt/2½pt cooking sauce (see Aromatic and Crispy Duck, page 174)

vegetable oil for deep-frying

Batter:

1 egg

5tbsp cornflour

2tbsp self-raising flour

■ PREPARATION ■

Parboil the duck in a pan of boiling water for about 5 minutes, then drain. Mix the ingredients for batter in a bowl until smooth.

■ COOKING ■

Heat the cooking sauce in a heavy pan. Add the duck and simmer gently for about 45 minutes. Remove the duck and drain thoroughly. Allow the duck to cool for 30 minutes, then remove the meat from the bones, leaving the meat in large pieces if possible. Turn the meat in the batter mixture until evenly coated. Heat the oil in a wok or deep-fryer. When hot, fry the battered duck for about 5 minutes. Drain.

■ SERVING ■

Place the large duck pieces on a chopping board and cut each piece into 3-4 pieces. Place a small bowl of Duck Sauce (see page 178) in the centre of a heated dish and surround with the fried duck pieces. Each piece of duck should be dipped in the sauce before eating.

Melon Chicken (*left*), an
attractive party dish; recipe
page 165.
Aromatic and Crispy
Duck (*above*), an
entertaining dish served
and eaten as Peking Duck;
recipe page 174.

1.75-2.25 kg/4-5 lb duck

vegetable oil for deep-frying

Cooking sauce:

1.5 lt/2½ pt good stock (see page 56)

6 tbsp sugar

6 slices fresh root ginger

10 tbsp soya sauce

4 tbsp yellow bean paste

6 tbsp dry sherry

6 pieces star anise

½ tsp five spice powder

¼ tsp pepper

AROMATIC AND CRISPY DUCK

This dish is served and eaten in the same way as Peking Duck – wrapped in a pancake along with shredded spring onions and cucumber and duck sauce. In a restaurant, this dish can be much more conveniently served than Peking Duck because a quantity of ducks can be pre-cooked in the marinade or cooking sauce and put aside. When required, they are simply deep-fried for 10-11 minutes and served; because of the final deep-frying, the duck meat will be invariably crisper and without the care and precise timing required when preparing and cooking traditional Peking Duck.

■ PREPARATION ■

Mix the ingredients for the cooking sauce together in a large saucepan. Clean the duck thoroughly and cut in half down the backbone. Place into the liquid and submerge.

■ COOKING ■

Simmer the duck gently for 2 hours. Remove from the cooking liquid and leave to cool. When required, heat the oil in a wok or deep-fryer. When hot, place the duck gently in the oil and fry for 10-11 minutes. Drain well.

■ SERVING ■

Place the duck on a large heated platter. Serve by taking the meat off the carcass at the table and wrapping it in pancakes. For the preparation of pancakes and duck sauce, see Peking Duck on page 178.

★ ★ ★ ★ ★

Cooking time: 2 hours 10 minutes

Serves: 6-8

Cooking method: simmer and deep-fry, p.45

Needs preparation beforehand

A main dish for a multi-dish dinner party

Illustrated on p.173

---

350 g/12 oz duck meat, breast and leg

3 young leeks

3 slices fresh root ginger

2 cloves garlic

4 tbsp vegetable oil

1½ tsp salt

15 g/½ oz lard

2 tsp soya sauce

2 tsp sugar

2 tbsp good stock (see page 56)

2 tbsp prepared English mustard

QUICK-FRIED DUCK IN SOYA AND MUSTARD SAUCE

■ PREPARATION ■

Cut the duck meat into 5 × 2.5 cm/2 × 1 inch strips. Wash and cut the leeks slantwise into 2.5 cm/1 inch sections. Shred the ginger. Crush the garlic.

■ COOKING ■

Heat 3 tablespoons of the oil in a wok or frying pan. When hot, fry the ginger and salt over high heat for 10 seconds. Add the duck meat and stir-fry for 1 minute. Remove the meat with a perforated spoon and put to one side. Add the remaining oil and reheat. Stir-fry the garlic and leeks for 1½ minutes, then remove with a perforated spoon and reserve. Add the lard to the wok or pan. When melted, add the soya sauce, sugar and stock. Stir together until a creamy bubbling mixture, then return the duck meat to the pan. Stir into the sauce, then add the

★ ★

Cooking time: about 8 minutes

Serves: 4-6

Cooking method: stir-fry, p.42

Easy to make

A very tasty dish which complements most others

leek mixture and toss quickly with the duck.

■ SERVING ■

Remove the contents from the wok on to a heated dish. Trickle the mustard over evenly and serve.

CANTONESE ROAST DUCK

Cantonese roast duck is the duck most often seen hanging in the windows of Cantonese restaurants abroad. The duck is filled with a sauce and basted with a different mixture several times during roasting.

■ PREPARATION ■

Wash and dry the duck. Rub the duck inside and out with the salt. Hang it up to dry for 2½-3 hours. Shred the ginger. Chop the garlic. Coarsely chop the spring onions. Mix the ginger, garlic and spring onion together with the remaining filling ingredients. Tie the neck of the duck securely so that there is no leakage. Place the duck in a large bowl, back side up, and pour in the filling mixture. Sew the skin up securely. Mix the basting ingredients together.

■ COOKING ■

Place the duck on a wire rack over a roasting tin filled with 4 cm/1½ inches of water. (In a restaurant, the bird is normally hung up to roast, tail end up.) Brush the duck with the basting mixture and roast in a preheated oven at 200°C, 400°F, Gas mark 6 for 30 minutes. Brush again with the basting mixture, reduce the oven temperature to 190°C, 375°F, Gas mark 5 and roast for 30 minutes. Brush the duck once more, reduce the oven temperature to 180°C, 350°F, Gas mark 4 and roast for a further 20 minutes.

■ SERVING ■

Drain the liquid from the duck into a large bowl. Place the duck on a chopping board and chop through the bones into 7.5 × 5 cm/3 × 2 inch pieces. Reassemble the duck on a heated serving dish. Boil the liquid from inside the duck in a small pan until reduced by a quarter. Pour this sauce over the duck. Serve hot or cold.

---

1 duck, about 1.5 kg/3½ lb

3 tsp salt

Filling:

3 slices fresh root ginger

3 cloves garlic

2 spring onions

3 tbsp soya sauce

¾ tbsp sugar

½ tbsp pounded Sichuan peppercorns

150 ml/¼ pt good stock (see page 56)

1 tbsp yellow bean paste

2 pieces star anise

1 tbsp broken dried tangerine peel

Baste:

150 ml/¼ pt boiling water

2 tbsp vinegar

2 tbsp soya sauce

2 tbsp honey

Peking Duck, the famous
dish for special occasions
that is such fun to eat.
Slices of Peking Duck are
wrapped in Chinese
pancakes with cucumber,
spring onions and sauce;
recipe page 178.

1.5-1.75 kg/3-4 lb duck

1 medium cucumber

1 bunch spring onions

Duck sauce:

2-3 tbsp vegetable oil

7-8 tbsp yellow bean paste

3 tbsp sugar

1 tsp sesame oil

Chinese pancakes

Garnish:

radish rose

PEKING DUCK

Peking duck is now a world famous dish, partly due to the way it is eaten and also the delicious flavours – a combination of crispy duck, fresh vegetables and tasty sauce all wrapped individually in Chinese pancakes.

■ PREPARATION ■

Wash and dry the duck thoroughly. Hang it up to dry in a well ventilated place overnight to dry the skin (at least 4-5 hours or if in a great hurry use a hair dryer). Cut the cucumber into matchstick-size shreds. Cut the spring onions into similar size shreds.

■ COOKING ■

Place the duck on a wire rack over a roasting dish. Place in a preheated oven at 200°C, 400°F, Gas Mark 6, for 1 hour 10 minutes. It is important to make sure the oven is correctly preheated for a good result. Do not open the oven door during the roasting, the duck requires no basting.

Meanwhile, to make the Duck Sauce, heat the oil in a small saucepan. When hot, add the yellow bean paste and stir over low heat for 2-3 minutes. Add the sugar and 3 tablespoons water and stir for another 2-3 minutes. Finally, add the sesame oil and stir for a further 30 seconds.

■ SERVING ■

Slice off the crispy skin with a sharp knife into 4 × 5 cm/1½ × 2 inch pieces and arrange on a heated plate. Carve the meat into similar size pieces and arrange on a separate heated plate. Brush each pancake with 1-1½ teaspoons duck sauce, and add a little shredded cucumber and spring onion. Place a little duck skin and meat overlapping on each pancake. Roll up, turning up one end of the pancake to stop the filling falling out. Eat using the fingers.

★ ★ ★ ★

Cooking time:
1 hour 10
minutes, plus
drying time

Serves: 6-8

Cooking method:
roast

Care is needed
with preparation
and timing

Excellent
centrepiece for a
dinner party

Illustrated on
pp.176-177

450 g/1 lb plain flour

1½ tsp sugar

1 tsp oil

CHINESE PANCAKES

■ PREPARATION ■

Sift the flour into a bowl and stir in the sugar, oil and 250 ml/8 fl oz warm water. Stir and mix with a pair of chopsticks or wooden spoon until smooth. Knead the dough for about 5 minutes using a little more flour, if necessary, to make a smooth, non-sticky dough, then form into 2 even 'sausages'. Cut each sausage into 8-10 pieces and roll each piece into a ball. Flatten each ball into a round. Brush the top of each round with oil and place another round on top to form a sandwich. Roll the pancakes together with a small rolling pin into a flat pancake about 15 cm/6 inches in diameter. Repeat the process until all the dough is rolled out.

★ ★ ★

Cooking time:
about 3 minutes
per 2 pancakes

Makes: 16-20

Cooking method:
dry-fry

These versatile
pancakes can hold
all kinds of fillings

■ COOKING ■

Heat a dry frying pan over medium heat. When hot, place a 'pancake sandwich' in the pan and shake the pan around. After 1½ minutes, turn the pancake over with a fish slice and cook the other side in the same way. The pancake should bubble and puff slightly. The pancake is ready when brown spots begin to show on the underside. Now, very gently peel the pancake sandwich apart into 2 pancakes. Fold each pancake in half and stack them up under a damp cloth. You can heat them in a steamer for a few minutes to soften before serving, if necessary.

DUCK CARCASS SOUP

★★

Cooking time: about 30 minutes

Serves: 6-8

Cooking method: boil

Easy to prepare

A good dish to end a meal

1 duck carcass

1.2-1.75 lt/2-3 pt water

1 kg/2 lb Chinese white cabbage

salt and pepper to taste

Duck Carcass Soup is the customary soup to serve after a Peking Duck dinner. In the winter in Peking, where the temperature seldom rises above freezing, to drink a large bowl of soup is ideal food.

■ PREPARATION AND COOKING ■

This soup is cooked and prepared in a short time. Simply boil the duck carcass in the water for 15 minutes. Cut the white cabbage into 7.5 cm/3 inch sections and add to the soup. Continue to cook for another 15 minutes. The only seasoning required is salt and pepper added to taste. If liked 1 tablespoon dried shrimps, 2 tablespoons wine vinegar and a crumbled chicken stock cube can be included. During the cooking, keep the soup boiling. The resulting soup will be very white. If not white enough, add a couple of tablespoons of milk. This soup is relatively light and is much appreciated after a rich meal. When the bowl of soup is drunk at the end of a lengthy meal, it should bring beads of perspiration to the forehead of every diner, an indication of the comfort and satisfaction from life and eating.

MEAT

肉類

Peking Mongolian Hot Pot (*left*); recipe page 211.
Sichuan Yu-hsiang Shredded Pork; recipe page 190.

PORK

Pork is used for cooking more frequently than any other type of meat in China, partly because it is so versatile. It can be short-cooked, quick stir-fried, or long steam-braised to produce highly delectable dishes. Pork can be cooked for its fresh sweet savouriness, its rich succulent tenderness or its crisp, crackling qualities; and its neutral flavour means that it can impart taste to other foods as well as receive and absorb them from numerous other ingredients.

The Chinese are thus unconcerned by the fattiness of pork, the effects of which are more than offset by their high intake of cereals and low consumption of dairy products. The problem of cholesterol – Western man's dietary preoccupation – has not arisen there.

The Chinese consider lean meat to be too dry for prolonged cooking, and prefer cuts like belly of pork (called 'five flower pork' by the Chinese, meaning that the meat consists of five layers of skin, lean, fat, lean, fat) which are used for long-steaming or stewing. This type of cooking produces the best gravies, which are wonderful to consume with rice and plain-cooked vegetables. The following pork dishes are probably the most commonly cooked in China and, therefore, probably the most widely eaten dishes in the world.

800g/1¾lb belly of pork
1½tbsp dark soya sauce
vegetable oil for deep-frying
3tbsp light soya sauce
3 slices fresh root ginger
300ml/½pt good stock (see page 56)
3tbsp dry sherry
1½tbsp sugar
3 pieces star anise

LONG BRAISED TUNG PO SOYA PORK

Su Tung Po, one of China's foremost poet, is reputed to have invented this dish, hence it bears his name.

PREPARATION
Cut the pork through the skin into 4 equal pieces. Plunge them into boiling water for about 5 minutes, then drain. Rub the pork, especially the skin, with the dark soya sauce. Heat the oil in a wok or deep-fryer. When hot, fry the pork pieces over a medium heat for about 3 minutes. Drain.

COOKING
Place the 4 pieces of pork, skin-side down, in a flat bottomed casserole and add the light soya sauce, ginger, stock, sherry, sugar and star anise. Bring to the boil, turn the pork pieces over several times. Place the open casserole into a steamer, with the pork skin-side down, for about 2 hours until tender.

SERVING
Serve the pork, skin-side up, in a heated deep dish, if liked, arranging 3 pieces in the bottom and the fourth piece on top across the others. Pour over the remaining sauce. The pork should be tender enough to break with a pair of chopsticks.

★★★
Cooking time: good 2 hours
Serves: 5-6
Cooking methods: deep-fry p.45 and braise
Quite easy to prepare but takes time to cook
Excellent served with rice and accompanied by lighter dishes and vegetables

CRISPY FIVE SPICE PORK

★★★

Cooking time: about 10 minutes

Serves: 5-6

Cooking methods: deep-fry p.45 and stir-fry p.42

An excellent starter

■ PREPARATION ■

Cut the pork into thick strips. Sprinkle and rub with the salt, five spice powder and cornflour. Leave to season for 30 minutes. Finely chop the ginger and garlic.

■ COOKING ■

Heat the oil in a wok or deep-fryer. When hot, fry half the pork strips over medium heat for 3½ minutes. Drain and place in a bowl. Fry the remaining pork strips for 3½ minutes, then drain and add to the bowl. Add the soya sauce and sugar to the pork, mixing well. Pour away the oil to use for other purposes, leaving 2 tablespoons. Reheat the wok or pan. When hot, stir in the ginger, garlic, sea salt and pepper over medium heat for 25 seconds. Pour the once-fried and seasoned pork into the pan. Turn and stir around quickly so that the pork is evenly coated by the spicy ingredients. Turn, toss and stir for 1 minute.

■ SERVING ■

Transfer to a heated serving dish. To serve, take a lettuce leaf, add a portion of pork, spoon on some duck sauce, then fold and wrap the lettuce up enclosing the pork. Eat with the fingers.

450g/1lb lean pork
1 tsp salt
½tsp five spice powder
1½tbsp cornflour
2 slices fresh root ginger
2 cloves garlic
vegetable oil for deep-frying
1½tbsp soya sauce
1 tsp caster sugar
2tsp sea salt
1½tsp pounded Sichuan peppercorns

Wrapping:
10-12 well-shaped lettuce leaves
6tbsp Peking Duck Sauce (see page 178)

CRISPY SKIN ROAST PORK

★★

Cooking time: 1½ hours, plus seasoning time

Serves: 5-6

Cooking method: roast

Takes a little time, but easy to prepare

Excellent with rice, accompanied by other savoury dishes

■ PREPARATION ■

Score the pork skin in a 2.5 cm/1 inch diamond pattern and rub in the ginger and salt. Leave to season for 2 hours. Bring a large pan of water to boil, add the pork and simmer for about 5 minutes. Remove, drain and wipe very dry.

■ COOKING ■

Put the pork on a rack with the skin side down. Place in a preheated oven at 200°C, 400°F, Gas Mark 6, and roast for about 45 minutes. Turn the pork over and paint on a mixture of honey and soya sauce. Reduce the oven temperature to 180°C, 350°F, Gas Mark 4, and roast again for about 45 minutes. By this time the skin should be very crisp and brown.

■ SERVING ■

Chop the pork into bite-size pieces. The crispy skin and the tenderness of the pork fat makes an interesting combination. Soya sauce may be used as a dip for the pork.

1.25kg/2½lb belly of pork
1½tsp ground ginger
3½tsp salt
1 tbsp honey
1½tbsp light soya sauce

Pearl-studded Pork Balls
(*above*), a steamed dish of
pork balls coated with rice;
recipe page 194.
Steamed Minced Pork
with Chinese Sausages
(*right*), an easy family dish
to serve with rice; recipe
page 187.

675g/1½lb meaty pork spare
   ribs

2 tbsp salted black beans

1 medium onion

2 cloves garlic

2 tbsp vegetable oil

½ tsp salt

2 tbsp good stock (see page 56)

2 tsp sugar

1½ tbsp light soya sauce

1½ tbsp dry sherry

1½ tbsp cornflour

1½ tbsp seeded chopped red
   chilli

CANTONESE STEAMED SPARE RIBS WITH BLACK BEANS

Chinese-style spare ribs differ from those usually served in the West mainly in that they are cut shorter, into 2.5-4 cm/1-1½ inch sections, so that can be eaten whole and the bone spat out! (Westerners need much practise to perfect this technique, if they wish to acquire the skill at all!) It also means that the cooking time is considerably shorter.

PREPARATION

Chop the spare ribs into 2.5-4 cm/1-1½ inch pieces. Place in a large pan of water, bring to the boil and simmer for 2 minutes. Drain well and place the spare ribs into a bowl. Soak the black beans in cold water to cover for 5 minutes. Drain and crush lightly. Peel and finely chop the onion. Crush the garlic. Heat the oil in a wok or frying pan. When hot, stir-fry the onion for about 30 seconds. Add the black beans, salt, stock, sugar, soya sauce and sherry and stir-fry for about 15 seconds. Pour the mixture into the bowl with the spare ribs and toss together. Mix in the cornflour.

COOKING

Transfer the spare ribs to a heatproof dish and sprinkle on the chilli and garlic. Place in a steamer and cook for 25-30 minutes.

SERVING

Spare ribs are often served as a dim sum item in the tea houses, where they are eaten as nibbles to accompany drinks. Included in a multi-course meal, this dish makes a delicious hot starter.

★★★

*Cooking time:
about 30 minutes*

Serves: 5-6

*Cooking method:
steam, p.49*

*Ideal snack or
starter*

Meat balls:

6 medium dried Chinese
   mushrooms

100g/4oz pork fat

100g/4oz pork skin

5 water chestnuts

2 spring onions

675g/1½lb minced lean pork

2 tbsp cornflour

1 egg

1½ tsp salt

1½ tbsp dark soya sauce

1 tbsp yellow bean paste

5 tbsp finely chopped shrimps

vegetable oil for deep-frying

1 Chinese white cabbage

900ml/1½pt good stock (see
   page 56)

LION'S HEAD MEAT BALLS IN CLEAR BROTH

'Lion's head' meat balls differ from ordinary meat balls in that they are much larger, cooked for much longer and are very succulent when prepared well.

PREPARATION

Soak the dried mushrooms in hot water to cover for 25 minutes. Drain. Discard the tough stalks and finely chop half the mushroom caps. Mince the pork fat and skin. Chop the water chestnuts and spring onions. Mix all the ingredients for the meat balls together in a large bowl, except the whole mushroom caps. Form the mixture into 3-5 large meat balls. Heat the oil in a wok or deep-fryer. When hot, add the meat balls, one by one, and fry gently for 6-7 minutes until brown all

★★★★

*Cooking time:
about 1½ hours*

Serves: 6-8

*Cooking methods:
deep-fry p.45 and
simmer*

*Rather time-
consuming*

*Serve with rice.
Goes well with
most dishes*

*Illustrated on
p.192*

over. Drain on absorbent kitchen paper. Cut the Chinese cabbage into large sections.

■ COOKING ■

Heat the stock and whole mushroom caps in a flameproof casserole or Chinese clay pot. When boiling, add the meat balls. Cover and simmer gently for 1 hour. Add the Chinese cabbage sections, cover and continue to simmer for about 20 minutes.

■ SERVING ■

Place the meat balls on a large heated serving dish and serve the soup separately. They are too large to eat whole and need to be eaten broken into quarters or pieces, then accompanied by rice.

★ ★

Cooking time:
30 minutes

Serves: 6-8

Cooking method:
steam, p.49

Easy to prepare

Good family fare

Illustrated on
p.185

STEAMED MINCED PORK WITH CHINESE SAUSAGES

■ PREPARATION ■

Cut the sausages slantwise into 4 cm/1½ inch sections. Mix the pork with the salt, pepper, soya sauce, cornflour and egg. Blend thoroughly until smooth. Cut the cauliflower into 5 cm/2 inch florets. Space the cauliflower evenly on the bottom of a deep heatproof dish. Cover with a thick layer of minced pork. Stud the top of the pork evenly with pieces of sausage.

■ COOKING ■

Place the dish in a steamer and steam for 30 minutes.

2 Chinese wind-dried sausages
450g/1lb minced pork
1 tsp salt
pepper to taste
1½ tbsp light soya sauce
1½ tbsp cornflour
1 egg
1 cauliflower

■

Deep-fried Crispy Fingers of Pork (*above*);
recipe page 191.
Opposite
Capital Spare ribs (*above left*); recipe page 196.
Sichuan Double Cooked Pork (*above right*);
recipe page 264.
Sichuan Hot Crispy Fried Shredded Beef (*centre
left*); recipe page 203.
Sliced Beef in Black Bean and Chilli Sauce (*centre
right*); recipe page 201.
Quick-fried Shredded Beef with Ginger and
Onions (*below left*); recipe page 201.
Soya-braised Pork – Long Cooked Version
(*below right*), dried squid and Sichuan pickles can
be used to flavour this dish; recipe page 196.

225g/8oz pork fillet

2 spring onions

2 slices fresh root ginger

2 fresh chillies

1 clove garlic, crushed

3-4 dried Chinese mushrooms

25g/1oz drained, canned bamboo shoots

2 egg whites

2 tsp cornflour

vegetable oil for deep-frying

1/2 tsp salt

1 tbsp yellow bean paste

1 tbsp good stock (see page 56)

1 tbsp dry sherry or rice wine

1 1/2 tbsp soya sauce

1 1/2 tbsp vinegar

1/2 tsp white pepper

2 tsp cornflour blended with 2 tbsp cold stock

1 tsp sesame oil

2 tsp red chilli oil or chilli sauce

1 tsp crushed Sichuan peppercorns

SICHUAN YU-HSIANG SHREDDED PORK

■ PREPARATION ■

Shred the pork fillet finely. Chop the spring onions, ginger, chillies, discarding the seeds, and garlic. Soak the dried mushrooms in boiling water to cover for 25 minutes. Drain and discard the tough stalks. Shred the mushroom caps. Shred the bamboo shoots. Put the pork in a bowl with the egg whites, cornflour and 1 tablespoon oil. Toss together very well.

■ COOKING ■

Heat the oil in a wok or deep-fryer. When medium hot, fry the pork for about 1 1/2 minutes. Add the bamboo shoots and mushrooms and stir for about 1 1/2 minutes. Drain and pour away the oil to use for other purposes. Reheat the wok or a pan with about 1 tablespoon oil. When hot, stir-fry the ginger, garlic, spring onions, salt and chillies for 1 minute. Add the bean paste, stock, sherry or wine, soya sauce, vinegar and white pepper. Stir and bring to the boil. Add the shredded pork and vegetables to the wok. Thicken the sauce with the blended cornflour. At the last minute, drizzle over the sesame oil and toss together.

■ SERVING ■

Transfer to a heated plate and sprinkle on the red chilli oil and crushed peppercorns.

★★★

Cooking time: about 10 minutes

Serves: 4-6

Cooking methods: deep-fry p.45 and stir-fry p.42

A spicy dish. Serve with rice and vegetables and other savoury dishes

Illustrated on p.181

3-4 lotus leaves

675g/1 1/2lb belly of pork, thick end

2 tbsp light soya sauce

vegetable oil for deep-frying

2 slices fresh root ginger

2 spring onions

1 1/2 tbsp oyster sauce

1/2 tsp salt

1 1/2 tsp sugar

1/4 tsp MSG (optional)

2 cloves garlic

3 tbsp ground rice

1 1/2 tsp sesame oil

STEAMED GROUND RICE-PORK WRAPPED IN LOTUS LEAVES

Although not considered haute cuisine, this is a prized dish in domestic cooking, beloved of all the connoisseurs of pork, which is 98 per cent of the Chinese population.

■ PREPARATION ■

Immerse the lotus leaves in warm water for 3-4 minutes to soften. Bring a large pan of water to the boil, add the pork and simmer for 10 minutes. Remove and drain. Rub the pork with the soya sauce. Heat the oil in a wok or deep-fryer. When hot, fry the pork for about 3 minutes. Drain. Cut the pork into 1 cm/1/2 inch slices. Finely chop the ginger and spring onions. Mix together the oyster sauce, salt, sugar, ginger, monosodium

★★★★

Cooking time: about 3 hours

Serves: 6-7

Cooking methods: deep-fry p.45 and steam p.49

Good family fare

Illustrated on p.209

glutamate, if using, garlic and spring onions. Add the ground rice and sesame oil. Mix in the pork slices and make sure they are evenly coated. Pile the slices neatly into a stack, then wrap in the softened lotus leaves. Tie securely with string.

■ COOKING ■
Place the parcel in a heatproof dish, put in a steamer and steam for 3 hours.

■ SERVING ■
When ready, drain away any excess water and serve straight from the lotus leaves. The pork will be tender and the ground rice will have soaked up any fattiness.

Note: The pork mixture can be wrapped in individual lotus leaf parcels.

DEEP-FRIED CRISPY FINGERS OF PORK

★★★
Cooking time: about 4-5 minutes per batch

Serves: 5-6

Cooking method: deep-fry, p.45

Quite easy to prepare

Good starter for a party meal

Illustrated on p.189

■ PREPARATION ■
Cut the pork into finger-size strips. Mix the salt, pepper, ginger, wine or sherry and sesame oil together. Add the pork and mix thoroughly. Leave to marinate for 10 minutes. To make the batter, mix the egg, flour and cornflour together. To make the dip sauce, heat the oil in a wok or pan. When hot, add the onion, garlic, chilli and ginger and stir for a few seconds. Add the rest of the dip sauce ingredients. Bring to the boil, then pour into a small heatproof bowl.

COOKING
Heat the oil in a wok or deep-fryer. When very hot, dip the pork fingers in the batter and put gently into the oil. Fry for about 3 minutes. Drain. Allow the oil to reheat, then fry the pork again for 30 seconds. Drain.

SERVING
Arrange the pork fingers on a heated plate and serve with the dip sauce. Sweet and sour sauce (see page 197) can also be used with these pork fingers, or a simple dip sauce of shredded fresh ginger root in vinegar.

675g/1½oz lean pork
1 tsp salt
¼tsp pepper
½tsp ground ginger
1 tbsp rice wine or dry sherry
1 tsp sesame oil
vegetable oil for deep-frying

Batter:
1 egg
5 tbsp plain flour
1½ tbsp cornflour

Dip sauce:
1½ tbsp vegetable oil
1½ tbsp chopped spring onion
2 tsp crushed garlic
2 tsp chopped fresh chillies
1½ tbsp chopped fresh root ginger
5 tbsp good stock (see page 56)
2 tbsp vinegar
2 tbsp light soya sauce
1 tsp salt
1 tsp sugar

Garnish:
radish rose
halved lemon slices

191

Quick-fried Shredded
Pork in Capital Sauce
(*above*), spoonfuls of pork
and rice can be wrapped in
lettuce leaves to eat with
the fingers; recipe page
193.
Lion's Head Meat Balls in
Clear Broth (*right*), serve
with rice to mop up the
juices; recipe page 186.

BARBECUE SPARE RIBS

★★★

*Cooking time:
50 minutes*

Serves: 5-6

*Cooking methods:
stir-fry p.42 and
stew p.46*

*Quite easy to
prepare*

*Can be served
alone or as a
starter*

*To reduce sauce,
p.46*

*Barbecue Spare Ribs evolved in the West comparatively recently.
Chinese ingredients and cooking methods are used to produce spare ribs
to suit the Western palate.*

■ PREPARATION ■

Separate the spare ribs. Parboil them in a pan of boiling water
for 5 minutes. Drain, sprinkle and rub them with the salt and
pepper. Heat the oil in a flameproof casserole. When hot, stir in
the ginger for 1½ minutes, then add the ribs. Turn and stir the
ribs for 4-5 minutes. Drain away all the excess oil. Cut the
spring onions into 5 mm/¼ inch sections.

■ COOKING ■

Add the sauce ingredients to the casserole, partly submerging
the ribs. Bring to the boil, stir and turn the ribs in the sauce over
high heat for 5 minutes. Reduce the heat to low, cover and
cook for 40 minutes, turning the ribs over after 20 minutes. If
there is a fair quantity of the sauce left in the casserole, raise the
heat to high and turn the ribs in the thickening sauce until the
sauce is well reduced. Sprinkle the ribs with the spring onions
and serve.

Ingredients
1.5 kg/3-3½ lb spare ribs
1½ tsp salt
pepper to taste
6 tbsp vegetable oil
3-4 slices fresh root ginger
3 spring onions
Sauce:
600 ml/1 pt good stock (see page 56)
1 chicken stock cube
3 tbsp soya sauce
1 tbsp yellow bean sauce
3 pieces star anise
6 tbsp dry sherry
2 tbsp sugar

QUICK-FRIED SHREDDED PORK

IN CAPITAL SAUCE

★★

*Cooking time:
about 6 minutes*

Serves: 4-6

*Cooking method:
stir-fry, p.42*

Easy to prepare

*Goes well with
other dishes for
family or party
meals*

*Illustrated
opposite*

*Yellow bean paste, stir-fried in oil with sugar and soya sauce etc, is
often referred to as Capital sauce as it is very popular in Peking.*

■ PREPARATION ■

Cut the pork into matchstick-size shreds. Mix the pork with
the salt, cornflour and egg white. Cut the spring onion into
1 cm/½ inch sections.

■ COOKING ■

Heat the oil in a wok or deep-fryer. When hot, add the pork,
separating all the shreds, and stir-fry for about 2 minutes.
Drain and pour off the oil to use for other purposes. Meanwhile, heat the 3 tablespoons oil in a wok or pan. When hot,
add the yellow bean paste, sugar, soya sauce and sherry. Stir
until smooth and glossy, then stir in the blended cornflour.
Bring back to the boil and add the pork. Stir in the spring
onions and sprinkle over the sesame oil.

■ SERVING ■

Serve on crispy rice flour noodles. If liked, wrap spoonfuls of
pork and rice in lettuce leaves to eat with the fingers.

Ingredients
350 g/12 oz fillet of pork
½ tsp salt
3 tbsp cornflour
1 egg white
2 spring onions
vegetable oil for deep-frying
Capital sauce:
3 tbsp vegetable oil
1½ tbsp yellow bean paste
1 tbsp sugar
½ tbsp dark soya sauce
1 tbsp dry sherry
½ tbsp cornflour blended with 2 tbsp water
1 tsp sesame oil

| 224g/8oz glutinous rice |
| 2 tbsp dried shrimps |
| 450g/1 lb minced pork |
| 1 tsp salt |
| 1½ tbsp finely chopped onion |
| 1 tbsp finely chopped fresh root ginger |
| 1 tbsp light soya sauce |
| 1 egg |
| 2 tbsp cornflour |

PEARL-STUDDED PORK BALLS

■ PREPARATION ■

Soak the rice in cold water to cover for at least 8 hours. Drain well. Soak the dried shrimps in hot water to cover for 25 minutes. Drain and finely chop. Place the pork in a bowl and add the dried shrimps, salt, onion, ginger, soya sauce, egg and 1½ tablespoons water. Combine thoroughly. Mix the soaked rice with the cornflour. Form the pork mixture into even-sized balls and wet each ball lightly with water. Roll the balls in the rice mixture and pat on lightly to get an even covering.

■ COOKING ■

Arrange the balls on a steaming tray in a steamer and steam vigorously for about 25 minutes.

■ SERVING ■

Serve on a heated dish and accompany with either a good quality soya sauce, tomato sauce or other mixed dip sauces (see page 211).

★★★★

Cooking time: 25 minutes

Serves: 4-6

Cooking method: steam, p.49

Takes time to prepare

Serve with a party meal

Illustrated on p.184

| 4 medium dried Chinese mushrooms |
| 4 tbsp dried shrimps |
| 2 spring onions |
| 2 slices fresh root ginger |
| 2 water chestnuts |
| 450g/1 lb minced pork |
| 1½ tbsp dry sherry |
| 2 eggs |
| ½ tsp MSG (optional) |
| 1 tsp salt |
| pepper to taste |
| vegetable oil for deep-frying |

CRISPY MEAT BALLS

While the meat balls in the Pearl-Studded Pork Balls are soft due to being steamed, these are crisp and crunchy as they are deep-fried. Crispy Meat Balls are smaller and suitable for accompanying drinks but they are also good served with boiled rice.

■ PREPARATION ■

Soak the dried mushrooms and dried shrimps separately in hot water to cover for 25 minutes. Drain. Discard the tough mushroom stalks and chop the caps roughly. Chop the shrimps, spring onions, ginger and water chestnuts. Mix the pork, mushrooms, shrimps, ginger, spring onions, water chestnuts, sherry, eggs, monosodium glutamate, if using, salt and pepper in a large bowl. Combine thoroughly, then form into small balls.

■ COOKING ■

Heat the oil in a wok or deep-fryer. When hot, add the meat balls, in 1-2 batches, and fry over medium heat for about 5 minutes or until golden brown. Drain.

★★★

Cooking time: 5 minutes per batch

Serves: 6-7

Cooking method: deep-fry, p.45

Fairly quick and easy to prepare

A good starter for a party meal

LONG-STEAMED KNUCKLE OF PORK

★ ★ ★ ★

Cooking time: about 2¾ hours

Serves: 8-10

Cooking methods: simmer, deep-fry p.45 and steam p.49

Lengthy cooking

Impressive dish for a party meal

■ PREPARATION ■

Bring a large pan of water to the boil. Add the knuckle of pork and boil for about 5 minutes, then remove and drain. Rub the skin and flesh with the dark soya sauce. Heat the oil in a wok or deep-fryer. When hot, fry the pork for about 5 minutes. Drain.

■ COOKING ■

Place the knuckle of pork in a flameproof casserole and add the light soya sauce, ginger, stock, salt, sugar and star anise. Bring to the boil and simmer for about 5 minutes. Turn the knuckle over and put on the lid. Place the casserole into a steamer and cook for 2½ hours, turning the knuckle over every 30 minutes.

■ SERVING ■

Serve the knuckle in a heated deep bowl with the sauce poured over the top. If liked, stir-fry about 450 g/1 lb spinach, then arrange it around the knuckle. A knife may be used to carve off the meat into bite-sized pieces but usually the meat is tender enough to remove with a pair of chopsticks.

1 knuckle of pork with skin on, about 2.25 kg/5 lb before boning, ask the butcher to remove the bone

2 tbsp dark soya sauce

vegetable oil for deep-frying

4 tbsp light soya sauce

3-4 slices fresh root ginger

600 ml/1 pt good stock (see page 56)

½ tsp salt

3 tbsp sugar

3 pieces star anise

DEEP-FRIED CRISPY PORK ROLLS

★ ★ ★ ★

Cooking time: 6-8 minutes

Serves: 4-6

Cooking method: deep-fry, p.45

A useful 'hot starter'

■ PREPARATION ■

Cut the pork into thin slices (about 7.5 × 5 cm/3 × 2 inch) and beat half a dozen times with a meat bat or rolling pin. Mix the salt, flour, sherry, monosodium glutamate, if using, and egg in a bowl. Toss the meat in this mixture. Cut the spring onions into 7.5 cm/3 inch sections. Roll a slice of pork around 2 pieces of spring onion. Secure each roll with a wooden cocktail stick, then coat in breadcrumbs.

■ COOKING ■

Heat the oil in a wok or deep-fryer. When hot, add the pork rolls, one at a time, and fry over medium heat for about 6 minutes until golden brown. Drain.

■ SERVING ■

Cut each roll on the slant into 2.5 cm/1 inch sections and arrange on lettuce leaves. These slices of pork may be served with a tomato sauce or with a salt and pepper dip. (see page 93)

675 g/1½ lb pork fillet

1 tsp salt

2 tbsp flour

1 tbsp sherry

½ tsp MSG (optional)

1 egg

4 spring onions

100 g/4 oz dry breadcrumbs

vegetable oil for deep-frying

6 crisp lettuce leaves

675g/1½–2lb belly of pork

300ml/½pt good stock (see page 56)

1½tbsp sugar

4tbsp soya sauce

SOYA-BRAISED PORK – LONG COOKED VERSION

■ PREPARATION ■

Cut the pork through the skin into 2.5 × 4 × 5 cm/1 × 1½ × 2 inch pieces.

■ COOKING ■

Bring 1.2lt/2pt water to the boil in a flameproof casserole. Blanch the pork for 3 minutes. Pour away the water. Add the stock, sugar and soya sauce to the casserole and bring to the boil. Cover and place the casserole in a preheated oven at 200°C, 400°F, Gas Mark 6, for 15 minutes. Remove the lid and stir the contents. Cover and cook for another 15 minutes, then stir again. Add a little more liquid if the sauce seems too thick. Reduce the oven temperature to 180°C, 350°F, Gas Mark 4 and continue to cook for a further 1½ hours.

Note: For extra flavour, add 3–4 slices fresh root ginger at the beginning of the cooking and 4–5 tablespoons rice wine when the contents are being stirred for the second time. Dried squid and hot Sichuan pickles can also be used to flavour this dish.

★ ★
Cooking time: 2-2¼ hours

Serves: 4-6

Cooking method: braise

Easy to prepare – lengthy cooking time

Excellent with rice and vegetable dishes for family meals

Illustrated on p.188

675g/1½lb meaty pork spare ribs

1½tsp salt

pepper to taste

vegetable oil for deep-frying

Sauce:

2tsp chopped fresh root ginger

2tsp chopped garlic

3tbsp yellow bean paste

2tsp sugar

2tbsp good stock (see page 56)

1½tbsp dark soya sauce

2tbsp dry sherry

1½tbsp hoisin sauce

1tbsp cornflour blended with 2tbsp stock

CAPITAL SPARE RIBS

■ PREPARATION ■

Chop the spare ribs into 2.5-4 cm/1-1½ inch pieces. Place in a large pan of water and bring to the boil. Simmer for 2 minutes, then drain. Sprinkle with the salt and pepper.

■ COOKING ■

Heat the oil in a wok or deep-fryer. When hot, fry the spare ribs over medium heat for about 8 minutes. Drain thoroughly and pour away the oil to use for other purposes, leaving 2 tablespoons. Heat the oil in the wok or a pan. When hot, stir in the ginger and garlic for about 15 seconds. Stir in the yellow bean paste and sugar. Add the stock, soya sauce, sherry and hoisin sauce and stir until smooth. Bring to the boil, return the spare ribs to the sauce and simmer for about 1 minute. Pour on the blended cornflour and stir until the sauce thickens.

★ ★
Cooking time: about 18 minutes

Serves: 5-6

Cooking method: deep-fry, p.45

Easy to prepare and cook

Serve as a starter

Illustrated on p.188

WHITE-COOKED SLICED PORK

★★

Cooking time: 45 minutes, plus cooling time

Serves: 4-6

Cooking method: simmer

Easy to prepare

1.5 kg/3 lb belly of pork
1 tbsp salt
4 slices fresh root ginger

■ PREPARATION AND COOKING ■

Bring 2.25 lt/4 pt water to the boil in a heavy saucepan or flameproof casserole. Place the pork in the pan and add the salt and ginger. Cover and simmer gently for 45 minutes. Remove the pork from the pan and cool for 5 × 7.5 cm/2 × 3 inch.

■ SERVING ■

Arrange the slices overlapping in a serving dish. Accompany with various simple dips such as: soya sauce, soya paste, chilli oil, sesame oil, chopped spring onions, shredded fresh root ginger, crushed garlic, vinegar, dry sherry.

SWEET AND SOUR PORK

★★★★

Cooking time: about 8 minutes

Serves: 4-6

Cooking methods: deep-fry p.45 and stir-fry p.42

Famous dish to serve as part of multi-course meal

1 kg/2 lb lean and fat pork
cornflour for coating
2 slices of canned pineapple or bamboo shoot
1 small green pepper
1 small red pepper
vegetable oil for deep-frying

Batter:
3 tbsp cornflour
3 tbsp self-raising flour
1 tsp salt
1 egg

Sweet and Sour Sauce:
2 tbsp sugar
3 tbsp vinegar
3 tbsp tomato purée
3 tbsp orange juice
1½ tbsp soya sauce
1½ tbsp cornflour blended with 4 tbsp water

■ PREPARATION ■

Cut the pork into 2.5 cm/1-in pieces and coat in cornflour. Coarsely chop the pineapple or bamboo shoot, green and red peppers. Mix the cornflour, flour, salt and egg into a smooth batter. Mix the sauce ingredients together until smooth. Add the pork pieces to the batter and coat evenly.

■ COOKING ■

Heat the oil in a wok or deep-fryer. When hot, fry the battered pork pieces for 3½ minutes. Remove and drain. Heat 2 tablespoons oil in another wok or frying pan. When hot, stir-fry the pineapple and peppers for a few seconds. Add the sauce and stir over medium heat until the sauce thickens and becomes translucent. Transfer the fried pork to the wok or pan containing the sweet and sour sauce. Stir and turn the pork in sauce over medium heat for 1 minute. (See pages 43–44 for step by step illustrations and instructions.)

BEEF

Interest in beef as a food is growing in China as the population gradually becomes more mobile and the impact of Western taste spreads, but as yet it is still only eaten by a minority. The Chinese Muslims, for example, who inhabit the great cattle-raising regions of Manchuria and the area north-west of Sinkiang, eat beef to the exclusion of pork, the consumption of which is forbidden by their religion. The majority of Chinese keep oxen, cows and buffalo in twos and threes as work animals, not for meat or as a source of dairy products, which few Chinese consume.

To a Chinese palate, beef tastes a trifle gamey and takes some getting used to. It can be cooked in the same way as pork, but it toughens more rapidly when subjected to heat and is not suitable for medium-length cooking: ie, 10-20 minutes. The majority of Chinese beef dishes are usually either very quickly stir-fried or cooked for a lengthy period by long simmering, long steaming or long red cooking.

Ingredients
450g/1lb beef steak, e.g. fillet, topside or sirloin
2-3 lambs' kidneys
½tsp salt
pepper to taste
1½tbsp cornflour
1 egg white
12 small button mushrooms or 100g/4oz canned straw mushrooms
50g/2oz drained, canned bamboo shoots
4 tbsp vegetable oil
3 slices fresh root ginger
15g/½oz lard
4 tbsp frozen peas
175g/6oz King prawns
1½tbsp light soya sauce
1 tbsp oyster sauce
2 tbsp good stock (see page 56)
1 tbsp dry sherry
1 tsp sesame oil

STIR-FRIED DICED BEEF
WITH KIDNEYS, SHRIMP AND MUSHROOMS

■ PREPARATION ■

Cut the beef into small cubes. Clean, then cut the smooth surface of each kidney with a criss-cross pattern. Cut the kidneys into similar sized cubes as the beef. Rub the beef and kidney with the salt and pepper. Toss evenly in the cornflour and coat in the egg white. Cut the button mushrooms in half or drain the straw mushrooms. Cut the bamboo shoots into cubes of similar size to the beef. Chop the prawns, if liked.

■ COOKING ■

Heat the vegetable oil in a wok or frying pan. When hot, stir-fry the beef, kidney and ginger over high heat for 1½ minutes, then drain, discarding the ginger. Add the lard to the pan. When hot, stir-fry the peas, prawns, mushrooms and bamboo shoots over high heat for 1 minute. Stir in the soya sauce, oyster sauce, stock and sherry and cook for 30 seconds. Return the beef and kidneys to the pan and stir-fry for another 30 seconds. Return the beef and kidneys to the pan and stir-fry for another 30 seconds. Sprinkle on the sesame oil.

■ SERVING ■

An unusual savoury dish suitable for nibbling as an accompaniment to wine, or to consume with rice as a main course dish.

★★★
Cooking time: about 8 minutes

Serves: 6-7

Cooking method: stir-fry, p.42

Fairly quick to prepare

Goes well with most dishes on a Chinese menu

Score kidneys p.39

★★★

Cooking time: about 10 minutes

Serves: 4-6

Cooking methods: deep-fry p.45 and stir-fry p.42

Quite easy to prepare

Good with most savoury and vegetable dishes

STIR-FRIED BEEF WITH CELERY

225 g/8 oz topside of beef
1 tsp salt
2 tbsp cornflour
1 egg white
4 sticks celery
2 spring onions
2 fresh chillies
2 slices fresh root ginger
vegetable oil for deep-frying
1 tsp pounded Sichuan peppercorns
1½ tbsp yellow bean paste
1 tbsp sugar
1 tbsp soya sauce
1 tbsp dry sherry
2 tbsp good stock (see page 56)
12 iceberg lettuce leaves or 12 Chinese pancakes (see page 178)

■ PREPARATION ■

Using a very sharp knife, cut the beef into thin slices, then cut again into matchstick-size shreds. Place in a bowl and mix with the salt, cornflour and egg white. Cut the celery into similar sized shreds as the beef. Cut the spring onions into 5 cm/2 inch sections. Finely shred the chillies, discarding the seeds. Shred the ginger.

■ COOKING ■

Heat the oil in a wok or deep-fryer. When hot, fry the beef for 2 minutes. Remove and drain off the excess oil. Pour away the oil to use for other purposes, leaving 1 tablespoon. Heat the wok or a frying pan with the oil. When hot, stir-fry the ginger, chilli, peppercorns, spring onion and celery for 1 minute. Add the bean paste, sugar, soya sauce, sherry, and stock and stir together over high heat for 30 seconds. Return the beef to the pan and stir-fry for 30 seconds.

■ SERVING ■

Transfer to a heated dish. To serve, place a small amount of beef and celery on to a lettuce leaf or pancake, roll up and eat.

★★

Cooking time: about 5-6 minutes

Serves: 4-6

Cooking method: stir-fry, p.42

Easy to prepare

Serve with rice. Complements most savoury dishes

QUICK STIR-FRIED BEEF WITH TOMATOES

450 g/1 lb beef steak, eg rump, fillet or sirloin
1 tsp salt
pepper to taste
2 tbsp cornflour
1 egg white
5 medium tomatoes
3 slices fresh root ginger
2 medium onions
4 tbsp vegetable oil
15 g/½ oz lard
1 tbsp soya sauce
1 tbsp dry sherry

This is a very popular beef dish in the summer in Peking where there is a profusion of tomatoes.

■ PREPARATION ■

Cut the beef into thin slices and rub evenly with salt and pepper. Toss in the cornflour and coat in the egg white. Cut each tomato into quarters. Shred the ginger. Peel and thinly slice the onions.

■ COOKING ■

Heat the oil in a wok or frying pan. When hot, spread the beef slices evenly over the surface of the pan and then stir-fry quickly over heat for 1 minute. Remove and set aside. Add the lard to the pan. When hot, stir-fry the ginger, onions and tomatoes for about 30 seconds. Add the soya sauce and sherry, return the beef to the pan and stir-fry all the ingredients for 30 seconds.

1 large sheet bean curd skin

225g/8oz beef fillet

½tsp salt

pepper to taste

1 tbsp cornflour

1 large ripe mango

2 slices fresh root ginger

1 tbsp oyster sauce

½tbsp light soya sauce

2tsp sugar

1 egg, beaten

vegetable oil for deep-frying

6tbsp hoisin sauce

12 iceberg lettuce leaves

MANGO BEEF

This is a departure from traditional Chinese cooking of beef, probably influenced by the cuisine of the South Seas, Singapore, Malaysia, Thailand, Vietnam and the Philippines.

▪ PREPARATION ▪

Soak the bean curd skin in hot water for 10 minutes. Cut the beef into 12 pieces and rub with the salt and pepper. Toss in the cornflour. Slice the mango flesh into 12 pieces. Shred the ginger. Place a few pieces of ginger over the top of the beef, then brush the beef with oyster sauce, soya sauce and sprinkle with sugar. Cover with a piece of mango. Cut the bean curd sheet into 12 pieces and use to wrap each mango, ginger and beef parcel up tightly. Seal the bean curd firmly with the beaten egg.

▪ COOKING ▪

Heat the oil in a wok or deep-fryer. When hot, fry the beef and mango parcels in batches for 2 minutes, then turn and fry for another 1 minute. Drain and keep the parcels warm as you fry the others.

▪ SERVING ▪

Heap the parcels on a heated dish. Serve with a spoonful of hoisin sauce and wrap in a lettuce leaf.

★★★★
Cooking time: about 3 minutes per batch

Serves: 4-6

Cooking method: deep-fry, p.45

Needs care and patience to make 'parcels'

An interesting dish to combine with others

450g/1lb beef steak, eg rump, fillet or sirloin

1 tsp salt

1½tbsp cornflour

1 egg white

3 slices fresh root ginger

3 leeks, about 225g/8oz

4tbsp vegetable oil

25g/1oz lard

1 tbsp light soya sauce

2tbsp good stock (see page 56)

1 tbsp prepared English mustard

2tsp red chilli oil

MUSTARD AND RED CHILLI OIL BEEF WITH LEEKS

▪ PREPARATION ▪

Cut the beef into very thin slices and rub with salt. Toss in the cornflour and coat in the egg white. Shred the ginger. Clean the leeks thoroughly and cut slantwise into 2.5cm/1 inch pieces.

▪ COOKING ▪

Heat the vegetable oil in a wok or frying pan. When hot, fry half the ginger for 30 seconds to flavour the oil. Add the leeks and stir-fry for 1½ minutes. Remove and set aside. Add the lard to the pan. When hot, stir-fry the beef for 1½ minutes. Add the soya sauce and remaining ginger, then return the leeks and stock to the pan. Toss together for another 30 seconds.

▪ SERVING ▪

Transfer to a heated serving dish. Drizzle the mustard and red oil evenly over the dish.

★★
Cooking time: about 10 minutes

Serves: 4-6

Cooking method: stir-fry, p.42

Quick and easy to make

A spicy dish that goes well with lighter dishes

Score kidneys, p.39

QUICK-FRIED SHREDDED BEEF WITH GINGER AND ONIONS

★★

Cooking time:
5-6 minutes

Serves: 4-6

Cooking method:
stir-fry, p.42

Quick and easy to prepare

Complements most savoury and vegetable dishes

Illustrated on p.188

■ PREPARATION ■

Using a very sharp knife, cut the beef into thin slices, then cut again into matchstick-size shreds. Sprinkle with the salt and pepper. Toss in the 1½ tablespoons cornflour and coat in the egg white. Peel and thinly slice the onions. Shred the ginger.

■ COOKING ■

Heat the oil in a wok or frying pan. When hot, stir-fry the beef over high heat for 1½ minutes. Remove and set aside. Add the lard to the pan. When hot, stir-fry the ginger and onions over high heat for 1½ minutes. Add the soya sauce, sugar and stock and stir together for 30 seconds. Return the beef, add the sherry and blended cornflour and continue to stir-fry for 30 seconds.

450g/1lb beef steak, eg rump or fillet
1 tsp salt
pepper to taste
1½tbsp cornflour
1 egg white
3 medium onions
3 slices fresh root ginger
4tbsp vegetable oil
25g/1oz lard
2tbsp soya sauce
1tbsp sugar
3tbsp good stock (see page 56)
1½tbsp dry sherry
2tsp cornflour blended with 2tbsp water

SLICED BEEF IN BLACK BEAN AND CHILLI SAUCE

★★★

Cooking time:
10 minutes

Serves: 4-6

Cooking method:
stir-fry, p.42

Easy to prepare

Serve with more lightly spiced dishes

Illustrated on p.188

■ PREPARATION ■

Cut the beef into thin slices and rub evenly with salt and pepper. Toss in the cornflour and coat in the egg white. Peel and thinly slice the onion. Finely chop the chillies. Cut the red and green peppers into 2.5cm/1 inch pieces. Soak the black beans in 4 tablespoons cold water for 3 minutes, then drain.

■ COOKING ■

Heat the oil in a wok or frying pan. When hot, stir-fry the beef over high heat for 1 minute. Remove and set aside. Add the lard to the pan. When hot, stir-fry the onion, black beans, chillies and peppers. Mash the softened black beans with a metal spoon against the edge of the wok or pan. Stir in the stock, sherry and soya sauce over high heat. Return the beef to the pan and mix well. Finally, add the blended cornflour to thicken the sauce. Stir all the ingredients for a further 30 seconds.

450g/1lb beef steak, eg rump, fillet or sirloin
¼tsp salt
pepper to taste
2tbsp cornflour
1 egg white
4tbsp vegetable oil
Sauce:
1 medium onion
2 dried chillies
1 small red pepper
1 small green pepper
1½tbsp salted black beans
15g/½oz lard
3tbsp good stock (see page 56)
1tbsp dry sherry
1tbsp soya sauce
½tbsp cornflour blended with 2tbsp water

3 medium onions
450g/1 lb good quality steak
1 tsp salt
1/4 tsp white pepper
1 1/2 tbsp light soya sauce
1 1/2 tbsp dark soya sauce
1/2 tbsp cornflour blended with 1 tbsp water
5 tbsp vegetable oil
2 tsp sugar
2 tsp dry sherry

QUICK-FRIED SHREDDED BEEF WITH ONIONS

■ PREPARATION ■

Peel and very thinly slice the onions. Thinly slice the beef, then cut into shreds. Add the salt, pepper, half of the soya sauces, the cornflour and 1 tablespoon of the oil to the beef; mix thoroughly.

■ COOKING ■

Heat the remaining oil in a wok or frying pan. When hot, stir-fry the onions for 1 minute. Push them to the side of the wok or pan and pour in the beef. Turn the beef and stir-fry for about 15 seconds. Sprinkle over the sugar, remaining soya sauces and sherry. When boiling, bring the onions in from the side of the pan and turn together with the beef. Turn and mix them evenly over a high heat. The whole process should not last more than 1 1/2 minutes after the beef has been added to the pan (the purpose is to keep the beef lightly cooked while strongly impregnated with the onion flavour).

Note: This dish is not suitable for reheating or keeping hot for long periods.

★★★

Cooking time: about 5 minutes

Serves: 4-6

Cooking method: stir-fry, p.42

Quick to prepare

Goes well with most dishes

800g/1 3/4 lb beef steak, eg fillet, sirloin or topside
2 slices fresh root ginger
1 1/2 tbsp soya sauce
1 1/2 tbsp hoisin sauce
1 tbsp Worcestershire sauce
1/2 tsp salt
1 1/2 tsp lightly pounded Sichuan peppercorns
1 green pepper
5 tbsp vegetable oil

SICHUAN PEPPERED BEEF MEDALLIONS

■ PREPARATION ■

Cut the beef at an angle into 4mm/1/6in thickness, then trim into medallion round shapes. Finely chop the ginger. Mix the soya, hoisin and Worcestershire sauces together and use as a marinade for the beef. Stir the salt, peppercorns and ginger into the marinade and leave the beef to season for about 30 minutes. Turn the beef over and marinate for a further 30 minutes. Cut the pepper into 2.5 cm/1 inch squares.

■ COOKING ■

Heat the oil in a wok or frying pan. When hot, add the beef pieces and space them evenly on the surface of the pan. Cook for 2 minutes, then turn them over and fry for another minute. Add the pepper and pour in any leftover marinade. Stir-fry for 30 seconds.

★★★

Cooking time: about 6 minutes, plus marinating time

Serves: 4–6

Cooking methods: shallow-fry and stir-fry, p.42

Quick to cook

Rather spicy, so best served with lighter, and less seasoned dishes

★★

Cooking time: about 8 minutes

Serves: 4-6

Cooking method: stir-fry, p.42

Easy to prepare

Accompany with other savoury and vegetable dishes

Illustrated on p.213

CANTONESE STIR-FRIED BEEF IN OYSTER SAUCE

450g/1lb beef steak, eg rump or fillet

1 tsp salt

pepper to taste

2 tbsp cornflour

1 egg white

3 slices fresh root ginger

100g/4oz mange tout or 3-4 spring onions

4 tbsp vegetable oil

1 tsp lard

1½ tbsp good stock (see page 56)

1 tbsp soya sauce

1½ tbsp oyster sauce

1 tbsp dry sherry

■ PREPARATION ■

Cut the beef into thin strips and mix with the salt and pepper. Toss in the cornflour and coat in the egg white. Shred the ginger. Cut each mange tout slantwise in half or cut the spring onions slantwise in 4cm/1½ inch sections.

■ COOKING ■

Heat the oil in a wok or frying pan. When hot, stir-fry the ginger in the oil to flavour. Add the beef and stir-fry over high heat for about 1 minute. Remove and set aside. Add the lard to the pan. When hot, stir-fry the mange tout or spring onions for 1-2 minutes. Add the stock and soya sauce, and continue to stir-fry for 30 seconds. Return the beef to the pan, add the oyster sauce and sherry and stir-fry over high heat for 30 seconds.

★★★★

Cooking time: about 15 minutes

Serves: 4-6

Cooking methods: deep-fry p.45 and stir-fry p.42

Care required in timing the cooking

A spicy dish, excellent with rice

Illustrated on p.188

SICHUAN HOT CRISPY FRIED SHREDDED BEEF

450g/1lb beef, eg rump, topside or fillet

3 eggs

1 tsp salt

100g/4oz cornflour

vegetable oil for deep-frying

Sauce:

3 medium carrots

4 slices fresh root ginger

3 spring onions

3 cloves garlic

2 fresh chillies

1 dried chilli

2 tbsp sugar

1½ tbsp soya sauce

3 tbsp vinegar

■ PREPARATION ■

Using a very sharp knife, cut the beef into thin slices, then cut again into matchstick-size shreds. Whisk the eggs, salt and cornflour to make a batter. Add the shredded beef and coat evenly. Cut the carrots and ginger into similar size shreds as the beef. Divide each spring onion into quarters lengthways, then cut into 4cm/1½ inch sections. Coarsely chop the garlic. Shred the chillies, discarding the seeds.

■ COOKING ■

Heat the oil in a wok or deep-fryer. When hot, fry the beef, stirring to keep the shreds separate, for 4 minutes. Remove with a perforated spoon and set aside. Reheat the oil, then fry the beef again to ensure it is crispy. Drain the beef on absorbent kitchen paper. Pour away the oil from the wok to use for other purposes, leaving 1 tablespoon. Heat the wok with the oil. When hot, stir-fry the carrots, spring onions, garlic, ginger and chillies over medium heat for 2½ minutes. Add the sugar, soya sauce, vinegar and finally the beef. Turn the ingredients around quickly over high heat for 15 seconds.

LAMB

Lamb is not eaten as often as beef in China. Indeed, the southern Chinese, especially the Cantonese, abhor mutton. Peking, on the other hand, has been called the 'Mutton Capital' and from Peking westwards, along the length of the old silk route, lamb and mutton are eaten almost exclusively. These meats are invariably cooked with quantities of strong-tasting vegetables, such as garlic, ginger, onion and leeks. Half of the restaurants in Peking reek of the smell of these vegetables being cooked and fried with the meat. The natives of Peking find the smell very inviting, but the majority of southerners would retreat a mile!

350g/12oz leg of lamb
2 spring onions
2 slices fresh root ginger
3 cloves garlic
4½ tbsp soya sauce
¾ tbsp yellow bean paste
7 tbsp vegetable oil
pepper to taste
3 tbsp dry sherry
350g/12oz lambs' liver
3 lambs' kidneys
1½ tbsp sesame oil

TRIPLE LAMB QUICK-FRY

■ PREPARATION ■

Cut the lamb meat into thin slices or cubes. Coarsely shred the spring onions, coarsely chop the ginger and garlic. Place the lamb in a bowl with 1½ tablespoons of the soya sauce, the yellow bean paste, 1 teaspoon of the oil, pepper to taste, 1 tablespoon of the sherry and the spring onions. Marinate for about 30 minutes. Cut the liver into similar size pieces as the lamb and place in another bowl with 1½ tablespoons soya sauce, 1 tablespoon sherry, 1 teaspoon oil, half the ginger and the garlic. Cut each kidney into 4 pieces and score the smooth side with a criss-cross pattern, if liked. Marinate in another bowl with 1½ tablespoons soya sauce, 1 tablespoon sherry, 1 teaspoon oil and the remaining ginger. Marinate the three types of lamb for 30 minutes.

■ COOKING ■

Place 3 tablespoons of the oil in a wok or frying pan. When hot, stir-fry the marinated lamb meat over high heat for 1½ minutes. Remove and set aside. Reheat the wok or pan with 1½ tablespoons oil. When hot, stir-fry the marinated liver over high heat for 1½ minutes. Remove and set aside. Finally, heat the remaining oil in the wok or pan. When hot, stir-fry the kidneys over high heat for 1 minute, then push them to the side of the pan. Add the sesame oil and return the lamb meat and liver to the pan. Mix together with the kidneys and stir-fry for another 30 seconds. Serve immediately.

Note: As can be seen from the above timing, it is very important that nothing is overcooked or undercooked. Therefore, make sure that all the ingredients are prepared before you commence cooking.

★ ★ ★ ★

Cooking time: about 6 minutes, plus marinating time

Serves: 6-7

Cooking method: multiple stir-fry, p.42

Requires care in cooking

Suitable for a family or party dinner

RED-COOKED LAMB

675-900 g/1½-2 lb shoulder or leg of lamb

3 tbsp oil

5-6 slices fresh root ginger

450 ml/¾ pt good stock (see page 56)

4 tbsp soya sauce

1 tsp sugar

1½ tbsp yellow bean paste

4 tbsp dry sherry

pepper to taste

Like most Chinese meats and poultry, lamb can be cooked with soya sauce. With lamb, less sugar is required than with pork, but much more ginger is added.

■ PREPARATION ■

Cut the lamb into 2.5 cm/1 inch pieces. Parboil the lamb in a pan of water for 3–4 minutes, then drain.

■ COOKING ■

Heat the oil in a wok or flameproof casserole. When hot, stir-fry the ginger for about 2 minutes to flavour the oil. Add the lamb and turn in the seasoned oil for 3–4 minutes. Add the stock, soya sauce, sugar, yellow bean paste, sherry and pepper. Bring to the boil and simmer gently for 1 hour, stirring occasionally. Serve directly from the wok or casserole at the table.

VARIATION
LONG BRAISED LAMB RED COOKED WITH CHINESE MUSHROOMS AND CHESTNUTS

This is a slightly fancier version of Red-Cooked Lamb, which with the addition of extra ingredients requires longer cooking. It is a dish for those who like rich, savoury food.

Soak 10–12 medium dried Chinese mushrooms in hot water to cover for 15 minutes. Discard the tough stalks. Boil 175 g/6 oz chestnuts for 15 minutes, then remove the skins. Add the mushrooms and chestnuts to the lamb casserole at the very beginning of cooking. Increase the stock to 600 ml/1 pint and the soya sauce to 5 tablespoons. Cook for 1½ hours. As with the previous recipe, the dish should be served directly from the casserole, and the diners help themselves. An ideal dish to accompany it is steamed buns (see page 240).

450g/1lb lean lamb, lightly frozen

8 tbsp vegetable oil

½ tsp salt

225g/8oz young leeks

1 tbsp soya sauce

1 tbsp yellow bean paste

¼ tsp pepper

1½ tbsp good stock (see page 56)

2 tbsp cornflour blended with 2 tbsp water

1 tbsp wine vinegar

1½ tsp sesame oil

2 tbsp finely chopped carlic

QUICK STIR-FRIED LAMB IN GARLIC SAUCE

■ PREPARATION ■

Cut the lamb into very thin slices, about 6 × 4 cm/2½ × 1½ inch. Place the meat in a bowl and marinate with salt and 2 tablespoons of the oil. Leave to season for 30 minutes. Cut the leeks slantwise into 2.5 cm/1 inch sections and clean thoroughly. Mix together the soya sauce, yellow bean paste, sherry, pepper, stock, blended cornflour, vinegar and sesame oil. Put aside for later use.

■ COOKING ■

Heat the remaining 6 tablespoons oil in a wok or frying pan. When very hot, stir-fry the garlic, then the lamb quickly over high heat for 20 seconds. Drain away any excess oil. Add the leeks and stir-fry quickly for 15 seconds. Pour in the soya sauce mixture and continue to stir-fry the ingredients over high heat for 15 seconds. Serve immediately.

Note: The success of the dish depends largely on the use of high heat and stir-fry with speed. The action produces a very Pekingese flavour.

★★

Cooking time: about 4-6 minutes, plus marinating time

Serves: 4-6

Cooking method: stir-fry, p.42

Quick to cook

Complements most Chinese dishes

675g/1½lb leg of lamb

225g/8oz pork skin

2 spring onions

3 cloves garlic

3 slices fresh root ginger

1½ tsp salt

pepper to taste

600ml/1pt good stock (see page 56)

3 tbsp white wine

1 tbsp light soya sauce

¼ tsp MSG (optional)

Dip sauce:

4 tbsp soya sauce

1 tbsp finely chopped fresh root ginger

1 tbsp finely chopped garlic

1 tbsp finely chopped spring onion

PEKING JELLY OF LAMB

This is a traditional Peking dish often used for eating with congee (rice gruel) or as an hors d'oeuvre item.

■ PREPARATION ■

Cut the lamb into 4 × 2.5 cm/1½ × 2 × 1 inch pieces. Cut the pork skin into smaller pieces. Parboil the lamb and pork skin in a pan of water for 2 minutes, then drain. Cut the spring onions into 2.5 cm/1 inch sections, keeping the green and white pieces separate. Thinly slice the garlic. Shred the ginger.

■ COOKING ■

Place the pork skin on the bottom of a heavy casserole and cover with the lamb. Add the salt, pepper, white parts of spring onions and the ginger. Pour in the stock and about 300 ml/½ pint water to cover the contents and bring to the boil. Reduce the heat to low, cover and simmer for 1¼ hours. Cool, then place in the refrigerator to encourage setting. The contents should be set after 3 hours. Remove the casserole from the refrigerator and peel away the pork fat and skin. Heat briefly to melt the jelly and then stir in the wine, soya sauce, monosodium glutamate, if using, garlic and green parts of the

★★★★

Cooking time: 1½ hours, plus setting time

Serves: 6-8

Cooking method: long simmer

Rather time-consuming to prepare

A good hors d'oeuvre or picnic dish

spring onions. Pour the lamb mixture into a rectangular mould (about 25 × 10 × 7.5 cm/10 × 4 × 3 inch) and leave in the refrigerator to set again. Mix the dip sauce ingredients together.

■ SERVING ■

Turn the mould out on to a serving dish and cut into 0.5 cm/¼ inch slices. Serve with the dip sauce.

★★★

Cooking time: about 10 minutes

Serves: 4-6

Cooking method: stir-fry, p.42

Fairly easy to prepare

Combines well with other Chinese dishes

STIR-FRIED LAMB AND LIVER

WITH BAMBOO SHOOTS, PEAS, LOTUS SEEDS AND GARLIC

■ PREPARATION ■

Soak the dried mushrooms, if using, in hot water to cover for 25 minutes. Drain and discard the tough stalks. Cut the lamb into small cubes. Cut the liver into similar sized cubes. Rub the salt into the lamb and liver. Toss in the cornflour. Coat in the egg white. Cut the bamboo shoots into cubes. Thinly slice the garlic. Blanch the lotus seeds in a pan of boiling water for 3 minutes, then drain.

■ COOKING ■

Heat 3 tablespoons oil in a wok or frying pan. When hot, stir-fry the lamb cubes over high heat for 1 minute. Remove and set aside. Heat the remaining tablespoon of oil in the wok or pan. When hot, stir-fry the cubed liver for 1 minute. Remove and set aside. Melt the lard in the wok or pan. When hot, stir in the garlic for 10 seconds, then add the bamboo shoots, peas, lotus seeds and mushrooms. Stir-fry over high heat for 2 minutes. Add the stock, soya sauce and sherry and continue to stir and turn for 1 minute. Return the lamb cubes and liver to the pan and stir-fry gently for 1 minute.

50g/2oz dried Chinese mushrooms or canned straw mushrooms, drained

350g/12oz leg of lamb

225g/8oz lambs' liver

1 tsp salt

1½tbsp cornflour

1 egg white

75g/3oz drained, canned bamboo shoots

4 cloves garlic

50g/2oz lotus seeds

4tbsp vegetable oil

20g/¾oz lard

75g/3oz green peas

3tbsp good stock (see page 56)

1½tbsp light soya sauce

1½tbsp dry sherry

1.5 kg/3 lb leg of lamb

4 slices fresh root ginger

4 cloves garlic

2 tsp salt

1/4 tsp pepper

3 tbsp vinegar

vegetable oil for deep-frying

Batter:

1 egg

4 tbsp cornflour

2 tbsp self-raising flour

Dip sauce:

3 tbsp sea salt

1 1/2 tbsp pounded Sichuan
  peppercorns

8 tbsp Peking Duck Sauce
  (see page 178)

8 tbsp wine vinegar mixed
  with 2 tbsp shredded fresh
  root ginger

MUSLIM DEEP-FRIED SIMMERED LAMB

■ PREPARATION ■

Cut the lamb into 6 × 1 cm/2½ × ½ inch strips. Parboil in a pan of water for 3 minutes, then drain.

■ COOKING ■

Place the lamb pieces at the bottom of a heavy pan. Add the ginger, garlic, salt and pepper and vinegar. Bring to the boil, reduce the heat and simmer gently for 45 minutes or until the sauce has completely reduced. Remove the lamb from the casserole and leave until cold. Whisk the batter ingredients in a mixing bowl. Use to coat each piece of lamb. Heat the oil in a wok or deep-fryer. When hot, fry the lamb pieces for about 3 minutes.

To make the dip sauce, heat the salt and pepper in a small dry frying pan over medium heat for 1½ minutes, stirring continuously. Divide into 2 small bowls. Add half the duck sauce and ginger-flavoured vinegar to each bowl.

■ SERVING ■

Arrange the lamb on a heated serving dish. Accompany with the dip sauce.

★★★

Cooking time:
about 1¼ hours

Serves: 4-6

Cooking methods:
simmer and deep-
fry, p.45

Not too difficult to
prepare

Adds variety to
menus of mostly
stir-fried dishes

---

675 g/1½ lb leg of lamb

½ tsp salt

pepper to taste

½ tbsp yellow bean paste

1 tbsp soya sauce

1 tbsp hoisin sauce

1 1/2 tbsp dry sherry

2 medium onions

6 slices fresh root ginger

2 spring onions

2-3 cloves garlic

4 tbsp vegetable oil

MARINATED LAMB
WITH ONION AND GINGER

■ PREPARATION ■

Cut the lamb into 5 × 2.5 × 0.5 cm/2 × 1 × ¼ inch thick slices. Sprinkle and rub with the salt and pepper. Mix the yellow bean paste, soya sauce, hoisin sauce and sherry together. Add this marinade to the lamb and leave to season for 30 minutes. Peel and thinly slice the onions. Shred the ginger. Cut the spring onions into 2.5 cm/1 inch sections. Coarsely chop the garlic.

■ COOKING ■

Heat the oil in a wok or frying pan. When hot, stir-fry the onion and ginger over high heat for 45 seconds, then push them to the sides of the wok or pan. Spread out the marinated slices of lamb in one layer at the centre of the pan and fry over high heat for 1¼ minutes on each side. Sprinkle with the spring onion and garlic. Bring in the onion and ginger from the sides and stir-fry for 1 minute.

★★★

Cooking time:
about 6 minutes,
plus seasoning
time

Serves: 4-6

Cooking methods:
shallow-fry and
stir-fry, p.42

Quick to cook

Combines well
with most
Chinese dishes

Steamed Ground Rice and
Pork in Lotus Leaves
(above), a full of flavour long
steamed dish; recipe page
190.
Quick-fried Shredded
Lamb and Leeks *(left)*,
accompany with a dip
sauce of your choice;
recipe page 210.

1.75-2.25 kg/4-5 lb neck of lamb
3 medium onions
2 dried chillies
4 slices fresh root ginger
4 cloves garlic
1.75 lt/3 pt water
3 tsp salt

Dip sauce:

9 tbsp soya sauce
2 tbsp finely chopped garlic
2 tbsp finely chopped fresh root ginger
2 tbsp finely chopped spring onions
2 tbsp finely chopped fresh coriander
1½ tbsp prepared English mustard
1½ tbsp wine vinegar
3 tbsp dry sherry
1 tbsp sesame oil
1 tbsp vegetable oil

MUSLIM LONG-SIMMERED LAMB
(OF THE LUNG FU SAI TEMPLE, PEKING)

As the lamb is cooked quite simply, the character of the dish comes largely from the dip sauce into which the lamb is dipped before eating.

■ PREPARATION ■
Cut the lamb into 5 × 2.5 × 0.5 cm/2 × 1 × ¼ inch thick slices. Parboil in a pan of water for 3 minutes, then drain. Peel and slice the onions. Shred the chillies, discarding the seeds. Shred the ginger. Crush the garlic.

■ COOKING ■
Place the lamb in a heavy flameproof casserole with a lid. Add the water, salt, onion, ginger, garlic and chilli. Bring to the boil, reduce the heat and simmer slowly for 3 hours, turning the contents every 30 minutes. Add more water if the sauce becomes too thick. Meanwhile, mix the dip sauce ingredients together.

■ SERVING ■
Serve the casserole at the table. The diners eat the lamb with the dip sauce and steamed buns (see page 240), which can be used to sandwich the meat after dipping in the sauce.

★★
Cooking time: 3 hours
Serves: 8-10
Cooking method: long simmer
Easy to prepare and lengthy cooking time
Normally eaten without accompaniment

---

225 g/8 oz leg of lamb
1 tsp salt
pepper to taste
3 slices fresh root ginger
225 g/8 oz young leeks
150 g/5 oz transparent pea starched noodles or ribbon noodles
2 tsp dried shrimps
3 tbsp vegetable oil
300 ml/½ pt good stock (see page 56)
½ chicken stock cube
2 tbsp light soya sauce
1½ tbsp dry sherry
1½ tbsp vinegar
1 tsp sesame oil

QUICK-FRIED SHREDDED LAMB AND LEEKS

■ PREPARATION ■
Cut the lamb into matchstick-size shreds and sprinkle with salt and pepper. Cut the ginger into similar shreds. Wash the leeks and shred. Soak the noodles in hot water for about 5 minutes, then drain. Soak the dried shrimps in hot water to cover for 10 minutes, then drain.

■ COOKING ■
Heat the oil in a wok or frying pan. When hot, stir-fry the ginger and leeks over high heat for 1 minute. Add the lamb and continue to stir-fry for 1 minute. Pour in the stock and add the crumbled stock cube, soya sauce, sherry, shrimps and vinegar. Bring to the boil, stirring. Simmer for 5 minutes, then add the noodles and simmer for a further 5 minutes. Sprinkle with sesame oil

★★
Cooking time: 15 minutes
Serves: 4-6
Cooking methods: stir-fry p.42 and simmer
Easy to prepare
Excellent just with rice
Illustrated on p.209

PEKING MONGOLIAN HOT POT

★ ★ ★ ★

Cooking and eating time: about 2 hours

Serves: 4-6

Cooking method: at table, in hot pot

Fairly time-consuming

A dish to be eaten without accompaniment

Illustrated on p.180

This dish was introduced into Peking in the 17th Century. It consists entirely of wafer thin slices of lamb which diners cook themselves by immersing them in boiling stock in a hot pot (fondue) at the table. For southerners this seems a primitive version of a hot pot, for in the south many different types of food are cooked in a hot pot, often including various kinds of seafood, different types of meat and vegetables. These all contribute to the flavour of the stock in the pot. In Peking they seem to prefer to keep the purity of flavour and only cook lamb. To cook this dish you will need a conventional Peking hot pot, made of brass and heated with charcoal, or an electric wok or an electric frying pan, capacity 1.75-2.25 lt/3-4 pt (see page 11).

■ PREPARATION ■

Thinly slice the partially frozen lamb with a razor sharp knife and lay the slices on saucers for each diner. The slices must be wafer thin or they will take too long to cook and will be tough. Shred spring onions and cut into 4 cm / 1½ inch sections. Clean and trim cabbage. Cut into 5 cm/2 inch pieces and place in 1-2 bowls. Blanch the noodles in a pan of boiling water for 3 minutes, then rinse under cold running water. Arrange in 2 bowls. Mix the 3 types of dip sauce and place in 3 small bowls on the table within easy reach of the diners.

■ COOKING ■

Bring 1.75 lt/3 pt of the stock to the boil in the hot pot. Add the salt, half the spring onions and half the ginger to the pot. After 15 seconds the diners can start cooking and eating. The diners pick up 2-3 slices of lamb in their chopsticks and dip them into the boiling stock for a few minutes to cook the lamb. Then the meat goes into the beaten egg and then into one of the dip sauces before being eaten.

After a few rounds of lamb have been eaten, each person may cook some noodles and cabbage in the stock. Unlike the meat, these are left to cook for a few minutes in the stock. After about half the food has been cooked, the host may add more stock to the pot, or add all the remaining ingredients and bring to the boil for about 4 minutes; the food will have formed a savoury soup to be drunk.

Ingredients
1.75-2.25 kg/4-5 lb lean lamb meat, lightly frozen
3 spring onions
1 small Chinese white cabbage
450 g/1 lb wheat flour noodles
100 g/4 oz transparent pea starched noodles
2-2.25 lt/3½-4 pt good stock (see page 56) or water
1½ tsp salt
4 slices fresh root ginger

Dip sauce 1:
10 tbsp soya sauce
2 tbsp finely chopped spring onion
1 tbsp finely chopped garlic
1 tbsp vegetable oil

Dip sauce 2:
8 tbsp wine vinegar
2 tbsp finely shredded fresh root ginger

Dip sauce 3:
6 tbsp sesame paste or peanut butter
2 tbsp sesame oil
2 tbsp water
1 tbsp soya sauce
1 tbsp chilli sauce
1 fresh egg, beaten and placed in front of each diner

Mongolian Barbecue of Lamb (*above*), an entertaining dish to be served in pancakes with cucumber, spring onions and sauce; recipe page 215. Long-steamed Wine-soaked Lamb with Tangerine Peel and Turnips (*left*), the lamb cooking liquid provides a delicious winey soup; recipe page 214. Cantonese Stir-fried Beef in Oyster Sauce (*right*), mange tout make a good alternative to spring onions; recipe page 203.

6 medium dried Chinese mushrooms
1 tbsp dried shrimps
175g/6oz transparent pea-starched noodles
2 slices fresh root ginger
2 cloves garlic
2 spring onions
3½tbsp vegetable oil
15g/½oz lard
1 tbsp drained, canned chopped winter pickles or snow pickles
225g/8oz minced lamb
2 tbsp light soya sauce
1 tbsp oyster sauce
1½tsp red chilli oil
4 tbsp good stock (see page 56)
1 tsp sesame oil

'ANTS CLIMBING UP TREES'
(STIR-FRIED LAMB WITH TRANSPARENT PEA-STARCHED NOODLES)

This recipe is so called because the finished dish of minced lamb with noodles is reminiscent of ants (lamb) climbing up trees (noodles). Although this dish is usually cooked with minced pork, minced lamb is equally good and some say even better.

■ PREPARATION ■

Soak the dried mushrooms and shrimps separately in hot water to cover for 25 minutes. Drain and discard the tough mushroom stalks. Finely chop the shrimp and mushroom caps. Cut the noodles into 7.5 cm/3 inch sections and soak in water to cover for 5 minutes. Drain. Shred the ginger. Crush the garlic. Coarsely chop the spring onions.

■ COOKING ■

Heat the vegetable oil in a wok or frying pan. When hot, stir-fry the shrimps, mushrooms and ginger over high heat for 30 seconds. Add the lard and garlic, half of the spring onions, the pickles and stir them around before adding the minced lamb. Stir-fry for about 2 minutes, then lower the heat and simmer for 3 minutes. Add the pea-starched noodles. Sprinkle them with soya sauce, oyster sauce, chilli oil and stock and the remaining spring onions. Toss all the ingredients together and sprinkle with the sesame oil.

★★★
Cooking time: 15 minutes

Serves: 4-6

Cooking methods: stir-fry p.42 and simmer

Quite easy to prepare

Goes well with most other Chinese dishes

575g/1½lb leg of lamb
350g/12oz turnips
1 dried tangerine peel
450ml/¾pt white wine
150ml/¼pt dry sherry
300ml/½pt water
5 slices fresh root ginger
1½tsp salt

LONG-STEAMED WINE-SOAKED LAMB
WITH TANGERINE PEEL AND TURNIPS

■ PREPARATION ■

Cut the lamb into 2.5 cm/1 inch cubes. Cut the turnips into similar size cubes. Parboil the lamb and turnips in a pan of water for about 3 minutes, then drain. Soak the tangerine peel in hot water for 5 minutes, then drain and break into small pieces.

■ COOKING ■

Put the lamb and turnip into a large heavy flameproof casserole with the wine, sherry, water, ginger, salt and tangerine peel. Bring to the boil, then place the casserole, covered, in a steamer and steam for 3 hours. If you do not have a large enough steamer, it is possible to cook the dish by placing the casserole into a pan containing 5 cm/2 inches water (a roasting tin will do) and then double boil the casserole for the same amount of time.

★★
Cooking time: 3 hours

Serves: 7-8

Cooking method: steam, p.49

Easy to prepare – lengthy cooking time

Serve with plenty of rice to mop up the soup

Illustrated on p.212

This dish is brought to the table and diners serve themselves. The soup in which the lamb and turnips are cooked is quite clear, extremely savoury and somewhat winey. It is an extremely good soup to drink after every mouthful of rice.

★ ★ ★ ★

Cooking time: about 2 hours, plus marinating time

Serves: 5-6

Cooking methods: steam p.49 and deep-fry p.45

8 Time and care needed in preparation

A main meal to eat unaccompanied

Illustrated on p.212

MONGOLIAN BARBECUE OF LAMB

Lamb is often eaten on the Steppes of Mongolia where it is sometimes barbecued over a big smouldering fire. This dish is a favourite among diners in my restaurant, where it is cooked in the following way.

■ PREPARATION ■

Cut the lamb along the grain into 6 long strips. Shred the ginger and spring onions. Mix with the peppercorns and salt and use to rub into the lamb. Mix the soya sauce, yellow bean paste, hoisin sauce, five spice powder and sherry and place in a bowl with the lamb. Marinate for 1–2 hours.

■ COOKING ■

Pack the seasoned lamb strips in a heatproof bowl, cover the top with foil. Place in a steamer and steam for about 2 hours or place the bowl in a pan containing 5 cm/2 inch of water and double boil for 2 hours. Remove from the bowl and leave to cool until required. When required, heat the oil in a wok or deep-fryer. When hot, fry the lamb for 4 minutes.

■ SERVING ■

Place the lamb on a chopping board and chop into bite-sized pieces while still hot. Serve the dish in the same way as Peking Duck. Spoon some duck sauce, on to a pancake or lettuce, then place on a few slices of lamb, followed by a little cucumber and spring onion. Form into a roll and turn up the end so nothing falls out, then eat.

1.5-1.75 kg/3-4 lb leg of lamb

4 slices fresh root ginger

5 spring onions

1 tbsp pounded Sichuan peppercorns

1 tbsp salt

3 tbsp soya sauce

1½ tbsp yellow bean paste

1½ tbsp hoisin sauce

¼ tsp five spice powder

2 tbsp dry sherry

vegetable oil for deep-frying

Wrapping and eating:

12 Chinese pancakes (see page 178) or lettuce leaves

2 small bowls of Peking Duck sauce (see page 178)

3 saucers of matchstick-size pieces of cucumber

3 saucers of shredded spring onions

DESSERTS

Frying Peking 'Toffee Apples' (*left*); recipe page 252.
Kiwi Fruit Salad with Mandarin and Lotus
Seeds (*above*); recipe page 223.

甜
品

DESSERTS

Desserts are not part and parcel of a normal Chinese meal, hence the scarcity of desserts on the menus of most Chinese restaurants. Most restaurant chefs concentrate on meats and savouries and tend to regard sweets as little more then confectionery. On the other hand, most Chinese banquets and party menus would include one or two sweet courses, which are sandwiched between the progression of numerous savoury courses.

It should not be assumed from this that Chinese sweets, cakes and confectioneries are limited in range. If you went to a Chinese market you would find stalls overflowing with bon bons, dried fruits and cakes which would do credit to the best confectionery shops in the West.

575g/1¼lb glutinous rice

65g/2½oz lard

75g/3oz sugar

about 25g/1oz nuts, eg almonds, walnuts, chestnuts or lotus seeds

6tbsp (optional) candied and dried fruits, eg ginger, cherries, angelica, mixed candied fruits, or dried lichee, or raisins or stoned date pieces

about 75g/3oz sweet bean paste

EIGHT TREASURE PUDDING

The candied and dried fruits provide the colourful pattern on this steamed pudding.

■ PREPARATION ■

Wash the rice and place in a saucepan. Cover with 1cm/½inch water. Bring to the boil and simmer gently for 11-12 minutes. Add half the lard and all the sugar, turn and stir until well mixed. Grease the sides of a large heatproof basin or bowl heavily with the remaining lard (lard must be cold). Stick the nuts and candied or dried fruits of your choice in a pattern on the sides of the basin in the lard, arranging the remainder at the bottom of the basin. Place a layer of sweetened rice in the basin, then spread a thinner layer of sweet bean paste on top of the rice. Repeat the layers, finishing with a rice layer. Cover the basin with foil, leaving a little room for expansion.

■ COOKING ■

Place the basin into steamer and steam steadily for 1 hour 10 minutes until cooked.

■ SERVING ■

Invert the basin on to a large round heated serving dish to turn out the pudding. Decorate with extra candied fruits etc, if liked.

★ ★ ★ ★

Cooking time: about 1¼ hours

Serves: 6-8

Cooking method: steam, p.49

Requires patience to prepare

Good dessert for Western palate

Illustrated on p.220

ALMOND 'TEA'

★★
Cooking time:
20-25 minutes

Serves: 5-6

Cooking method:
simmer

Easy to make

Ideal after multi-
course meal

This is a sweet hot dessert drink, which we Chinese enjoy drinking slowly after a multi-course savoury meal.

175g/6oz blanched almonds
100g/4oz long grain rice
4 tbsp sugar
1 tsp almond essence
6 tbsp milk
1½ tbsp cornflour blended with 3 tbsp water

■ PREPARATION ■

Grind the almonds and rice in a blender or food processor. Add 600 ml/1 pint water and blend until smooth. Add the sugar, almond essence and another 300 ml/½ pint water. Stir together until well blended.

■ COOKING ■

Transfer the almond mixture to a heavy-based pan and slowly bring to the boil, stirring. Simmer very gently for 10 minutes, stirring constantly. Add the milk and blended cornflour. Continue to cook and stir for a further 5 minutes.

■ SERVING ■

Serve in small bowls, in small quantities at a time, as it is likely to be very hot.

PEARS IN HONEY SAUCE

★★★
Cooking time:
25 minutes, plus
chilling time

Serves: 6

Cooking method:
simmer

Quite easy to
make

Refreshing dessert

Illustrated on
p.221

6 firm, ripe pears
4 tbsp runny honey
4 tbsp sweet liqueur, eg Chinese Rose Dew, kirsh, cherry brandy, crème de menthe
4 tbsp sugar

■ PREPARATION ■

Peel the pears, leaving on the stalks and a little of the surrounding skin. Blend the honey with the liqueur, 1 tablespoon of the sugar and 2 tablespoons water.

■ COOKING ■

Stand the pears in a flat bottomed pan and barely cover with water. Bring slowly to the boil. Add the remaining sugar and simmer gently for 20 minutes. Refrigerate the pears with a quarter of the sugar water for 2 hours, discarding the remaining sugar water.

■ SERVING ■

Stand each pear in a small bowl. Spoon over a little sugar water, then pour about 2 tablespoons of the honey sauce over each pear. Chill for another 30 minutes before serving.

225g/8oz canned water
 chestnuts, drained

175-225g/6-8oz caster sugar

175-225g/6-8oz water
 chestnut flour

4tbsp corn oil

3tbsp vegetable oil

WATER CHESTNUT 'CAKE'

These cakes are quite unique in texture. For although they have the appearance and feel of slices of firm jelly, you will experience a crunchy sensation when you bite through the shreds of water chestnut in the jelly.

■ PREPARATION ■
Cut the water chestnuts into matchstick-size shreds.

■ COOKING ■
Place the water chestnuts in a saucepan, add the sugar and 450ml/¾ pint water. Bring to the boil. Stir in the water chestnut flour and add another 450ml/¾ pint water. Stir and mix well, then simmer for 5 minutes. Add the corn oil, stir and bring once more to the boil. Reduce heat to very low and simmer gently for 5 minutes. Pour the mixture into a square cake tin or Swiss roll tin. Place the tin in a steamer and steam for 30 minutes. Remove from the steamer and leave to cool.
When cold, the 'cake' is like a firm jelly with streaks of water chestnut inside. Cut into pieces about the thickness of bread slices. Heat the vegetable oil in a frying pan. When hot, fry each slice of chestnut 'cake' for 2½ minutes on each side. Serve hot or cold.

★★★
Cooking time: about 1 hour

Serves: 5-6

Cooking methods: simmer, steam p.49 and shallow-fry

Usually served as a dim sum item

1 recipe Almond 'Tea' (see
 page 219)

1 envelope plain gelatine

150ml/¼pt evaporated milk

ALMOND JUNKET

■ PREPARATION AND COOKING ■
Repeat the Almond Tea recipe until the almond mixture is brought to the boil. Meanwhile, sprinkle the gelatine over a bowl containing 5-6 tablespoons water. Place the bowl in a pan of hot water to dissolve the gelatine. Instead of adding the 300ml/½ pint water, stir in the dissolved gelatine. Bring slowly to the boil, stirring constantly. Simmer very gently for 10 minutes. Mix in the evaporated milk. Simmer for a further 5 minutes, stirring. Pour the almond mixture into a square deep-sided dish. Leave to cool for 30 minutes, then chill in the refrigerator.

■ SERVING ■
After 1½-2 hours, the mixture will be set. Cut the junket into squares, triangular wedges or diamond shapes. They can be served on their own, mixed with other jellies or added to a fruit salad. Their distinctive appeal lies in their nutty flavour.

★★★
Cooking time: about 30 minutes, plus cooling and chilling time

Serves: 5-6

Cooking method: simmer

Delicious with fruit

Illustrated on p.220

YUAN HSAIO OR NEW YEAR DUMPLINGS

★ ★ ★ ★

Cooking time: about 5-6 minutes per batch, plus firming time

Serves: 6-7

Cooking method: simmer

Time-consuming to make

Traditional dessert at Chinese New Year

Dough skin:
100 g/4 oz glutinous rice flour

Filling:
1½ tbsp vegetable oil
1½ tbsp sesame paste or peanut butter
1½ tbsp sugar
3 tbsp sweet red bean paste

These dumplings came to be served as New Year dumplings because they are smooth, round and full – symbolic of good fortune. However, they are also deceptive because each has a heart of sesame paste and very hot sugar is often twice as hot as the exterior of the dumplings and the liquid in which they are served. Therefore, give them the time to cool a little before eating.

■ PREPARATION ■

Add 300 ml/½ pint water to the rice flour, mix and squeeze with your hand into a rough dough. Add more water slowly and gradually until the dough is smooth and does not flake in the hand as you knead and mix. Form and roll it into a long 46 cm/18 inch sausage. Cut into 18 pieces and press each piece of dough into a round. Heat the oil in a pan. When hot, pour it over the sesame paste. Stir it in until the paste becomes softer and pasty. Add the sugar and red bean paste. Stir until well blended. Place the mixture in a refrigerator for 30 minutes to become firm. Divide the filling into 18 pieces. Place each piece of filling on a dough round. Fold it over to wrap the filling completely, then roll into a ball.

■ COOKING ■

Heat 1 litre/2½ pints water in a large saucepan. Add the dumplings to the boiling water, a few at a time. Bring to the boil and simmer over medium heat for 5-6 minutes. When the dumplings will rise to the top. Remove the dumplings with a perforated spoon.

■ SERVING ■

Divide the dumplings between 6 bowls and cover with the cooking water.

KIWI FRUIT SALAD
WITH MANDARIN AND LOTUS SEEDS

★

Preparation time: 8 minutes

Serves: 4-6

Easy to prepare

Illustrated on p.217

225-275 g/8-10 oz lotus seeds
275 g/8 oz canned mandarin oranges
2-3 kiwi fruit

■ PREPARATION ■

Drain the lotus seeds and mandarin orange segments, reserving the orange juice. Peel the kiwi fruit and slice the flesh. Place the lotus seeds, mandarin segments and Chinese gooseberry slices in a serving dish. Spoon over the reserved juice and mix together gently.

DIM SUM

Wontons, see pages 230–231, can be deep–fried (*left*);
see also page 238. Lotus Leaf Savoury Rice *(above)*; recipe page 70.

點

心

DIM SUM

Dim sum are Chinese snacks or 'small eats' which are consumed between meals. The Chinese tradition of eating dim sum is becoming increasingly popular both at home and abroad. So widespread is the popularity of these snacks that institutions have grown up which serve only or mainly dim sum. Indeed, a good proportion of the large Chinese Cantonese restaurants in Western cities such as London, New York, Toronto, San Francisco and Los Angeles serve dim sum throughout the day until dusk. Dim sum are generally served from heated trolleys, which are pushed through the restaurant so the customer may choose what he likes.

They are rarely eaten with rice, and consist mainly of crispy deep-fried items which Westerners take to readily, or steamed items which are often served in steam baskets. These latter are picturesque and succulent, and are thought to constitute healthy eating.

In the warmer south, dim sum are prepared and eaten in tea houses and small restaurants and even outdoors rather than at home. In north China, which has severe weather during a good part of the year, and where people eat out much less often, the preparation and eating of dim sum remains largely a domestic activity. There the whole family, from the very old to the very young, will gather together and make dim sum (mostly steamed or poached dumplings or Chiaotzus and steamed and stuffed buns or Bao tzus) by the hundred. Domestic dim sum take the place of a full-scale meal and are usually prepared and eaten during festivals and holidays when there are more hands available.

There are scores of different dim sum, many of them fancy, but the main line consists of no more than a score of items. Northern dim sum are less well known in the West than those from the south, there being many more Cantonese restaurants abroad. The southern Cantonese dim sum are undoubtedly daintier and require more skill to make than those from the north. For practical reasons we shall confine ourselves to those dim sum which can be readily made at home.

Peking Kuo–Tieh dumplings are fun to make for a celebration meal. The same dumplings can be simmered, then drained and eaten with a spicy sauce (Red Chilli Oil Dumplings), but these are steamed and then shallow-fried.

1 After mixing the flour with boiling then cold water, the dough is gathered with the hand.

For recipe see Peking Kuo-tieh Dumplings, p. 241

For recipe see Red Chilli Oil Dumplings, p. 268

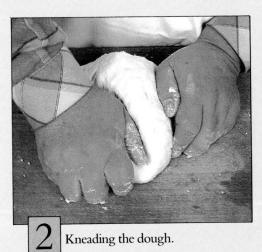

2 Kneading the dough.

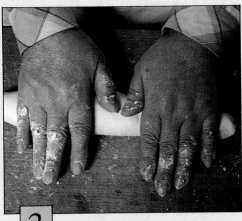

3 Rolling the dough into a sausage shape before cutting it into small pieces.

4 Flouring the pieces of dough.

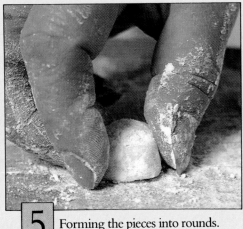

5 Forming the pieces into rounds.

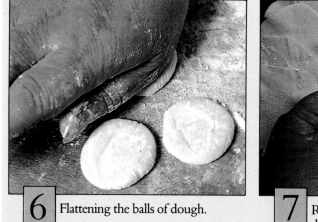

6 Flattening the balls of dough.

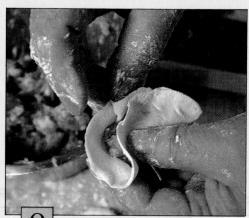

7 Rolling out each round of dough.

8 Filling the centre of each round.

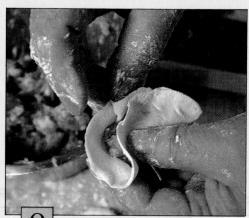

9 Folding over the dough and pinching the edges firmly to seal.

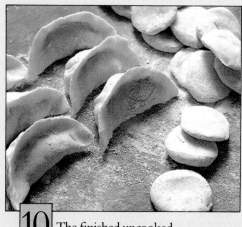

10 The finished uncooked dumplings and flattened dough.

11 Shallow-frying the dumplings.

Steamed buns and dumplings are an important part of northern Chinese cooking and are a popular breakfast or snack sold at roadside stalls for people going to work.

Stuffed wontons are easy to make because wonton skins are sold ready-made at many good Chinese food stores. But whether you buy or make the skins, fried or steamed wontons make a tasty snack. Alternatively, wontons can be simmered for a delicious addition to soup.

To filling 20 wonton skins:
3-4 oz minced pork
4 tbsp minced shrimps
2 tbsp chopped spring onion
Salt and pepper
1 tbsp rice wine
1 tbsp finely chopped fresh root ginger

Allow about 4 wontons per person

1 Adding rice wine to the stuffing mixture.

2 Adding ginger to the mixture.

3 Adding water to the mixture.

4 Stirring well to form an evenly flavoured mixture.

5 Filling the centre of the wonton skins. (Allow about 1 teaspoon of filling per wonton.)

6 Wetting and joining the edges, pressing to seal.

7 Folding the wontons over.

Deep-fried Crispy Wontons are illustrated on p. 238

Wonton Soup is illustrated on p. 234

8 Wontons in their traditional shape.

9 Adding the wontons to simmering stock or soup. Simmer for about 10 minutes.

The final cooked wontons.

Dough skin wrappers:

1 egg

225 g/8 oz plain flour

½ tsp salt

120 ml/4 fl oz water

cornflour

SPRING ROLL WRAPPERS

★★★
Preparation time:
about 30 minutes,
plus resting time

Spring roll wrappers or pancakes are generally available at the majority of major Chinese supermarkets, but they can also be easily made at home. Spring roll wrappers can vary greatly in size. The daintier smaller ones are no more than 7.5 cm/3 inch long, while some can reach 25 cm/10 inch in length.

■ PREPARATION ■

Lightly beat the egg. Sift the flour and salt into a large bowl. Make a well in the centre and mix the beaten egg and water into the flour. Stir with a wooden spoon to form a smooth dough. Place the dough on a floured board and knead for 10 minutes until smooth. Cover with a damp cloth and leave to rest for about 30 minutes. Roll the dough into a 30 cm/12 inch sausage, then cut into 4 cm/1½ inch pieces. Dust with cornflour and flatten with the palm of your hand. Roll as thinly as possible, then trim to 15 × 18 cm/6 × 7 inch rectangles. Dust with cornflour and stack them up.

350 g/12 oz lean pork or
  chicken meat

2 slices fresh root ginger

75 g/3 oz drained, canned
  bamboo shoots

8 medium dried Chinese
  mushrooms

2 spring onions

3 tbsp vegetable oil

1 tsp salt

2 tbsp soya sauce

100-150 g/4-5 oz bean sprouts

1 tbsp cornflour blended with
  2 tbsp water

beaten egg for sealing

vegetable oil for deep-frying

SPRING ROLL FILLINGS

★★★★
Cooking time:
45 minutes for
filling,
3¾-4½ minutes
per batch of spring
rolls

Serves: 6-8

Cooking methods:
stir-fry p.42 and
deep-fry p.45

Fairly easy to
make with practice

Useful side dish
with soya-based dip
sauce

Illustrated on
pp.235 and 266

Almost any mixture of meat and vegetables can be used as fillings for spring rolls. They will need to be shredded and quickly stir-fried, then left to cool before wrapping in the pancakes as fillings. The most popular ingredients for fillings are the following:

■ PREPARATION ■

Cut the pork or chicken into matchstick-size shreds. Cut the ginger and bamboo shoots into similar or finer shreds. Soak the dried mushrooms in hot water to cover for 25 minutes. Drain and discard the tough stalks. Cut the mushroom caps into fine shreds. Divide the spring onions lengthwise in half, then cut into 1 cm/½ in sections.

■ COOKING ■

Heat the 3 tbsp oil in a wok or frying pan. When hot, stir-fry the ginger, salt, mushrooms and shredded meat over high heat for 1¼ minutes. Add all the other ingredients, except the cornflour, and stir-fry for 1 minute. Pour in the blended cornflour, stir and turn for another 30 seconds. Remove from the heat and leave to cool before using as a filling.

■ FILLING THE PANCAKES ■

Take 2 tablespoons of filling and spread across each pancake just below the centre. Fold the pancake up from the bottom by raising the lower corner to fold over the filling. Roll the filling over once, and bring in the 2 corners from the side to overlap each other. Finally fold the top flap down, sealing with a little beaten egg. Stack the spring rolls as you make them, placing them so that the weight of the pancake rests on the flap that has just been sealed.

■ COOKING THE PANCAKES ■

Fry the pancakes soon after they have been made, as otherwise they may become soggy. Heat the oil in a wok or deep-fryer. When hot, fry not more then 5-6 pancakes at a time for 3¾-4½ minutes until golden brown and crispy. Once fried, they can be kept crispy in the oven for up to 30 minutes. Or store them in the refrigerator for a day after an initial frying of 2½ minutes, then re-fry them for 3 minutes when required.

■ SESAME PRAWNS ON TOAST ■

★★★★

Cooking time: about 4 minutes per batch

Serves: 7-8

Cooking method: deep-fry, p.45

Quite easy to make

Excellent party starter

Illustrated on p.239

225 g/8 oz peeled prawns

50 g/2 oz pork fat

1 tsp salt

pepper to taste

½ tsp ground ginger

1 tbsp dry sherry or white wine

1½ tbsp finely chopped spring onion

1 egg white

2 tsp cornflour

6 slices bread

100 g/4 oz sesame seeds

vegetable oil for deep-frying

These toasts make an excellent starter and can be used as canapés for a cocktail party.

■ PREPARATION ■

Chop and mix the prawns and pork fat into a paste in a bowl. Add the salt, pepper, ginger, sherry or wine, spring onion, egg white and cornflour. Mix together thoroughly. Spread the mixture very thickly on the top of the slices of bread. Spread the sesame seeds evenly over the surface of a large plate or a small tray. Place each piece of bread, spread side down, on the sesame seeds. Press gently so that each slice has a good coating of seeds.

COOKING

Heat the oil in a wok or deep-fryer. When hot, fry the slices of bread, spread-side down (only 2-3 slices of bread can be fried at a time) for 2½ minutes. Turn over and fry for a further 1½ minutes. Drain on absorbent kitchen paper.

■ SERVING ■

When all the slices of bread have been fried and drained, place each piece of bread on a chopping board, cut off and discard the crusts. Cut the coated and fried bread slices into 6 rectangular pieces (the size of fish fingers) or into 4 triangles. Arrange them on a heated serving dish and serve hot.

Steamed buns (*above*), a
tempting savoury snack.
Wonton Soup (*left*),
wonton–making needs
practise to perfect; recipe
page 231.
Spring Rolls (*right*), serve
these famous deep–fried
savoury rolls as a snack or as
part of a multi-course
meal; recipe page 232.

12 quails' eggs (drained if necessary)
350g/12oz shelled shrimps, fresh or frozen
50g/2oz pork fat
2 egg whites
1 tsp salt
1/4 tsp pepper
1/4 tsp MSG (optional)
1 tbsp cornflour
1 tsp dry sherry
1/2 tsp sesame oil
1 tsp finely chopped spring onion
6 slices thin white bread
1 1/2 tbsp finely chopped carrot
1 1/2 tbsp finely chopped coriander leaves
vegetable oil for deep-frying

QUAILS' EGGS ON SHRIMP TOASTS

This is a more elaborate version of the popular Sesame Prawns on Toast. They make very attractive and appealing canapés at any cocktail party.

■ PREPARATION ■

Place the eggs in a pan of water. Bring to the boil and simmer for 4 minutes. Drain and plunge into cold water. Chop the shrimps and pork fat together to form a smooth paste. Place them in a bowl and add the egg whites, salt, pepper, monosodium glutamate, if using, cornflour, sherry, sesame oil and spring onion. Mix together until smooth. Shell the quails' eggs and cut in half lengthwise. Spread each piece of bread evenly with the prawn mixture, then cut each slice of bread into 4 pieces. Press half a quails' egg into the mixture and a pinch of chopped carrot at one end and chopped coriander at the other end.

■ COOKING ■

Heat the oil in a wok or deep-fryer. When hot, lower the slices of bread, in batches, shrimp-side down, into the oil. Fry for 1 1/2 minutes, then turn over gently and fry for a further minute. Turn them once again and fry for another 15 seconds. Remove and drain on absorbent kitchen paper.

★★★★
Cooking time: about 3 minutes per batch

Serves: 6-8

Cooking method: deep-fry, p.45

A little time-consuming to prepare

Use good quality soya, or soya, chilli and ketchup as a dip sauce

Attractive canapé

15g/1/2oz dry yeast
300ml/1/2pt warm water
1 tsp sugar
400g/14oz self-raising flour
Filling:
6 dried Chinese mushrooms
450g/1lb minced pork
2 tbsp light soya sauce
1 tsp salt
1 tsp sugar
1/2 tsp pepper
1/4 tsp MSG (optional)
2 tbsp water
1 Chinese white cabbage
2 tsp sesame oil

BAO TZU STEAMED BUNS

■ PREPARATION ■

Mix the yeast with 4 tablespoons warm water and the sugar. Leave until frothy – about 10 minutes. Sift the flour into a large bowl. Make a well in the centre. Pour in the yeast mixture with remaining 250ml/8floz warm water. Mix and knead the dough. Leave in a warm place until the dough doubles in size. Knead well, then leave to rise until about half the size again. For the filling, soak the dried mushrooms in hot water to cover for 25 minutes. Drain and discard the tough stalks. Chop the mushroom caps into 0.5cm/1/4 inch pieces. Put the minced pork in a large bowl. Add the soya sauce. Mix half the salt, the sugar, pepper, monosodium glutamate, if using, and water together. Add to the meat mixture. Wash the cabbage and blanch whole in a saucepan of boiling water for 30 seconds. Squeeze the cabbage dry and cut into small pieces. Mix the mushrooms and cabbage together with remaining salt, 2 teaspoons sesame oil and then mix with the minced pork. Divide dough into 28-30 balls. Roll each ball into 7.5cm/3inch flat rounds. Put 1 tablespoon meat filling on each round. Gather up the edges. Pinch the dough together to enclose the filling.

★★★★
Cooking time: 12 minutes

Serves: 10-12

Cooking method: steam, p.49

Fairly easy to make with practice

Tasty snack

Illustrated on p.266

■ COOKING ■

Put the buns in a steamer on greased paper, about 2.5 cm/1 inch apart. Steam for 12 minutes.

BAO TZU STEAMED BUNS
STUFFED WITH SWEET BEAN PASTE

★★★★

Cooking time: 12 minutes

Serves: 10-12

Cooking method: steam, p.49

Fairly easy to make with practice

Eat as snack

15 g/¹/₂ oz dry yeast

300 ml/¹/₂ pt warm water

1 tsp sugar

400 g/14 oz self-raising flour

sweet bean paste

■ PREPARATION ■

Mix the yeast with 4 tablespoons warm water and the sugar. Leave until frothy, about 10 minutes. Sift the flour into a large bowl, make a well in the centre. Pour in the yeast mixture with remaining 250 ml/8 fl oz warm water. Mix and knead the dough. Leave in a warm place until the dough doubles in size. Knead well, then leave to rise until about half the size again. Take a piece of dough (about 2-3 tablespoons), knock back and knead again for a few minutes. Form it into a cup or shell. Stuff each bun with 2 teaspoons sweet bean paste. Gather up the dough to enclose the filling. Leave to prove for 15-20 minutes.

■ COOKING ■

Place the buns in a steamer on greased paper, 7.5 cm/1 in apart. Steam for 12 minutes.

Crispy Wontons (*above*). Wontons (page 231)
can be deep-fried for 2½-3 minutes and served
with a dip sauce or Sweet and sour sauce, found
on page 197.
Steamed Siu Mai (*above right*), steamed
dumplings filled with a savoury mixture of
prawns, pork and vegetables; recipe page 240.
Peking Kuo-tieh Steamed and Sautéed
Dumplings (*centre right*), a Northern dim sum
dumpling filled with a pork mixture; recipe
page 241.
Sesame Prawns on Toast (*below right*), serve as a
sumptuous starter or as part of a buffet spread;
recipe page 233.

250ml/8 fl oz boiling water
450ml/3/4 pint cold water
1 tsp dry yeast
1 tbsp caster sugar
450g/1 lb self-raising flour
3 tbsp vegetable oil

LOTUS LEAF SHAPED STEAMED BUNS

Serve these buns with rich saucy dishes.

■ PREPARATION ■

Mix the boiling water with cold water, sprinkle over the yeast and stir in ½ teaspoon of the sugar. Cover and stand for 3 minutes until the yeast froths. (If the bubbling does not take place, discard and start again with new yeast.) Sift the flour into a large bowl and gradually stir in yeast mixture with 1 tablespoon of the vegetable oil and the rest of the sugar to form a soft dough. Knead until the texture becomes elastic. Leave the dough in a warm draught free place for 2-3 hours until the dough doubles in size. Knock back the dough to reduce it to the original size. Cover with a damp cloth and leave for another 20-30 minutes. When risen turn out the dough and knead again. Roll into a 4cm/1½ inch thick roll. Cut dough into 2.5cm/1 inch sections, roll into a ball and flatten with the hand. With a rolling pin, roll the dough into 7.5cm/3in rounds. Brush oil on half of the top. Fold the other half over and score a criss-cross pattern on top. Pinch in slightly around the edge at intervals to form it into the shape of a lotus leaf.

■ COOKING ■

Place the buns in a heatproof dish in a steamer and steam over high heat for 6 minutes.

★★★★
Cooking time: 6 minutes
Serves: 5-6
Cooking method: steam, p.49
Fairly easy to make after practice
Ideal accompaniment to rich meaty dishes with lots of sauce

---

6 dried Chinese mushrooms
2 drained, canned bamboo shoots
100g/4oz peeled prawns
1 spring onion
2 eggs
350g/12oz minced pork
2 tbsp peas
½ tsp salt
pinch of MSG (optional)
pinch of white pepper
½ tsp sugar
2 tbsp vegetable oil
2 tbsp cornflour
1 tsp sesame oil
100g/4oz wonton skins

STEAMED SIU MAI

■ PREPARATION ■

Soak the dried mushrooms in hot water to cover for 25 minutes. Drain and discard the tough stalks. Chop the mushroom caps. Finely chop the bamboo shoots, prawns and spring onion. Lightly beat the eggs. Mix the pork, mushrooms, bamboo shoots, prawns, peas and egg together in a bowl. Add the salt, spring onion, monosodium gluta-mate, if using, white pepper, sugar, vegetable oil, cornflour and sesame oil and combine together thoroughly. Place 1¼ teaspoons of the meat and vegetable mixture in the centre of a wonton skin. Gather the edges up to form a kind of 'flower pot' with an open top.

■ COOKING ■

Place the dumplings into a steamer and steam for 10-11 minutes. Serve very hot.

★★★★★
Cooking time: 10-11 minutes
Serves: 6-7
Cooking method: steam, p.49
Time-consuming to make
Serve with soya-based dip as starter or side dish
Illustrated on p.239

★★★★

Cooking time: about 20 minutes

Serves: 8-10

Cooking method: part fry and part steam, p.49

Requires practice to perfect

Traditionally served with dip of fresh grated root ginger with vinegar

Illustrated on p.239

PEKING KUO-TIEH STEAMED AND SAUTEED DUMPLINGS

Both this and Red Chilli Oil Dumplings (see page 268) are Northern Dim Sum. The ingredients used for Kuo-Tieh Dumplings are the same, the only differences being the dip sauce and the way in which the dumplings are cooked.

■ PREPARATION ■

Sift the flour in a bowl and mix in the boiling water. Leave for 5 minutes. Add the cold water, then knead well.

For the stuffing, finely chop the ginger and spring onions. Mince the pork and shrimps together. Add the ginger, spring onions, salt, soya sauce, sugar and 1 tablespoon water. Mix together well. Finely chop the Chinese cabbage and season lightly with salt, pepper and monosodium glutamate, if using. Add to the pork mixture, combining well.

Form the dough into a long roll and then cut off about thirty 2.5 cm/1 inch pieces. Roll each piece into a flat pancake and then place a teaspoon of the pork stuffing in the centre. Fold the pancake in half to form a half circle and seal the edges. Repeat the process until all the ingredients are used.

■ COOKING ■

Heat 3 tablespoons vegetable oil in a wok or frying pan over medium heat. When hot, tilt the pan so that the surface is evenly coated in oil. Arrange the dumplings evenly over the surface and fry over high heat for 2½ minutes, until the bases of the dumplings are browned. Pour 600 ml/1 pint hot water down the side of the pan. Cover and continue to cook over high heat until almost all the water has evaporated. Add 2 tablespoons hot vegetable oil down side of the pan. Lower the heat and continue to cook, covered, until all the water has evaporated. Remove from the heat. Use a fish slice or spatula to gently loosen the dumplings from the bottom of the pan. Place a large serving dish face-down over the dumplings. Quickly turn the pan and dumplings over on to the dish, so that the browned side of the dumplings is face upwards.

■ SERVING ■

Transfer the dumplings to a heated serving plate and keep warm while you prepare the dip sauce. Mix all the dip sauce ingredients together and pour over the dumplings.

Dough skin:
350g/12oz plain flour
600ml/1pt boiling water
5tbsp cold water

Stuffing:
2 slices fresh root ginger
2 spring onions
225g/8oz lean pork
100-150g/4-5oz shrimps, fresh or frozen, shelled
1tsp salt
1tbsp light soya sauce
1tsp sugar
225g/8oz Chinese white cabbage
pinch of pepper
pinch of MSG (optional)
5tbsp vegetable oil

Dip sauce:
2tbsp shredded fresh root ginger
5tbsp vinegar
2tbsp soya sauce (optional)

REGIONAL CUISINE

Spring Onion Pancakes – chef's version; recipe page 250.

地區性烹飪法

Regional Cuisine

CHINA IS ABOUT the same size as the continental United States, and may be divided into four regions: Peking, Shanghai, Sichuan and Canton. As you will see, each region has its own distinctive ways of cooking, so that dishes from Shanghai are as different from those of Sichuan as Coney Island hot dogs are from the Creole cooking of Louisiana.

▨ PEKING AND THE NORTH ▨

Peking is to China what Paris is to France: the many cultural threads of the country are drawn to the capital. All the various provincial styles of cooking are represented in Peking though the most common dishes have drawn their inspiration locally. These use regional produce and seem to reflect local culinary traditions and the harsh northern climate.

The huge numbers of sheep kept in the region have had a far greater influence on local cooking than dishes from the emperor's palace, so it is not surprising that the Chinese have nicknamed Peking 'Mutton City'. Mutton and lamb and the extensive use of ginger, leeks, garlic and spring onions give northern cooking a stronger, more robust character than in the rest of the country. The meals also seem heavier because steamed wheat buns, noodles and Chinese pancakes are served more often than rice. These substantial fillers are eaten as side dishes, seasoned with sauce, or are served with the many local slowly simmered or braised dishes to mop up the richly flavoured sauces.

There are fewer fresh vegetables in Peking and the surrounding area, especially in the winter months, than in the warmer regions to the south, though huge crops of the familiar Chinese, or Tientsin, cabbage are grown as they keep well through the winter. To make up for the lack of variety, there is a comparatively greater use made of pickled and preserved vegetables.

Northern China was once overrun by Tartar hordes from nearby Mongolia, then ruled for many years by Mongolian emperors such as Genghis and Kublai Kahn. Their influence on northern cooking can be seen in the local preference for less sophisticated foods such as roasted and barbecued meat dipped in strong-tasting sauces and condiments. Even when stir-frying the huge, delicately flavoured prawns caught off the Shantung coast, thick savoury soya paste is favoured over lighter seasonings.

The region's two most famous dishes, Peking Duck and Mongolian Hot Pot, also originated from the Tartars. Though its skin is crispy and the meat is juicy, the duck is simply cooked, then rolled up in a pancake with a piquant sauce and crunchy vegetables. For Mongolian Hot Pot, thinly sliced lamb is cooked at the table in boiling stock sometimes containing noodles and cabbage. The meat is dipped into

THE REGIONS OF CHINA

JILIN

NEI MONGOL (INNER MONGOLIA)

Tonghua
Shenyang
LIAONING

GOBI DESERT

Peking
PO HAI
Luda

Huhhot
Yellow R.
Yantai
Tianjin
Weihai

ORDOS DESERT
HEBEI
YELLOW SEA

GANSU
Shijiazhuang
Qingdao
Dezhou
Jinan

SHANXI
SHANDONG
Grand Canal
JIANGSU

Yinchuan
Taiyuan
Fen
He R.
Weishan
Kaifeng
Yangzhou
EAST CHINA SEA
PACIFIC OCEAN

NINGXIA HUIZU
Fenyang
Gaoyou
Pukow
Zhenjiang

Great Wall
Zhengzhou
Hongze
Suzhou

Xining
Wei R.
Luoyang
Huai R.
Shanghai

Lanzhou
HENAN
Chao
Hefei
Nanjing
Tai
Hangzhou

Fengxiang
Xi'an
ANHUI
Shaoxing

SHAANXI
Qimen
COOKERY SCHOOLS

HUBEI
Yangtse R.
Jinhua
Northern/Peking

BASIN OF SICHUAN
Yangtse Gorges
Wuhan
Jiujiang
Jingdezhen
ZHEIJIANG
Peking

Min R.
Jialing R.
SICHUAN
Dongting
LU SHAN
Poyang
WUYI MOUNTAINS
Shandong

Chengdu
Tuo R.
Nanchang
JIANGXI
FUJIAN
Fuzhou
Eastern/Shanghai

Chonqing
Changsha
Quanzhou
TAIWAN
Shanghai

HUNAN
Longyan
Huaiyang

GUIZHOU
Hengyang
Dong'an
Xiamen
Suzhe

Renhuai
Zhangzhou
Hangzhou

Guiyang
NAN LING
Chao'an
Shantou
Fukien

Xuanwei
Guilin
Bei Jiang
Dong Jiang
Western/ Sichuan

Kunming
Liuzhou
Huizhou
Sichuan

Dian Chi
GUANGXI ZHUANGZU
Xi Jiang
(Pearl R.)
HONG KONG
Southern/Canton

YUNNAN
Nanning
Guangzhou (Canton)
Guangzhou (Canton)

Puer
GUANGDONG
Dong Jiang

Shantou

Haikou
SOUTH CHINA SEA

HAINAN

one of several strong sauces and afterwards the righly flavoured stock is shared as soup to end the hearty one-dish meal.

■ SHANGHAI AND THE EAST ■

Shanghai, the gateway to eastern China, is one of the largest cities in the world and centuries ago was the first seaport opened to traders from the West. This made the area one of the most affluent in China. Situated along with the other main cities of the region on the Yangtze River delta where China's great river flows into the East China Sea, Shanghai also marks the boundary between north and south China.

The lush region is very fertile and the climate is temperate with mild seasons. This seems to be reflected in the nature of eastern cooking, which is full of fresh-water produce and the bounty of abundant rice harvests. The many rivers, streams and ponds provide fish and shellfish in plenty. A wide range of vegetables thrive on the intensively irrigated land as well as millions of ducks which are reared every year. There are also many pig and poultry farms. These foods are tender, their flavours are

245

A colourful and varied
selection of dishes from the
Shanghai region, which
covers a wide range of
cooking techniques from
succulent long-steamed
pork knuckle and steamed
whole fish with garnish
and savoury white sauce to
quick, lightly stir-fried
dishes such as prawns and
tomato wedges with mange tout
sections, and bean curd
with chopped prawns.

delicate, so the seasonings used with them are mild.

This does not mean that the cooking is simple or unsophisticated. Generally speaking, Shanghai and eastern Chinese dishes are slightly sweet and rich both in the amount of fat and in the variety and quality of other ingredients used. They are also known for their elaborate presentation.

As in northern China, steamed wheat buns and plain noodles are widely eaten here. The buns, however, are smaller, with delicate stuffings such as crab eggs, young bamboo shoots or minced pork with aspic. The region's enormous rice crop is not wasted, for much of it is used in vinegar and in wine. China's finest rice vinegar is a dark aromatic one called Chinkiang after the town in which the vinegar is made. It, as well as rice wine, is produced in great quantity. Known as 'yellow wine' because of its pale golden colour, the most famous one in China, Shaoshing, comes from a town of that name just south of the Yangtze River. Rice wine is naturally used in many local dishes such as those red-braised, a cooking method whereby fish, meat or poultry cooks slowly in a mixture of rice wine and dark soya sauce until the mixture reduces and can be served spooned over rice and noodles.

One of the most common sights along the Yangtze River is the transplanting of rice from the nursery to the paddy field, which is always done by hand. By comparison, running a market stall seems positively tranquil, especially between sales.

■ SICHUAN AND THE WEST ■

Known as the rice bowl of China, Sichuan and the other fertile provinces of the western part of the country are over a thousand miles from the sea and surrounded by high mountains and deep river valleys. This is the home of well over one hundred million people who, due to their geographical location and reasonably prosperous peasant background, have produced dishes with a remarkably sophisticated range of flavours. Fresh foods such as pork, river fish and vegetables are combined with smoked, pickled and dried ingredients, while in the same dish sour, sweet and salty flavours are carefully balanced with chillies.

The chilli-hot aspect of Sichuan, Hunan and other western Chinese food is the one that is best known to people outside China. Fresh and dried chillies are used by the people of western China both for health and a good table. Much of the year the weather is extremely humid and the people believe that perspiring wards off illness. They also believe that instead of burning the taste buds, chilli stimulates them to be more sensitive to a full range of flavours and after-tastes.

The winter in this part of China is mild, so cultivation is possible all year long. Besides rice, wheat, corn, citrus fruit and Sichuan peppercorns are major crops. Mushrooms, cloud ears and other fungi, both wild and cultivated, as well as bamboo grow in great profusion on the largely agricultural, well irrigated land.

As the western provinces were so isolated from the busy sea and river trade carried on gave a strong flavour to ingredients used in many of their dishes. Perhaps for this became essential. The smoking, pickling, spicing and drying that of necessity went on gave a strong flavor to ingredients used in many of their dishes. Perhaps for this reason the western Chinese palate became appreciative of the more pungently flavoured vegetables such as onions, garlic, fresh ginger, spring onions, chillies and peppers as well as nutty aromatic ones such as sesame oil, sesame seeds and sesame butter and peanuts. When used in conjunction with salty soya bean products such as soya sauce, soya paste, bean curd cheese and black beans, these ingredients produce the piquant spiciness characteristic of many western Chinese dishes. The Chinese outside this region have understandably adopted the best of them so that now, even in the West, people can enjoy the pleasure of western Chinese cooking.

■ CANTON AND THE SOUTH ■

As far as food is concerned, the Cantonese are easily the most indulgent people in China. They and the other southern Chinese live in a semi-tropical region where the soil is so fertile that two rice crops a year are grown and people can also engage in small-scale fruit and fish farming. A great variety of green leafy vegetables are grown and meat is readily available from a large selection of reared animals, including pigs, cattle and poultry.

Fresh seafood is an enormously important element in their cooking as the south has the longest coastline of any region in China. All along the coast vast quantities of fish and shellfish are brought in including prawns, scallops, crabs, eels, and crayfish as well as more exotic delicacies such as abalone, sea cucumber, shark – and shark's fin. Probably it is such variety that has inspired southern Chinese cooks to incorporate seafood flavours through oyster sauce, shrimp sauce and shrimp paste into meat and even vegetable dishes. This juxtaposition of flavours creates highly savoury dishes and clever cooks are not beyond introducing meats such as a shredded chicken into basically seafood dishes.

That being said, southern Chinese dishes generally are not highly seasoned. Endlessly creative, the cooks aim at cooking very fresh foods together to bring out the best in each of them, adding only a few condiments to enhance the mixture. The Cantonese are especially partial to stir-frying.

Egg rather than plain noodles are used in many dishes, but rice is eaten at every meal including the variously-flavoured soft rice gruel, congee, usually served for breakfast. Served with plain boiled rice are an enormous number of meat and vegetable dishes, usually three or four at both lunch and dinner. Even so, the greedy southern Chinese make time and room for tea and savoury snacks called dim sum. These are pastry tidbits stuffed with meat, seafood and vegetable mixtures, then sautéed, deep-fried or steamed.

3 large spring onions

350g/12oz plain flour

300ml/½pt boiling water

65g/2½ lard

5 tbsp cold water

1¼ tbsp large grain sea salt

SPRING ONION PANCAKES

These pancakes, often included as a Northern dim sum item, are more aromatic and tasty than one would imagine. They are normally eaten on their own, or they can be eaten to supplement other savoury dishes. The strong presence of onion and the occasional sharpness of the sea salt grains in the crispy dough give them an unexpected simple appeal.

■ PREPARATION ■

Coarsely chop the spring onions. Sift the flour into a large bowl. Slowly add the boiling water and 15g/½oz of the lard. Stir with a fork or a pair of chopsticks for 3 minutes. Mix in the cold water and knead for 2 minutes. Leave the dough to stand for 30 minutes. Form and roll the dough into a long roll and cut into 10 equal sections. Roll each piece into a ball and press the ball into a flat pancake. Sprinkle the pancake evenly with salt and chopped spring onion. Fold it up from the sides to form a ball again, then press again into a pancake.

■ COOKING AND SERVING ■

Heat the remaining lard in a wok or frying pan. When hot, spread the pancakes evenly over the pan and fry over low heat for 2½ minutes on either side, until golden brown.

★★★★

Cooking time: 5 minutes each

Serves: 5-6 (makes 10)

Cooking method: shallow-fry

Needs practice to perfect

A good starter

Illustrated on p.243

100g/4oz lean pork

4 medium dried Chinese mushrooms

50g/2oz wood ears

3 stalks golden needles (tiger lily buds)

3 spring onions

4 eggs

5 tbsp vegetable oil

2½ tbsp light soya sauce

½ tsp sugar

2½ tbsp good stock (see page 56)

1 tbsp dry sherry

1 tsp sesame oil

EGG FLOWER PORK – MU SHU ROU

This dish is often used as a pancake filling, and served like Peking Duck (see page 178).

■ PREPARATION ■

Cut the pork into matchstick-size shreds. Soak the dried mushrooms and wood ears in hot water to cover for 25 minutes. Drain, discard the tough stalks, then cut the mushroom caps into similar size shreds as the pork. Cut the golden needles and spring onions into 2.5cm/1 inch section. Beat the eggs lightly with a fork.

■ COOKING ■

In the cooking of this dish, it is best to use 2 woks or frying pans – one small and one large. Heat 2 tablespoons of the oil in the larger pan. When hot, stir-fry the mushrooms and pork for 1½ minutes. Add the wood ears, spring onions and golden needles. Stir together for 1 minute, then add the soya sauce, sugar and stock. Toss together for another minute, remove from the heat. Heat the remaining vegetable oil in the smaller pan and pour in the beaten eggs. Heat steadily over low heat until set and then stir to break up the eggs into 1cm/½ inch pieces. Transfer the eggs to the larger pan and reheat. Sprinkle on the sherry and sesame oil. Stir and turn over high heat for a few seconds and serve.

★★★

Cooking time: about 6-8 minutes

Serves: 4-6

Cooking method: stir-fry, p.42

Quick to cook

Illustrated opposite

北京和北方

575g/1¼lb white fish fillets,
  eg sole, plaice, carp,
  halibut etc

1½tsp salt

2tbsp cornflour

1 egg white

vegetable oil for deep-frying

Sauce:

3 slices fresh root ginger

2 spring onions

25g/1oz lard

2tbsp light soya sauce

1½tbsp wine vinegar

1tsp sugar

3tbsp good stock (see page 56)

2tbsp rice wine or dry sherry

½ chicken stock cube

½tbsp cornflour blended with
  1½tbsp water

PEKING
SLICED FISH IN
'STANDARD SAUCE'

■ PREPARATION ■

Cut the fish into 5 × 2.5 cm/2 × 1 inch slices. Rub with the salt. Dust with the cornflour. Coat with the egg white. Shred the ginger. Cut the spring onions into 1 cm/½ inch shreds.

■ COOKING ■

Heat the oil in a wok or deep-fryer until very hot. Remove from the heat and leave to cool for 30 seconds. Add the fish slices, one by one, to the oil and fry for 1 minute. Return the pan to the heat and fry for 1 minute. Remove the fish and drain. Heat the lard in a wok or frying pan. When hot, stir-fry the ginger and spring onion for a few seconds. Add the soya sauce, vinegar, sugar, stock, wine or sherry and crumbled stock cube; mix well. Finally, stir in the blended cornflour and bring to the boil. Add the fish to the sauce and spread the slices out. Baste a few times with the sauce.

■ SERVING ■

Transfer the fish to a heated dish. Pour the sauce over.

★★★

Cooking time:
about 10 minutes

Serves: 5-6

Cooking methods:
deep-fry p.45 and
stir-fry p.42

Quite easy to
prepare

Goes well with
most other
Chinese dishes

---

5 medium cooking apples

2tbsp sesame seeds

Batter:

100g/4oz plain flour

120ml/4floz cold water

1 egg

vegetable oil for deep frying

Sugar coating:

225g/8oz sugar

2tbsp vegetable oil

PEKING
'TOFFEE APPLE'S

This is an infinitely more refined version of the Toffee Apple than those often encountered at fairgrounds.

■ PREPARATION ■

Mix the flour with the water and beaten egg. Beat to a smooth batter. Peel and core the apples. Cut each apple into 5-6 equal pieces. For the sugar coating, heat the sugar and oil in a small saucepan. Stir continuously until the sugar has melted and blended with the oil. Keep hot. Dip the apple pieces in the batter, then sprinkle with sesame seeds.

■ COOKING ■

Heat the oil in a wok or deep-fryer. Fry the battered apple pieces in batches for 2½ minutes. Drain. When all the apple pieces have been fried and drained, add 2-3 pieces at a time to the hot sugar coating. Pull them out one at a time with a pair of wooden chopsticks, then dip quickly into a bowl of ice-cold water. Retrieve immediately and set aside. (This makes the sugar coating brittle, and prevents the batter from becoming soggy.) Repeat with all the apple pieces.

★★★★★

Cooking time:
2½ minutes per
batch

Serves: 6-8

Cooking method:
deep-fry, p.45

Needs practice to
perfect

One of the few
Chinese desserts
easily acceptable to
Western palates

Illustrated on
p.254

SERVING

Either divide the toffee apples into individual dishes, as in the West, or pile them on to a large serving dish for the diners to help themselves.

★ ★ ★

Cooking time: about 20 minutes

Serves: 5-6

Cooking method: stir-fry, p.42

Interesting and fairly easy to prepare

Good as part of a multi-dish meal

RIVAL OF CRAB

OR SAI PAN HSIA

This recipe is said to have been a favourite of the Empress Dowager. For, when she wanted crab in the winter, and it was unavailable in the North at this time of year due to the severity of the weather, she was presented with this dish instead.

PREPARATION

Cut the fish into cubes. Sprinkle and rub with the salt. Beat the eggs with a fork in a bowl for 10 seconds. Beat 1 egg yolk with 1 tablespoon water for 6–7 seconds. Beat the remaining egg yolk with the tomato purée for 6–7 seconds in a separate bowl. Finely chop the ginger. Cut the spring onions into 0.5 cm/¼ inch shreds. Mix the sauce ingredients together until smooth.

COOKING

Heat the lard and the oil in a wok or frying pan. When hot, stir-fry the ginger and spring onion over medium heat for 15 seconds. Add the fish cubes, turn and gently stir them quickly for 30 seconds. Stir in the beaten eggs and mix with the fish. When the eggs are about to set, pour or drop in the yolk and water mixture, then sprinkle over the yolk and tomato purée mixture. Scramble lightly and turn the contents over. Add the sauce mixture and continue to turn and scramble gently and lightly for 1½ minutes. Transfer the mixture to a heated dish.

225g/8oz white fish

1½tsp salt

4 eggs

2 egg yolks

1 tbsp water

1¼tbsp tomato purée

2 slices fresh root ginger

1 spring onion

25g/1oz lard

1½tbsp vegetable oil

Sauce:

1 tbsp cornflour

4 tbsp good stock (see page 56)

1 tbsp shrimp sauce

½tbsp oyster sauce

1 tsp salt

2 tbsp dry sherry or white wine

Peking 'Toffee Apples' (*left*), apple pieces coated in a brittle sugar coating; recipe page 252.
Quick Fry of Three Sea Flavours (*above right*), prawns, scallop and squid are the three flavours; recipe page 260.
Multi-coloured Prawn Balls (*below right*), coated in crumbled noodles, shredded cabbage and carrot, serve this attractive party dish on a bed of cucumber slices; recipe page 256.

2 slices fresh root ginger
225g/8oz peeled prawns
50g/2oz pork fat
2 egg whites
1/2 tsp salt
pepper to taste
2 tbsp cornflour
1 tsp dry sherry or white wine
1/2 tsp sesame oil
2 leaves green cabbage
1 carrot
2 radishes (optional)
50g/2oz rice flour noodles
vegetable oil for deep-frying

▉MULTI-COLOURED PRAWN BALLS

▉ PREPARATION ▉

Finely chop the ginger. Finely chop the prawns with the pork fat. Place the mixture in a bowl. Add the egg white, salt, pepper, cornflour, ginger, sherry and sesame oil. Mix thoroughly. Shred the cabbage finely. Finely chop the carrot. Peel the radishes, if using, and chop the red skin.

Heat the oil in a wok or deep-fryer. When hot, add the rice flour noodles – they will puff up immediately. Remove and drain. Crumble the noodles and mix with the cabbage, carrot and radish. Spread the mixture over a large dish or tray.

Form the pork fat and prawn paste into small balls, using about 2-3 teaspoons of the mixture at a time. Roll them over the finely chopped vegetable and noodle mixture to take on a multi-coloured coating.

▉ COOKING ▉

Reheat the oil in the wok or deep-fryer. When hot, gently fry the prawn balls in batches for 2½-3 minutes until cooked through and crispy. Drain.

★★★★

Cooking time: 2½-3 minutes per batch

Serves: 5–6

Cooking method: deep-fry, p.45

Good as a light attractive starter

Illustrated on p.255

225g/8oz spring greens or cabbage
2 tsp salt
4½-5½ tbsp vegetable oil
2 eggs
2 spring onions
450g/1lb cooked rice (see page 68)
2 tbsp chopped ham
1/4 tsp MSG (optional)

▉SHANGHAI EMERALD FRIED RICE

▉ PREPARATION ▉

Wash and finely shred the cabbage. Sprinkle with 1½ teaspoons of the salt. Toss and leave to season for 10 minutes. Squeeze dry. Heat 1½ tablespoons of the oil in a wok or pan. When hot, stir-fry the cabbage for 30 seconds. Remove from the pan. Add 1 tablespoon oil to the wok or pan. When hot, add the beaten eggs to form a thin pancake. As soon as the egg sets, remove from the pan and chop. Chop the spring onions.

▉ COOKING ▉

Heat 2-3 tablespoons oil in a wok or saucepan. When hot, stir-fry the spring onion for a few seconds. Add the rice and stir with the spring onion. Reduce the heat to low, stir and turn until the rice is heated through. Add the cabbage, egg and ham. Stir and mix them together well. Sprinkle with monosodium glutamate, if using, and remaining salt. Stir and turn once more, then sprinkle with remaining egg.

★★★

Cooking time: about 8 minutes

Serves: 4-6

Cooking method: stir-fry, p.42

Quite easy to prepare

Serve with other savoury dishes for an informal meal

Illustrated on p.258

★★★

Cooking time:
about 5-6 minutes

Serves: 5-6

Cooking methods:
deep-fry p.45 and
stir-fry p.42

Quick to cook

Serve with any
combination of
dishes

Illustrated on
p.259

STIR-FRIED CHICKEN WITH BABY CORN
ON CRISPY NOODLES

PREPARATION

Cut the chicken into 0.5 cm/¼ inch cubes. Rub with the salt. Dust with cornflour. Coat with the egg white. Chop each baby corn into halves or quarters. Dice the bamboo shoots. Mix all the sauce ingredients together in a bowl.

COOKING

Heat the oil in a wok or deep-fryer. When hot, add the rice noodles; they will puff up immediately. Remove and drain. Place and press level on a large heated serving dish. Pour away the oil to use for other purposes, leaving 4 tablespoons. Reheat the wok or pan. When hot, stir-fry the chicken for 30 seconds. Add the ham, bamboo shoots, corn, peas and mushrooms, stir-fry over medium heat for 1 minute. Pour in the sauce, stir and turn together for about 30 seconds, until boiling and thickened.

SERVING

Pour the chicken and corn mixture over the crispy noodles.

225 g/8 oz chicken breast meat

½ tsp salt

1 tbsp cornflour

½ egg white

6 baby corns

100 g/4 oz drained, canned bamboo shoots

vegetable oil for deep-frying

50 g/2 oz rice flour noodles

100 g/4 oz diced ham (optional)

3 tbsp peas

100 g/4 oz button mushrooms

Sauce:

1 tsp salt

pepper to taste

½ tbsp light soya sauce

4 tbsp good stock (see page 56)

½ tsp sugar

2 tbsp dry sherry or white wine

1 tbsp cornflour blended with 3 tbsp water

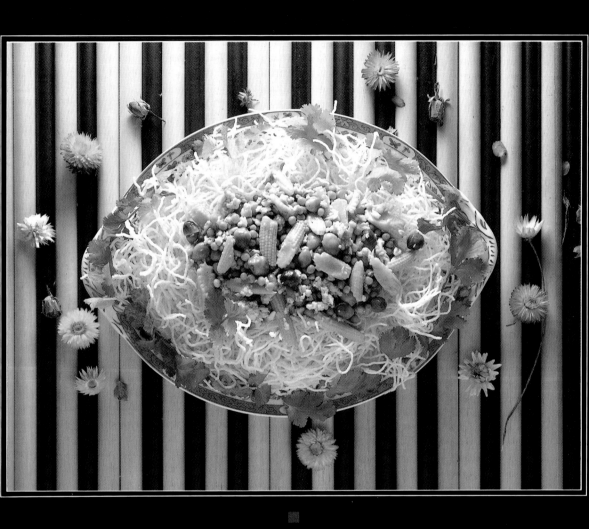

Crab Meat with Cream of
Chinese Cabbage (*above
left*), a light dish to serve as
part of a multi-dish meal;
recipe page 96.
Shanghai Emerald Fried
Rice (*below left*), a simple
yet useful rice dish
garnished with chopped
egg; recipe page 256.
Stir-fried Chicken with
Baby Corn on Crispy
Noodles (*above*), a colourful
main course dish; recipe
page 257.

100g/4oz large peeled
  prawns
6 medium scallops
75-100g/3-4oz squid
1½tsp salt
pepper to taste
6tbsp vegetable oil
2 slices fresh root ginger
1 medium fresh green chilli
2 spring onions
2 cloves garlic
1 carrot
1 stalk celery
2tbsp good stock (see page 56)
1tbsp light soya sauce
2tbsp Chinese wine-lee paste
1tsp sesame oil

QUICK FRY OF THREE SEA FLAVOURS

If wine-lee paste is unavailable, substitute 1½ tablespoons dry sherry and ½ tablespoon brandy mixed with 1 teaspoon cornflour.

PREPARATION

Cut each prawn into 3 sections and the scallops in half. Clean the squid under running cold water and score with criss-cross cuts 1 cm/½ inch apart, then cut into similar size pieces as the prawn sections. Sprinkle on the salt, pepper and 1½ teaspoons of the vegetable oil. Finely shred the ginger and chilli, discarding the seeds. Cut the spring onions into 1 cm/½ inch shreds. Finely chop the garlic. Thinly slice the carrot and celery.

COOKING

Heat 4 tablespoons of the oil in a wok or frying pan. When hot, stir-fry the prawns, scallops and squid over high heat for 1½ minutes. Remove with a perforated spoon. Pour in the remaining oil, reheat and add the ginger, garlic, spring onions, carrot, celery and chilli. Stir-fry quickly over high heat for 30 seconds, then pour in the stock, soya sauce and wine-lee paste. When boiling, return the 'three sea flavours' and stir together for about 1 minute. Sprinkle over the sesame oil.

★★★
Cooking time:
5-6 minutes

Serves: 4-6

Cooking method:
stir-fry, p.42

Scoring squid,
p.41

Quick to cook

Illustrated on
p.255

上
海
和
東
方

CHINESE MUSHROOM SOUP WITH SPARE RIBS

★★

Cooking time:
1 hour 20 minutes

Serves: 5-6

Cooking method:
simmer

Easy to prepare
but requires time
to cook

Serve the soup at
the beginning or in
the middle of a
Chinese meal

The spare ribs can
be eaten as a
supplementary
main course

1.25 kg/2½ lb pork spare ribs

12 large or medium dried
  Chinese mushrooms

2 slices fresh root ginger

1 tsp salt

pepper to taste

1 tbsp light soya sauce

600 ml/1 pt good stock (see
  page 56)

1½ chicken stock cubes

PREPARATION

Cut the spare ribs into individual ribs, then chop into 5 cm/2 inch lengths. Parboil them for 3 minutes in a saucepan of boiling water. Drain. Soak the dried mushrooms in hot water to cover for 25 minutes. Drain and discard the tough stalks. Cut half the mushroom caps in half. Shred the ginger.

COOKING

Place the spare ribs and ginger in a heavy saucepan or casserole. Add 900 ml/1½ pints water. Bring to the boil and simmer for 5 minutes, skimming away any scum. Reduce the heat, then add the salt, pepper and soya sauce and simmer gently for 45 minutes. Stir in the mushrooms, stock and the crumbled stock cubes. Continue to cook gently for 30 minutes.

SERVING

Serve the soup in a tureen. It is customary in China for the diners to ladle out the soup to drink from their own rice bowls, then to pick out the spare ribs and eat, first dipping into a dip sauce (soya sauce mixed with a little chilli and sesame oil).

Pork Balls
Chrysanthemum Style
(*above*), coated in strips of
egg omelette; recipe
page 269.
Red-cooked Oxtail (*left*),
for special occasions cut
the carrots attractively;
recipe page 268.
Bang Bang Chicken
(*right*), an easy to make
starter or main dish; recipe
page 265.

300 ml/½ pt vegetable oil

50/2 oz rice flour noodles

Milk mixture:

6 egg whites

300 ml/½ pt milk

4 tbsp unsweetened evaporated milk

1¼ tbsp cornflour

½ tsp salt

pepper to taste

75 g/3 oz crabmeat

Garnish:

1½ tbsp chopped ham

1½ tbsp chopped coriander leaves

FRIED 'MILK' WITH CRAB MEAT ON CRISPY NOODLES

■ PREPARATION ■

Beat the egg whites with a fork in a bowl for 20 seconds. Add the milk, evaporated milk, cornflour, salt and pepper. Beat together until smooth.

■ COOKING ■

Heat the oil in a wok or frying pan. When hot, continue heating for 10 seconds over medium heat. Drop the rice flour noodles into the hot oil. The noodles will crisp and froth up into a great mass. Remove the noodles immediately on to absorbent kitchen paper to drain. Pour away the oil to use for other purposes, except 2 tablespoons. Reheat the wok or pan. When hot, stir-fry the crab meat for 30 seconds, breaking it up into smaller pieces and shreds. Pour in the milk and egg white mixture. Turn and stir slowly, scraping up continuously from the bottom, until the mixture thickens and sets.

■ SERVING ■

Spread the crispy noodles on the base of a heated serving dish. Pour the crab mixture over the noodles. Sprinkle with the chopped ham and coriander.

★★★

Cooking time: about 10 minutes

Serves: 5-6

Cooking methods: deep-fry p.45 and stir-fry p.42

Combines well in a multi-course meal

675 g/1½ lb belly of pork

1 medium onion

2 red or green peppers

2 dried chillies

2 spring onions

4 tbsp vegetable oil

Sauce:

2½ tbsp dark soya sauce

1½ tbsp light soya sauce

1½ tbsp hoisin sauce

2 tbsp good stock (see page 56)

1½ tbsp tomato purée

1½ tbsp chilli sauce

1½ tbsp sugar

SICHUAN DOUBLE COOKED PORK

■ PREPARATION ■

Place the pork in a large saucepan of water. Bring to the boil and simmer for 30 minutes. Leave the pork to cool in the water for another 30 minutes. Remove, drain and slice the pork very thinly. Peel and thinly slice the onion. Cut the peppers into small pieces. Seed and shred the chillies. Cut the spring onions into 5 cm/2 inch sections.

■ COOKING ■

Heat the oil in a wok or frying pan. When hot, stir-fry the onion for about 1 minute. Add the pork and stir-fry for 2 minutes. Stir in the sauce ingredients. Bring to the boil, add the peppers and chillies and stir for another 2 minutes.

★★★

Cooking time: 35 minutes, plus cooling time

Serves: 4-6

Cooking methods: simmer and stir-fry, p.42

A spicy dish that goes well with rice and vegetable dishes

Illustrated on p.188

BANG BANG CHICKEN

★ ★ ★ ★

Cooking time:
35 minutes, plus
cooling time

Serves: 8-10 (as a
starter)

Cooking method:
simmer

Quite easy to
make

An excellent cold
starter

Illustrated on
p.263

1 medium cucumber

1.5 g/3 lb chicken

3 slices fresh root ginger

3 tsp salt

Sauce:

5 tbsp peanut butter

2½ tbsp sesame oil

2 tsp sugar

1 tsp salt

4 tbsp good stock (see page 56)

1½ tbsp red chilli oil

▨ PREPARATION ▨

Scrape the cucumber and cut into large matchstick-size shreds.
Mix all the sauce ingredients together in a bowl, except the red
chilli oil, until well blended.

▨ COOKING ▨

Place the chicken in a saucepan of water with the ginger and
salt. Bring to the boil, cover and simmer for 35 minutes. Allow
the chicken to cool in the water for 45 minutes. Remove the
chicken and drain well. Place on a chopping board and chop off
the wings and legs, leaving the body. Chop the body into 2
pieces. Give each piece of chicken several *bangs* with the back or
side of the chopper to loosen the meat. Remove the meat from
the bones or carcass and cut into large matchstick-size shreds.

▨ SERVING ▨

Arrange the shredded cucumber on the base of a large serving
dish. Pile the shredded chicken on top. Pour the sauce over the
chicken and sprinkle with the red chilli oil. Alternatively, serve
on a bed of shredded lettuce and spring onion.

TRIPE, SQUID AND PEA SOUP

★ ★ ★

Cooking time:
about 2½ hours,
including cooking
tripe

Serves: 4-6

Cooking method:
simmer

Takes time to
prepare

A soup of
character served in
the Chinese or
Western style

225 g/8 oz dried squid

3 tsp salt

3 slices fresh root ginger

350-450 g/12 oz-1 lb tripe
(pork or beef)

350 g/12 oz green peas

900 ml/1½ pt good stock (see
page 56)

1 chicken stock cube

1½ tbsp cornflour blended
with 4 tbsp water

salt and pepper to taste

1 tsp sesame oil

*The presence of shredded tripe and dried squid in this green-coloured
soup gives it an unmistakable Chinese flavour.*

▨ PREPARATION ▨

Soak the dried squid in warm water to cover for 3 hours. Place
the salt and ginger in a saucepan with 1.2 litres/2 pints water.
Bring to the boil and add the tripe. Simmer for 1½ hours.
Drain the tripe and squid, then cut into matchstick-size shreds.
Purée the peas in a liquidizer.

▨ COOKING ▨

Place the squid in a saucepan with 300 ml/½ pint boiling water.
Simmer until the liquid in the pan has been reduced by half,
about 15 minutes. Add the tripe and stock and simmer gently
for 30 minutes. Add the pea purée and crumbled stock cube.
Heat and stir gently for 10 minutes. Add the blended cornflour
and salt and pepper to taste. Stir in the sesame oil. Contue to
cook for 2 minutes, stirring.

■

Red Chilli Oil Dumplings
(*left*), a good starter or
snack served with a hot
spicy dip sauce; recipe page
268.
Bao Tzu Steamed Buns
(*centre*), a savoury or sweet
filled steamed dim sum;
recipe page 236.
Mini Spring Rolls (*right*),
these delicious savouries can
be made in all sizes; recipe
page 232.

Hainan Chicken Rice
(*above*), a useful family
dish; recipe page 272.

Dough skin:
350g/12oz plain flour
600ml/1pt boiling water
5tbsp cold water

Stuffing:
2 slices fresh root ginger
2 spring onions
225g/8oz lean pork
100-150g/4-5oz shrimps
1tsp salt
1tbsp light soya sauce
1tsp sugar
225g/8oz Chinese white
  cabbage
pinch of pepper
pinch of MSG (optional)

Dip sauce:
2tbsp red chilli oil
1tbsp soya sauce
1tbsp finely chopped garlic
1tbsp finely chopped spring
  onion

RED CHILLI OIL DUMPLINGS

These dumplings make a good starter to a multi-course meal or they can be eaten on their own as a snack. The hot spicy dip sauce adds considerable zest to the dish. (To prepare the dumplings, see p.227-228, steps 1-10.)

PREPARATION

Sift the flour in a bowl and mix in the boiling water. Leave for 5 minutes. Add the cold water, then knead well.

For the stuffing, finely chop the ginger and spring onions. Mince the pork and shrimps together. Add the ginger, spring onions, salt, soya sauce, sugar and 1 tablespoon water. Mix together well. Finely chop the Chinese cabbage and season lightly with salt, pepper and monosodium glutamate, if using. Add to the pork mixture, combining well.

Form the dough into a long roll and then cut off about thirty 2.5cm/1 inch pieces. Roll each piece into a flat pancake and then place a teaspoon of the pork stuffing in the centre. Fold the pancake in half to form a half circle and seal the edges. Repeat the process until all the ingredients are used up.

COOKING

Bring a large saucepan of water to the boil and add the dumplings, 6 at a time. Simmer over medium heat for 5 minutes, then drain.

SERVING

Transfer the dumplings to a heated serving plate and keep warm while you prepare the dip sauce. Mix all the dip sauce ingredients together and pour over the dumplings.

★★★★
Cooking time: about 25 minutes

Serves: 8-10 (makes 30)

Cooking method: poach

Dumplings take time to make

A good starter dish

Illustrated on p.266

---

2 garlic cloves
2.25-2.75kg/5-6lb oxtail
  (ask butcher to cut into
  sections)
2-3 young carrots
3 slices fresh root ginger
1tsp salt
6tbsp soya sauce
1½tbsp hoisin sauce
4tbsp dry sherry
150ml/¼pt good stock (see
  page 56)
2tsp sugar
2tbsp peas (optional)

RED-COOKED OXTAIL

PREPARATION

Crush the garlic. Clean the oxtail. Cut the carrots slantwise into 0.5cm/¼ inch slices. Blanch the oxtail for 3-4 minutes in a pan of boiling water. Drain and place in a heavy saucepan or flameproof casserole with the garlic, ginger, salt, soya sauce, hoisin sauce and carrots. Add 900ml/1½ pints water.

COOKING

Bring the contents of the pan to the boil, cover and simmer very gently for 1½ hours. Turn the contents every 30 minutes. Add the sherry, stock and sugar and continue to simmer gently for further 1 hour, turning the contents after 30 minutes. Add

★★
Cooking time: about 2½ hours

Serves: 4-6

Cooking method: simmer

Easy to prepare, lengthy cooking

Illustrated on p.262

四
川
和
西
方

the peas 10 minutes before the end of the cooking time. (If cooked in the oven, cook at 150°C, 300°F, Gas Mark 2 for 3 hours.)

Illustrated on p.262

★★★★

Cooking time: about 8 minutes

Serves: 5-6

Cooking method: deep-fry, p.45

Take time to prepare

Serve with a party meal

Illustrated on p.262

PORK BALLS CHRYSANTHEMUM STYLE

4 medium dried Chinese mushrooms
2 slices fresh root ginger
75g/3oz shrimps
1 spring onion
225g/8oz minced pork
4 tbsp cornflour
1½ tsp salt
pepper to taste
½ tsp MSG (optional)
1 egg white
4 eggs
vegetable oil for deep-frying

■ PREPARATION ■

Soak the dried Chinese mushrooms in hot water to cover for 25 minutes. Drain and discard the tough stalks. Finely chop the mushroom caps. Finely chop the ginger, shrimps and spring onion. Place the minced pork in a bowl and add the ginger, shrimps, mushroom, spring onion, cornflour, salt, pepper, monosodium glutamate, if using, and egg white. Mix together until smooth and then make into small meat balls. Beat the eggs. Heat 3 tablespoons oil in a flat-bottomed pan. When hot, pour in a quarter of the beaten egg and make a thin omelette. Repeat this process 3 more times with the rest of the egg. Cut the 4 egg omelettes into fine strips. Spread out the egg strips and then roll the meat balls in them. Press the egg strips on to the balls firmly.

■ COOKING ■

Heat the oil in a wok or deep fryer. When hot, gently fry the meatballs, in 2 batches if necessary, for about 4 minutes or until brown and crisp. Drain.

■ SERVING ■

Serve the pork balls on a bed of shredded lettuce surrounded by orange slices; for a party, surround with chrysanthemum flowers.

地
區
性
烹
飪
法

Ho–Fen Noodles with
Beef in Black Bean Sauce
(*above*), a substantial dish
with a rich flavoured sauce;
recipe page 273.
Cha Siu Roast Pork (*above
right*), marinated, roasted
pork with carrot flower
garnish; recipe page 274.
Crab Meat Soup (*below
right*), a light soup with
crab meat, bean curd and
spinach or lettuce; recipe
page 275.

1.5 kg/3¼-3¾ lb chicken

2 tsp salt

pepper to taste

450 g/1 lb long grain rice

2 medium onions

350 g/12 oz broccoli or spring
greens

100 g/4 oz green peas
(optional)

2 chicken stock cubes

1½ tsp sesame oil

Sauce:

3 spring onions

4 cloves garlic

4 tbsp good soya sauce

1 tbsp red chilli oil

HAINAN
CHICKEN RICE

★ ★ ★ ★

*Cooking time:
about 1¼ hours*

Serves: 4-6

*Cooking method:
simmer*

*Useful family dish
to be eaten
unaccompanied*

*Illustrated on
p.267*

This is a useful family dish which can be eaten on its own by a family or party of 4-6 people without the need of being supplemented, as is usual in China, by at least 2-3 other dishes.

■ PREPARATION ■

Chop the chicken through the bones into 30 large bite size pieces. Rub with salt and pepper. Wash and measure the rice. Place in a saucepan and add an equal amount of water. Bring to the boil, cover, reduce the heat and simmer for 5-6 minutes. Remove from the heat and leave the rice to cook and absorb all the water, covered, for 10 minutes. Thinly slice the onions. Chop the broccoli into 5 cm/2 inch pieces . Finely chop the spring onions and garlic.

■ COOKING ■

Place the chicken pieces in a large saucepan of boiling water and blanch for 3 minutes. Drain and place them in a large heavy saucepan or flameproof casserole. Pour in 1.75 litres/3 pints of water and add the onions. Bring to the boil, reduce the heat and simmer gently for 45 minutes. Add the broccoli or spring greens, peas, if using, and crumbled stock cubes to the pan and simmer for 5 minutes. Remove the chicken pieces and vegetables and put aside. Pour three-fifths of the stock into a separate saucepan (to use as a soup for the diners). Add the partially cooked rice to the remaining chicken stock in the heavy pan or casserole. Place over low to medium heat and cook gently for 10-15 minutes until the rice has absorbed all the stock. Just before the end of cooking time, arrange the chicken pieces and vegetables on top.

■ SERVING ■

Heat the stock in the saucepan. Adjust the seasonings, and sprinkle with half the chopped spring onion and the sesame oil. Mix the ingredients for the sauce together and pour it over the chicken in the casserole. Divide and serve in as many small bowls as there are diners.

HO-FEN NOODLES WITH BEEF IN BLACK BEAN SAUCE

★ ★ ★

Cooking time: about 12 minutes

Serves: 5-6

Cooking methods: simmer, and stir-fry, p.42

Quite easy to prepare

Excellent as part of a multi-dish meal for hearty appetites

Illustrated on p.270

Ingredients
350g/12oz Ho-Fen rice flour noodles
2 medium onions
2 slices fresh root ginger
450g/1lb lean beef, such as rump or topside
1½tbsp cornflour
1 egg white
1 medium to large red pepper
2 cloves garlic
3 spring onions
4tbsp vegetable oil

Sauce:

65g/2½oz lard
1½tbsp salted black beans
2tbsp soya sauce
1½tbsp oyster sauce
1½tbsp chilli sauce
4tbsp good stock (see page 56)
1½tbsp cornflour blended with 3tbsp water

Ho-Fen noodles are flat ribbon rice flour noodles. If unavailable use any rice flour noodles.

PREPARATION

Place the noodles in a saucepan of boiling water and simmer for 5-6 minutes. Drain and rinse under running cold water to keep separate. Thinly slice the onions. Cut the ginger into thin shreds. Soak the black beans in water to cover for 5 minutes. Drain and coarsely chop. Cut the beef into thin 4 × 1 cm/ 1½ × ½ inch strips. Dust and rub with the cornflour. Coat with the egg white. Slice the red pepper. Crush the garlic. Cut the spring onions into 5 cm/2 inch sections.

COOKING

Heat the oil in a wok or large frying pan. When hot, stir-fry the onion, ginger and garlic over medium heat for 3-4 minutes until the onions are soft. Push them to the sides of the pan. Add the beef to the centre of the pan and stir-fry for 1 minute. Push to the side of the pan. Add 40 g/1½ oz of the lard to the centre of the wok or pan. When melted, add the black beans and stir and mash them into the fat. Add the soya sauce, oyster sauce, chilli sauce and stock. Stir together until the sauce boils. Add the blended cornflour and stir to thicken, mixing the sauce well. Bring the onion and beef into the centre of the pan and mix with the sauce. Remove half the beef mixture from the wok or pan and put aside. Add the noodles to the wok, then turn and mix with the beef mixture.

SERVING

Transfer the well coated noodles to a heated serving dish. Heat the remaining lard in the wok or pan. When hot, stir-fry the red pepper and spring onion over high heat for 30 seconds. Return the reserved beef mixture, stir and mix well, for 30 seconds. Spoon over the noodles. Alternatively, serve the beef mixture on the plain noodles.

1 kg/2 lb fillet of pork

Marinade:

2 tbsp dark soya sauce

1 tbsp yellow bean paste

1 tbsp hoisin sauce

1 tbsp oyster sauce

1 tbsp sugar

1½ tbsp vegetable oil

1 tbsp red bean curd cheese

Garnish:

carrot flowers

CHA SIU ROAST PORK

This special way of rapid roasting marinated meat, practised mainly by the southern Cantonese, can be applied to all kinds of good cuts of meat.

■ PREPARATION ■

Cut the pork into 2 strips, about 5-6.5 cm/2-2½ inch thick and 15 × 18 cm/6-7 inch long. Mix the ingredients for the marinade in a large bowl. Add the 2 pieces of pork and rub thoroughly with the marinade. Leave to marinate for 30 minutes.

■ COOKING ■

Place the 2 strips of pork on a wire rack over a roasting tin filled with 4 cm/1½ inch of water to catch the drips. Place in a preheated oven at 220°C, 425°F, Gas Mark 7, and roast for 7-8 minutes. Reduce the oven temperature to 180°C, 350°F, Gas Mark 4 (to avoid burning) and roast for another 12-13 minutes. By this time the meat will be coated with the dark marinade.

■ SERVING ■

Remove the pork and cut across the grain into 1 cm/½ inch thick slices. The distinguishing feature of pork so rapidly roasted is that each slice or pork has a dark rim of well cooked pork with even darker encrustation of marinade, surrounding a centre of lighter cooked pork. The contrast between the well cooked and lighter cooked meat not only provides visual appeal but also an appetizing difference in flavour. Serve Cha Siu pork in overlapping slices on a bed of lightly stir-fried vegetables – bean sprouts or spinach.

★ ★

Cooking time: about 20 minutes, plus marinating time

Serves: 6-8

Cooking method: roast

Simple to prepare

Serve with vegetables and stir-fry dishes at a family meal or dinner party

Illustrated on p.271

1 kg/2 lb pork spare ribs

6 medium plums

1 tbsp salted black beans

3 tsp sugar

2½ tbsp soya sauce

1½ tbsp oyster sauce

1 tbsp vegetable oil

STEAMED SPARE RIBS WITH PLUMS

■ PREPARATION ■

Chop the spare ribs into 2.5 cm/1 inch sections. Stone the plums and cut each in half. Soak the black beans in hot water for 5 minutes, then drain. Place all the ingredients in a heatproof dish. Turn and mix thoroughly.

■ COOKING ■

Cover the dish well with foil. Place in a steamer and steam vigorously for 1 hour.

★ ★

Cooking time: 1 hour

Serves: 4-6

Cooking method: steam, p.49

Easy to prepare

Serve with any combination of dishes

SOYA CHICKEN IN AROMATIC OIL

★★★

Cooking time: about 25 minutes

Serves: 7-8

Cooking methods: stir-fry p.42 and fast simmer

Quite easy to prepare

Useful dish at a meal for a large number of diners

| 1.5 kg/3½-4 lb chicken |
| 2 medium onions |
| 4 cloves garlic |
| 4 slices fresh root ginger |
| 2 spring onions |
| 50 g/2 oz lard |
| 3 tbsp vegetable oil |
| ¾ tbsp star anise |
| 1½ tsp sesame oil |
| Sauce: |
| 300 ml/½ pint good stock (see page 56) |
| 3 tbsp soya sauce |
| 1 tsp salt |
| 1 tbsp sugar |

▇ PREPARATION ▇

Chop the chicken through the bones into 20-24 bite-size pieces. Place in a flameproof casserole. Thinly slice the onions. Coarsely chop the garlic. Shred the ginger. Cut the spring onions into 1 cm/½ inch shreds.

▇ COOKING ▇

For the aromatic oil, heat the lard and oil in a small saucepan or frying pan. When hot, stir-fry the sliced onion, ginger, garlic, peppercorns and star anise for 4-5 minutes. Pour the seasoned oil through a sieve over the chicken pieces. Place the casserole over medium heat and stir-fry the chicken pieces in the aromatic oil for 4-5 minutes. Add the stock, soya sauce, salt and sugar. Bring to the boil, then cook over high heat for 10-12 minutes, stirring all the time, until the sauce is reduced to less than one quarter. Sprinkle with the spring onion and sesame oil.

CRAB MEAT SOUP

★★

Cooking time: about 10 minutes

Serves: 5-6

Cooking methods: stir-fry p.42 and simmer

Easy to prepare

A substantial soup for a starter or as part of a main meal

Illustrated on p.271

| 175-200 g/6-7 oz crab meat, fresh or frozen |
| 2 slices fresh root ginger |
| 2 spring onions |
| 1 cake bean curd |
| 225 g/8 oz young spinach |
| 2 tbsp vegetable oil |
| 900 ml/1½ pt good stock (see page 56) |
| 1 chicken stock cube |
| 1 tsp salt |
| pepper to taste |
| 2 tbsp cornflour blended with 5 tbsp water |

▇ PREPARATION ▇

Flake the crab meat, thawing first if necessary. Coarsely chop the ginger. Cut the spring onions into 1 cm/½ inch shreds. Cut the bean curd into cubes. Wash the spinach, removing any tough stems and discoloured leaves.

▇ COOKING ▇

Heat the oil in a wok or saucepan. When hot, stir-fry the ginger and spring onion for 30 seconds. Add the crab meat and stir-fry for 15 seconds. Pour in the stock. Add the crumbled stock cube and the salt and pepper. Bring to the boil, stirring. Add the spinach and bean curd. Bring contents to the boil again, stirring, then simmer gently for 2 minutes. Stir in the blended cornflour and cook until thickened.

How to Choose and Order Chinese Food

WHEN CHOOSING CHINESE FOOD the average Westerner is faced with several problems. None of these is insurmountable or even difficult, given a few very simple guidelines.

The first aim of any Chinese meal is harmony and variety – in colour, texture, flavour, method of cooking and food materials.

A Chinese meal is essentially a hot buffet. A group of dishes is served on the table at the same time, to be shared by everyone. Dishes are only served singly if one person is eating alone. Even at a formal banquet or dinner party, the dishes are served in groups, one after the other. Chinese hors d'oeuvres consist of four to eight dishes all served at once, for example.

■ CHOOSING FOR A SMALL GROUP ■
OF FOUR TO SIX PEOPLE

In China people generally eat in groups: family groups, groups of friends, groups of colleagues. And Chinese food is best eaten in this way, for only then can you enjoy a variety of dishes.

Usually you should order one more dish than there are people: four dishes for three people, five dishes for four people. It is only when you are entertaining particularly lavishly that you have two extra dishes.

It is not until you have more than five or six dishes that you should start duplicating the order of one or two particular favourites. Normally you will want to avoid overcrowding the table by duplicating dishes, and it is only when the dishes become too small to be shared by all the people around the table that you should think of doubling any order.

You should ensure variety by selecting dishes from the range of foods available. When you have ordered a chicken dish, next order a fish. When you've ordered a meat dish, then select a vegetable. If you choose a seafood dish, next pick a bean curd or tofu dish. After rice, order noodles, especially if everybody's hungry and bulky food is required.

The next thing that you should bear in mind is the method of cooking. Try to achieve as much variety as possible here also. After you've ordered a stir-fried dish, order something that has been cooked longer: a red-cooked dish or one that has been braised for a long time in a clay pot or casserole. After ordering a deep-fried crispy dish, pick a steamed dish. And after selecting a highly spiced dish, order a lightly cooked, fresh-tasting dish.

Texture is closely related to the method of cooking employed. Most deep-fried dishes are crispy. Steamed or simmered dishes are tender. But stir-fried dishes can be soft or crunchy, or a combination of both, depending on their ingredients. Try to

■

The following menu suggestions should help you select dishes that combine to produce meals that are well balanced in terms of flavour and texture. All the dishes mentioned may be found in the recipe sections in the book. The wines listed are suggestions only and are in no way obligatory. Beer, China tea or, indeed, mineral water, are equally suitable to be served as accompaniments to a Chinese meal.

MENU FOR 2 PEOPLE
Hot and Sour Soup
(recipe page 63)
Long-Braised Tung Po Soya Pork
(recipe page 182)
Cantonese Stir-Fried Beef in Oyster Sauce
(recipe page 203)
Fu-Yung Cauliflower
(recipe page 97)
Rice

Suggested wines: A white wine such as Chablis Premier Cru or Pouilly Fuissee

MENU FOR 4 PEOPLE
Cantonese Steamed Spare Ribs with Black Beans
(recipe page 186)
Steamed Fish with Garnish
(recipe page 126)
Deep-Fried Crispy Prawn Balls
(recipe page 134)
Peking Diced Chicken Stir-Fried in Capital Sauce
(recipe page 156)
Crab Meat with Cream of Chinese Cabbage
(recipe page 96)
Rice

Suggested wines: A Loire wine such as white Sancerre Chavignol Reserve de Mont Damnes 1983 or red Sancerre Chavignol 1982

MENU FOR 4 PEOPLE
Peking Sliced Fish Pepper Pot Soup
(recipe page 65)
Braised Pea-Starched Noodles
(recipe page 82)
Quick-Fried Mange Tout
(recipe page 85)
Cantonese Roast Duck (half portion)
(recipe page 175)
Lion's Head Meat Balls
(recipe page 186)
Quick-Fried Chilli Prawns
(recipe page 143)

Suggested wines: A Provençale white wine such as Castel Roubine or an Australian or Californian Chardonnay such as Rosemount or Mondavi

MENU FOR 6-8 PEOPLE
Chicken and Straw Mushroom Soup
(recipe page 60)
'Ten Treasure' Tapestry Noodles
(recipe page 83)
Aromatic and Crispy Duck
(recipe page 174)
Sichuan Braised Aubergine
(recipe page 96)
Sautéed Fish Steaks with Garnish
(recipe page 123)
Deep-Fried King Prawns
(recipe page 136)
Red-Cooked Chicken
(recipe page 148)
Steamed Ground Rice-Pork in Lotus Leaves
(recipe page 190)
Rice

Suggested wines: A light red wine such as Beaujolais Village and Joseph Drouhin 1983 or a white wine such as Château Carbonnieux 1982

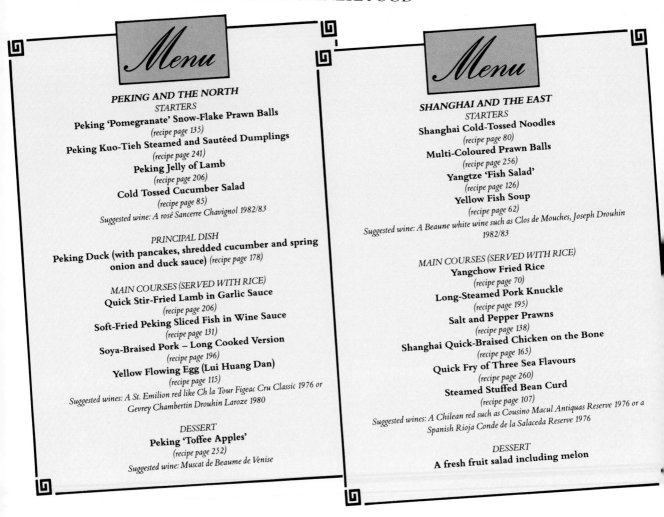

Menu

PEKING AND THE NORTH
STARTERS
Peking 'Pomegranate' Snow-Flake Prawn Balls
(recipe page 135)
Peking Kuo-Tieh Steamed and Sautéed Dumplings
(recipe page 241)
Peking Jelly of Lamb
(recipe page 206)
Cold Tossed Cucumber Salad
(recipe page 85)
Suggested wine: A rosé Sancerre Chavignol 1982/83

PRINCIPAL DISH
Peking Duck (with pancakes, shredded cucumber and spring onion and duck sauce) *(recipe page 178)*

MAIN COURSES (SERVED WITH RICE)
Quick Stir-Fried Lamb in Garlic Sauce
(recipe page 206)
Soft-Fried Peking Sliced Fish in Wine Sauce
(recipe page 131)
Soya-Braised Pork – Long Cooked Version
(recipe page 196)
Yellow Flowing Egg (Lui Huang Dan)
(recipe page 115)
Suggested wines: A St. Emilion red like Ch la Tour Figeac Cru Classic 1976 or Gevrey Chambertin Drouhin Laroze 1980

DESSERT
Peking 'Toffee Apples'
(recipe page 252)
Suggested wine: Muscat de Beaume de Venise

Menu

SHANGHAI AND THE EAST
STARTERS
Shanghai Cold-Tossed Noodles
(recipe page 80)
Multi-Coloured Prawn Balls
(recipe page 256)
Yangtze 'Fish Salad'
(recipe page 126)
Yellow Fish Soup
(recipe page 62)
Suggested wine: A Beaune white wine such as Clos de Mouches, Joseph Drouhin 1982/83

MAIN COURSES (SERVED WITH RICE)
Yangchow Fried Rice
(recipe page 70)
Long-Steamed Pork Knuckle
(recipe page 195)
Salt and Pepper Prawns
(recipe page 138)
Shanghai Quick-Braised Chicken on the Bone
(recipe page 165)
Quick Fry of Three Sea Flavours
(recipe page 260)
Steamed Stuffed Bean Curd
(recipe page 107)
Suggested wines: A Chilean red such as Cousino Macul Antiquas Reserve 1976 or a Spanish Rioja Conde de la Salaceda Reserve 1976

DESSERT
A fresh fruit salad including melon

order as wide a variety of textures as possible.

Soups and semi-soups are essential lubricants which help wash down bulky foods. The sensation of washing a mouthful of food with a savoury soup is peculiar to Chinese eating. In Western cuisine, soups and solids are rigorously segregated. But again, the incorporation of soups and semi-soups into the main meal add variety in texture.

Variety in flavour and differences in the degree of flavour and spiciness are all factors you should bear in mind when choosing dishes. Again, select as wide a range as possible.

When eating, aim for this variety too. After a meat dish you will naturally gravitate towards a seafood flavour or a vegetable dish. After a spicy dish, try a bite of a fresh, natural-tasting dish. After a hot dish, try a cold dish. After a dry dish, a soup dish. The possible sequences and combinations are almost endless.

Four Regional Menus
These are all intended as full-scale Chinese dinners, which are usually for 8–10 people.

■ CHOOSING FOR ONE ■

Occasionally you may find yourself dining alone, in which case it will not be possible to order a variety of tastes and textures. In this situation a Chinese will choose a soup and a composite rice or noodle dish which contains meat, fish or vegetables. An extra meat, fish or vegetable dish might be ordered to make a lavish meal. But for the Chinese the soup would be essential, while an American might prefer to wash the meal down with a soda, a beer or a glass of wine.

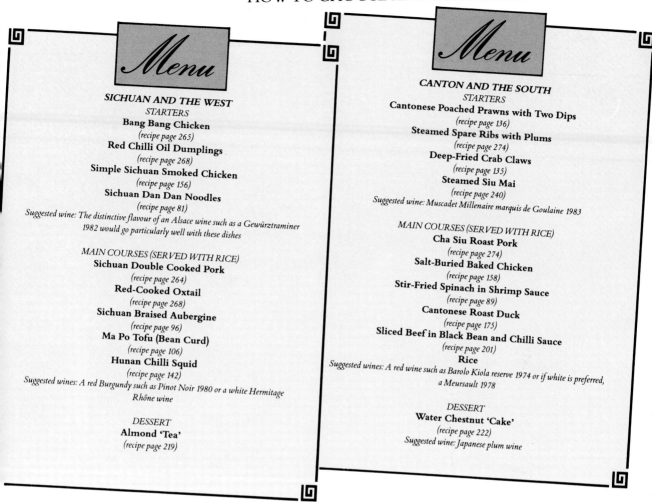

Menu

SICHUAN AND THE WEST
STARTERS
Bang Bang Chicken
(recipe page 265)
Red Chilli Oil Dumplings
(recipe page 268)
Simple Sichuan Smoked Chicken
(recipe page 156)
Sichuan Dan Dan Noodles
(recipe page 81)
Suggested wine: The distinctive flavour of an Alsace wine such as a Gewürztraminer 1982 would go particularly well with these dishes

MAIN COURSES (SERVED WITH RICE)
Sichuan Double Cooked Pork
(recipe page 264)
Red-Cooked Oxtail
(recipe page 268)
Sichuan Braised Aubergine
(recipe page 96)
Ma Po Tofu (Bean Curd)
(recipe page 106)
Hunan Chilli Squid
(recipe page 142)
Suggested wines: A red Burgundy such as Pinot Noir 1980 or a white Hermitage Rhône wine

DESSERT
Almond 'Tea'
(recipe page 219)

Menu

CANTON AND THE SOUTH
STARTERS
Cantonese Poached Prawns with Two Dips
(recipe page 136)
Steamed Spare Ribs with Plums
(recipe page 274)
Deep-Fried Crab Claws
(recipe page 135)
Steamed Siu Mai
(recipe page 240)
Suggested wine: Muscadet Millenaire marquis de Goulaine 1983

MAIN COURSES (SERVED WITH RICE)
Cha Siu Roast Pork
(recipe page 274)
Salt-Buried Baked Chicken
(recipe page 158)
Stir-Fried Spinach in Shrimp Sauce
(recipe page 89)
Cantonese Roast Duck
(recipe page 175)
Sliced Beef in Black Bean and Chilli Sauce
(recipe page 201)
Rice
Suggested wines: A red wine such as Barolo Kiola reserve 1974 or if white is preferred, a Meursault 1978

DESSERT
Water Chestnut 'Cake'
(recipe page 222)
Suggested wine: Japanese plum wine

◼ CHOOSING FOR TWO ◼

In the Western world people often dine out as a couple and regularly eat with one friend or colleague. Here I recommend the selection of at least three dishes: a meat dish, a fish or seafood dish and a vegetable dish.

If that is not enough, have both a fish dish *and* a seafood dish. You will also need a rice or noodle dish and a soup—though the latter is not mandatory if you are drinking wine or beer.

In that case you may consider exchanging the soup for a starter. Try a light dish like a pancake roll, a dim sum dish or even spareribs which can be eaten Western style, with your fingers. The Chinese never eat spareribs as a main course to complement a rice or noodle dish.

If you are extra hungry, have both a rice and a noodle dish. In this case take your noodles as a simple chow mein which is fried noodles cooked with bean sprouts and shredded meat. That will satisfy the largest of appetites.

◼ CHOOSING FOR A DINNER PARTY ◼

We are dealing here with a dinner party of more than six people, otherwise refer back to the section on 'Choosing for a small group of four to six people' and add and duplicate dishes as necessary.

At a dinner party the number of dishes should exceed the number of people by three or four portions. As a result the table should appear like a grand buffet – a hot

buffet at that. There should not be less than eight to ten separate dishes served, with several of these being double or triple servings. This means that you can have whole chickens, ducks and fish, and piles of vegetables and meat-filled dumplings.

If you are employing an outside caterer for your dinner party, it may be advisable to have the dishes brought to the table in two or three stages. This will stop the table becoming too overcrowded, with too many choices at once. And unless you have a round table with a Lazy Susan not everyone will be able to sample every dish.

■ ORDERING FOR A BANQUET ■

Cold dishes and Chinese hor d'oeuvres can be arranged on the table before the guests are seated. This should then be followed by three or four hot starter dishes.

These should be in small serving dishes – not more than 20cm/8 inches in diameter. They are designed to stimulate the appetite rather than satisfy it.

Between the starters and the main courses, you can have a soup served. This acts as punctuation and helps slow down the proceedings. A Chinese banquet is meant to proceed at a leisurely pace.

Following the soup will be the main courses – or the 'big dishes' as they are known in China. These may consist of whole ducks, chickens, geese, fish or lobster, along with one or two mixed dishes – like seaslugs with meatballs or stuffed mushrooms – and a large dish of glistening vegetables.

Just when the diners are beginning to feel a little full, a large dish of noodles should arrive. These are there to make sure that no one goes away hungry.

Then, when your guests are beginning to feel that the meal is almost over, a bowl of fruity or sweet soup should arrive. This is not a dessert though; it is another punctuation which heralds another series of dishes.

Groups of four to six medium-size dishes should then be served, with a small bowl of rice provided for each person. These dishes should all be fairly plain dishes with no overwhelming spices or flavourings. They are meant to settle the stomach after the spicy dishes served earlier. It is only then that a large bowl of fresh fruit should be served to mark the end of the banquet.

Naturally you will have to discuss the details of your banquet with the caterers. But if you feel that the meal outlined here is too much, eliminate the hors d'oeuvres and stop the meal after the sweet soup.

■ WESTERN WINE AND CHINESE FOOD ■

The combination of these two vast territories of epicurean delight is still very much in the exploratory stage. In China there is only one word, 'Jiu', which covers beer, wine and liquor. And in Hong Kong, Singapore and Taiwan you'll see well-heeled Chinese still at restaurant tables with several bottles of whiskey, drinking it as if it were table wine. Many believe that Scotch is a brand of British wine that should be gulped down by the tumblerful. The Chinese are either great drinkers, or they do not drink at all. So you should not set great store by their opinion of wines.

On the other hand, Western wine experts rarely have an extensive knowledge of Chinese cuisine. So far the marriage between Western wine and Chinese food is still largely virgin territory which remains to be explored by men and women of discerning palates.

In my opinion, though, there is no doubt that wine does go very well indeed with Chinese food. In some of the more elaborate menus in this book, I shall list some of the Western wines that I feel best suit the particular menu and the Chinese dishes involved.

■
A typical large Chinese family meal, where all the dishes are shared from the centre of the table

Index

■ ACKNOWLEDGEMENTS ■

The author wishes to thank Barbara Croxford for the competence and
efficiency of her editing; Mrs D. Liang, Madam C.W. Fei and
Miss Elaine Ngaan for preparing such elegant dishes for photography;
and, the photographer, David Burch for his unstinting efforts to
make every dish an artistic creation.

The publishers wish to thank the following for the loan of china,
glassware, kitchen equipment and provisions:
Cheong-Leen Supermarkets, Tower Street, London WC2
The Reject China Shop, Beauchamp Place, London SW1
Liberty, Regent Street, London W1
David Mellor (kitchen supplies), Covent Garden, London WC2

Additional photographs were taken by Stephanie Colasanti (pages 6-7,
9, 15, 242-3, 248-9) and Michael Freeman (page 280).